REPRESSION
OF HERESY
IN MEDIEVAL
GERMANY

RICHARD KIECKHEFER

UNIVERSITY OF PENNSYLVANIA PRESS
1979

Library of Congress Cataloging in Publication Data

Kieckhefer, Richard.
    Repression of heresy in medieval Germany.

    (The Middle ages)
    Bibliography: p.
    Includes index.
    1. Heresies and heretics—Germany. 2. Germany—
Church history—Middle Ages, 843–1517. I. Title.
II. Series.
BR854.K53 1979   273'.6   76-65112
    ISBN 0-8122-7758-9

To the memory of
John T. Ferguson, IV

Contents

Preface

Much of the historical literature on the repression of medieval heresy grew out of Protestant-Catholic polemics, and derived its relevance from this polemical context. Historians and their readers were interested in knowing about the subject because of the light it purportedly shed on Catholicism in general and on the position of Protestantism vis-à-vis Catholicism. But in an ecumenical age there is less zeal among Protestants for exposing the enormities of the whore of Babylon, and few Catholics are eager to exert themselves in defense of the medieval Church. Thus, the traditional reasons for interest in medieval repression no longer inspire much enthusiasm. During the 1950s the McCarthy hearings may have been partly responsible for a new kind of interest in matters inquisitorial, but this approach, too, now seems dated. And yet the general topic of repression has scarcely become irrelevant in today's world. As Amnesty International and other organizations remind us repeatedly, principles of toleration are by no means flourishing in contemporary society; indeed, in nations throughout the world, forms of repression—intimidation, imprisonment, torture, and execution—have become common which are far more brutal and systematic than their medieval counterparts. The problem of intolerance is perennial, though its forms may vary. It would be hazardous to draw conclusions from one historical period and apply them hastily to another. Medieval inquisitors, whose primary goal was at least ostensibly the salvation of the heretic's soul, operated quite differently from agents of twentieth-century police states. But the prevalence of repression in the modern world should at least arouse interest in historical precedents within our own culture as well as in other cultures, and should provoke concern about certain basic questions. What sorts of conditions lead to repression? What circumstances favor growth of toleration? And given a society that makes use of repression, what factors have augmented or restricted the extent of its effectiveness and brutality? The present work is intended in part as a modest contribution toward answering especially the last of these questions.

From the perspective of ecclesiastical history, this study addresses a different kind of question. The history of the Western Church in the high and late Middle Ages has traditionally been seen as a story of increasing central control. Beginning with the reforming popes of the eleventh century, the papacy gradually asserted its power in diverse areas: judicial proceedings, appointment to benefices, taxation, control of councils, and so forth, across the entire scope of ecclesiastical life. After many years of local resistance, the Great Schism led in the late Middle Ages to the conciliar movement, which sought to limit papal power, but the drive toward centralization has been seen as essentially a success. This, too, is a general topic that should be of interest at a time when Catholics and Protestants alike are reassessing the role of the papacy and re-examining the historical roots of papal power. But quite apart from its contemporary relevance, the subject is important simply for an understanding of the medieval Church. The present study will examine one of the many areas in which the papal Curia became involved, and will inquire whether this involvement served, or was intended to serve, the cause of centralized papal authority. Thus, it will seek to shed light on one aspect of this vital theme in Church history.

The repression of heresy in medieval Germany is by no means an overworked topic. To be sure, research on the heretics themselves has progressed, with intermittent slack periods, ever since the late nineteenth century, when scholars such as J. J. I. von Döllinger and Herman Haupt began to ferret out relevant manuscripts and piece together the evidence. In recent years the impetus has been carried forward by Herbert Grundmann, Ernst Werner, Alexander Patschovsky, Robert Lerner, Dietrich Kurze, Martin Erbstösser, and others. There has never been much attention given, however, to the related topic of the repression of heresy. The chapter on Germany in the early work of H. C. Lea remains the only general survey of the subject. Around the turn of the century, Paul Flade published various works on the agencies of repression and on specific instances of prosecution, though his work must be used with caution. There have been other articles and monographs on particular trials. Hermann Heimpel has edited the records of some highly important cases, with an extensive apparatus that sheds light both on the heresies in question and on the background and procedures for repression. Still, most of the work on antiheretical efforts in Germany has been incidental to studies of the various heretics and heretical movements. Unfortunately, this kind of incidental treatment has resulted in an understanding of repressive action which in my view needs to be revised. The present book is intended specifically to contribute toward discussion of the topic by suggesting a new interpretation of the evidence.

In view of this limited purpose, I have sought to avoid giving an encyclopedic account of my subject. I have generally refrained from retelling in detail narratives given in other English studies, and I have not considered myself obliged to comment on every instance of repression known to scholars. Instead, I have tried to sketch as briefly as possible the course of antiheretical action during each period, analyzing in detail only those trials that were especially significant. In particular, I have dwelt on cases that are somehow relevant to the thesis of this study, whether as evidence for my interpretation or as potential counterevidence. This method has its inevitable drawbacks, especially for specialists in medieval heresy and repression, and to these individuals I offer my apologies. Yet even for the sake of such specialists, it seemed to me useful to highlight the main interpretative contributions that I have to make. I emphasize my purposes in this regard because otherwise the arrangement of chapters might suggest that I am trying to give an exhaustive, chronologically arranged account of all the material. Although the chapters in this study are arranged chronologically, the primary focus within each chapter is analytic. In other words, I have tried to state concisely the distinctive features of heresy and repression of heresy during three main periods.

For similar reasons I have not attempted to examine with equal thoroughness every aspect of the topic. The subject at hand can be approached from at least four perspectives: social, legal, doctrinal, and institutional. For the sake of the nonspecialist reader I have tried to provide enough information from each of these areas that the general context will be clear. But I have attended most systematically to the ecclesiastical institutions, and it is in this area alone that I have sought to advance knowledge of the subject. Thus, I have not found it useful to discuss the social context extensively. It is not that I lack interest in the social dynamics of repression. I am simply not convinced that the prosecution of heretics arose primarily in response to social pressures; I contend that in most cases it came instead principally from clerical initiative, and owed more to the convictions and policies of individuals than to the dynamics of social class. Nor have I given sustained attention to legal questions. In early drafts of my work I included a great deal of material on law and procedure, but in revision I deleted it because it proved more distracting than useful. Legal and judicial aspects of repression were essentially the same in Germany as elsewhere, and any reader seeking detailed information on the subject can readily find it. I trust that what I have retained will give some idea of the general legal outlines, and will prove sufficient when legal questions bear upon my central thesis. Likewise, I have relegated to a minor place the intellectual content of heresies and of the orthodox response to heretics. I acknowledge the great interest and importance of this topic, but detailed examination of it would only distract from the essential concerns at hand. Furthermore, there are already numerous studies that cover the heretics and their beliefs admirably. Thus, while I have endeavored to provide the necessary background from these other areas, I have focused mainly on those specific workings of ecclesiastical institutions and ecclesiastical politics on which I hope to have made some more or less original contribution. My choice of emphasis is not arbitrary or subjective, but is determined by my judgment as to what constitute the essential and determinative factors that explain how and why heretics were prosecuted in Germany. And while my judgment on this matter is of course fallible and subject to challenge, I trust that it rests upon some reasonable grounds.

There is one methodological matter which, while perhaps elementary, may require comment. Many of the early studies of heresy and its repression engendered needless confusion by relying on derivative chronicles for their information. During the late Middle Ages there was a vast proliferation of chronicles in the German towns. The authors were by and large reliable when they reported events of their own times, though the structure of most of their works leaves a great deal to be desired. For example, they would routinely report meteorological information, or give names of the local burgomasters, at random junctures, disregarding the context in which they deposited such information. Their worst fault, however, was that to supplement their accounts they borrowed earlier material from preceding chroniclers in a grossly irresponsible fashion. If one chronicler referred to heretics without specifying the sect to which they belonged, a later chronicler would be sure to remedy the omission, usually by gratuitous conjecture. If an early author followed his account of a trial with a wholly

unconnected reference to the burgomaster, some later writer, postu-
lating a link between one datum and the other, would invent some
role for the burgomaster to have played in the proceedings. And the
further one traces down the stemma of derivative chronicles, the
more likely one is to find stereotyped accusations about antinomian
orgies. At times one suspects that the later chronicler may have had
independent information, but more often than not this conjecture
proves highly unlikely. Far more commonly, the additions of later
chroniclers are demonstrably wrong. Scholars who trust these derivative accounts do so at their own risk. It might seem needless to call
attention here to this basic methodological problem, except that it
has so often been overlooked in studies of the present subject. As a
matter of principle, I have relied on contemporary chronicles and
excluded derivative ones. With only a few exceptions, I have not felt
it necessary to give specific justification for this procedure.

In the course of my research I have become indebted to many
people. Foremost among them are three scholars who have given me
abundant encouragement and guidance. The late John T. Ferguson,
to whose memory this book is dedicated, aided in countless ways,
both as teacher and as friend. His untimely death impoverished historical scholarship, but his example still serves to inspire his students
to make up in part for the loss. Alexander Patschovsky and Robert E.
Lerner also gave generously of their time and of their expert knowledge, corrected errors and oversights I made, and furnished the opportunity to reformulate and clarify my conclusions. I have learned
a great deal from them both personally and through their writing.
If on occasion I have taken exception to their views, my disagreement
should not distract from the very high respect that I have for their
work. I am grateful furthermore to Gerald Strauss, Ilse Bulhof,
Oliver H. Radkey, and Stanley N. Werbow for their reading and
advice. Their comments have been consistently helpful. And I have
profited from conversation and correspondence with Walter L. Wakefield and Howard Kaminsky.

The research for this work would have been impossible without
the grant that I received from the Deutscher Akademischer Austausch-
dienst for an enjoyable year of work in Munich. During that year
I made considerable use of the kind and efficient services of the
librarians for the Monumenta Germaniae Historica. I am deeply
grateful for their aid, and also for the services of the Bayerische
Staatsbibliothek, the Universitätsbibliothek München, the Fürstlich
Oettingen-Wallerstein'sche Bibliothek und Kunstsammlung, die Ba-
yerisches Hauptstaatsarchiv, the Österreichische Nationalbibliothek,

the Stadtarchiv Augsburg, the Stadtarchiv Speyer, and the Stadtarchiv Ulm. My visits to these libraries and archives were all rewarding, even when they proved unfruitful for my research.

I am especially pleased to thank my wife, Margaret, who fostered my work with an unending flow of coffee, and whose support and tolerance have been a godsend.

1

Introduction

By the eve of the Reformation it was clear that the papal inquisitors in Germany had little respect from their contemporaries, and met with abuse particularly from the emerging humanist movement. In the course of the famous trial of John Reuchlin, the humanist Crotus Rubeanus issued a parody of these inquisitors, in the form of a treatise on inquisitorial procedure. "Armed with the whole armor of God," the author advised, "the Inquisitor shall smile like a dog showing his teeth, contort his face, protrude his lips, and wave his arms with fingers outspread." If the heretic threatened to entangle the inquisitor in discussion of Scripture, the inquisitor should stamp his feet, "for a riot on behalf of the Church is meritorious if it proceeds from the right intention according to Aristotle."[1] This particular instance of ridicule is in some ways extreme, yet examples of disrespect are not limited to the period just before the Reformation. From the very outset, papal inquisitors encountered difficulty in enforcing their will in Germany. They frequently suffered contempt and assault both from those they accused and from the general populace. To be sure, some of the papal inquisitors appointed for German territories were respected by their contemporaries, and were highly effective in their efforts against heretics. But even if one assumes that the conspicuously inept inquisitors formed a small minority, there is reason to think that they had strong influence on the general image of papal inquisitors in Germany. In any event, papal inquisitors never gained the degree of power and respect in Germany that they enjoyed at least for a time in such areas as southern France. Perhaps the most significant question to be answered in this connection is whether papal inquisitors throughout Germany suffered from the excesses of a few of their colleagues, or whether the clear instances of failure are manifestations of some underlying weakness in the machinery for repressing heresy.

H. C. Lea argued that papal inquisitors were only weakly established in Germany because they met resistance from native authorities.[2] He suggested that popes appointed inquisitors as tools for the augmentation of papal power over Germany, and that the emperor Charles IV fostered these inquisitors as a means toward the ends of both papacy and empire. In other words, repression of heresy was in Lea's eyes a program imposed on Germany by the highest levels of political authority, and the ends that it served were mainly political. Consequently, Lea argued, papal inquisitors as agents of one political force encountered resistance from political rivals. Opposition to inquisitors arose not only from the heretics who came under attack, but from the ruling figures of Germany: princes, magistrates, archbishops, and bishops. The keenest resistance is supported to have come from the Rhenish prelates, who reacted against encroachment on their jurisdiction and allegedly set up their own Inquisitions in an effort to forestall papal inquisitors, and thus to maintain their own judicial rights.

Lea's interpretation has dominated the historical literature, both in Germany and in the English-speaking world. Granted, his thesis has not been perpetuated in a formal body of directly pertinent literature, for the simple reason that there has been scarcely any literature dealing specifically with the general topic of repression in Germany. But when scholars have had occasion, in whatever context, to touch upon the subject, they have generally invoked Lea's interpretation or something closely resembling it.[3] With the significant exception of Joseph Hansen, who planned to write a book showing that inquisitors were firmly established in Germany, no one has seriously challenged Lea's views.[4] Indeed, in a general appraisal of Lea, H. R. Trevor-Roper has remarked that "It is inconceivable that his work on the Inquisition, as an objective narrative of fact, will ever be replaced," and the respect that Lea's work still commands carries over to his interpretation of the situation in Germany.[5]

Yet Lea's analysis is not wholly unproblematic. During the late Middle Ages the political fragmentation of Germany made German lands peculiarly susceptible to papal intervention in certain respects;

it was especially in Germany that late medieval popes enforced their will in the dispensation of benefices and the collection of revenues.[6] Why, then, should the political situation in Germany result in a strong measure of successful resistance to papal inquisitors? Nor is it clear exactly how popes and emperors were to profit from the foothold of power that papal inquisitors would provide. And perhaps most importantly, when one searches the sources for proof that Germans resisted the establishment of inquisitors, one finds that this basic assumption dissolves. There were indeed cases in which individuals sought to protect defendants whom they judged innocent, but there was no general opposition from either ecclesiastical or secular authorities to the fundamental policy of repression under papal auspices. When inquisitors met resistance, it was almost always because they had exceeded the bounds of commonly recognized regular and justifiable prosecution. The real question, then, is why papal inquisitors were so prone to irregular action. It remans evident that papal inquisitors were not, for the most part, a significant force in the religious life of Germany. But the reasons for their lack of influence must be sought more within their own institutional structure than in their relations with native authorities.

The first step toward clarification must lie in an examination of the crucial term, "the Inquisition." Historians for generations have spoken about the power wielded by the Inquisition, and have attempted to assess the extent of that power. But what, if anything, was the Inquisition? There were several kinds of judge delegated in medieval law to carry out inquisitions, or trials in accordance with inquisitorial procedure. Some of these, such as the episcopal *officiales*, had duties other than the repression of heresy; others were specifically entrusted, with either episcopal or papal authority, to seek out heretics, and these judges were known by the technical term *inquisitor heretice pravitatis*.[7] In addition, during the later Middle Ages even secular courts began to adopt inquisitorial procedures, and occasionally they used them against persons whom they referred to as heretics. It has long been customary in the historical literature to refer to all such judicial agents, or at least the ecclesiastical ones, as constituting "the Inquisition." But such usage can only serve to obscure the real and significant differences between one kind of judge and another. H. C. Lea states explicitly, and other scholars have assumed, that these differences were negligible, but following chapters will attempt to show that this is not the case.[8] In any event, there was no institutional bond that united all papal and episcopal inquisitors within a single agency. To refer to all such inquisitors collectively as constituting "the Inquisition" is to engage in an abstraction, and a dangerously misleading one.

Is it more useful, then, to speak of episcopal inquisitors alone, or of papal inquisitors by themselves, as making up an Inquisition? In several known cases, probably even the majority, episcopal inquisitors were commissioned *ad hoc* when the problem of heresy became known.[9] Nor is there evidence that these inquisitors commonly retained their commissions or titles after the immediate problems were resolved.[10] In general, then, bishops do not appear even to have maintained standing inquisitors, much less standing Inquisitions. Papal inquisitors, by contrast, held long-term appointments; they were delegated routinely to seek out heretics or to act in the event that a sect might come to light, and not to proceed against some specific person or group that had already aroused attention. Furthermore, their offices were continuous; when an inquisitor was appointed, he was typically entering into an office that had existed before his term and would continue afterward. Yet there were two other criteria of an institution that were lacking, both in Germany and in other parts of Europe. First, there was no structure of authority to ensure regularity or propriety of function. Inquisitors were appointed by their superiors in the Dominican order (or, for certain other parts of Europe, the Franciscan order), and were answerable ultimately to the papal Curia. In other words, they entered into two highly centralized ecclesiastical institutions, but not a specifically judical institution that could be labeled "the Inquisition."[11] Second, there was no mechanism to assure interaction of personnel; that is, there was no provision for routine mutual consultation, meetings, shared use of physical facilities, or collective expression of policy. Inquisitors for two cities or regions might take it upon themselves to share information or cooperate in other ways, but they did so as autonomous agents, without institutional provisions to direct them toward interaction.[12] Despite the antiheretical zeal of churchmen, institutional sophistication was as yet lacking for an Inquisition in any strict sense.

Nor is there clear evidence that contemporaries thought of inquisitors, papal or episcopal, in Germany or elsewhere, as forming an Inquisition. When Gregory IX began to appoint members of the mendicant orders to act against heresy in the 1230s, he referred to them individually rather than collectively—that is, as "inquisitors" rather than as an "Inquisition," and this usage remained standard through most of the thirteenth century.[13] Later, especially in the fourteenth century, the term *officium inquisitionis heretice pravitatis* ("office of inquisition of heretical pravity") came into common use, but the context usually requires, or at least allows, this phrase to be construed as referring to a function, activity, or jurisdiction entrusted to individual inquisitors.[14] In other words, the "office of inquisition" was the function of carrying out inquisitorial justice against heretics, rather than an institution established for this purpose. On rare occasions one finds contexts that do suggest that contemporaries may have been thinking of either an institution or an abstraction when they used this term, but this atypical usage is inconclusive.[15] In these circumstances, it would perhaps be advisable to avoid speaking of even papal inquisitors as if they formed a suprapersonal agency, or an Inquisition.

The matter is more than merely verbal. The lack of institutional sophistication made for a real weakness in the orthodox response to heresy. For lack of effective direction, papal inquisitors tended either to remain inert or to dissipate their energies attacking religious eccentrics, marginally heretical groups (such as beghards and beguines), political subjects, witches, and other elements which posed little if any danger to the organized Church. The annals of Dominican history in Germany are replete with the names of inquisitors who are not known to have taken action against heretics.[16] They bore their titles proudly—there would otherwise be scarcely any indication that some of them were inquisitors—but their zeal for the *negotium fidei* was less than ardent. They were handicapped by assignment to territories far too broad for effective surveillance; an inquisitor was routinely charged with an entire ecclesiastical province, or even more than one province. In this respect they were unlike the inquisitors of southern Europe, who were generally responsible for only a diocese, or perhaps two or three of the relatively small southern dioceses.[17] Presumably, if there had been some kind of antiheretical institution in Germany, a genuine Inquisition, these men would have attended systematically to the extermination of those heretics who were at hand. The authorities within this institution might have seen to it that the individual inquisitors applied themselves their duties. But as it was, they allowed themselves to be distracted by the numerous other tasks that were assigned to them as academicians, administrators in the Dominican order, and so forth.[18] Even when they did bestir themselves to action, however, the papal inquisitors in Germany focused their energies on the fringe elements in society. In the majority of cases, though certainly not all, it was papal inquisitors who proceeded against beghards and beguines, witches, and political subjects. And their action tended to be marked by a high degree of arbitrariness, which frequently aroused opposition from contemporaries.

One might argue that the success of papal inquisitors in southern Europe shows that tight institutional structure was not needed for regular and effective prosecution. And the comparison between northern and southern Europe does indeed lead to a significant qualification: when contemporaries perceived heresy as an urgent problem, even weakly organized inquisitors could muster enough zeal and support to carry out a strong attack on heretics. In areas such as southern France and northern Italy, heresy was not only endemic but politically controversial, and the situation called for systematic action. Under these circumstances, papal inquisitors could be effective even without institutional structure. But in Germany, as later chapters will endeavor to show, the problem of heretics was not so overwhelmingly clear and serious a threat to the Church. There were almost certainly fewer heretics, though the contrast is impossible to establish statistically. In any event, heresy was not *perceived* as such an overwhelming danger, at least in ordinary times. If one examines the sources of the period—literacy as well as documentary—one finds that the problem of heresy was only to a very minor degree in the consciousness of Germans. Granted, there were times when the threat of irregular and uncontrolled devotion caused German churchmen to overreact, and to brand as heresy movements that were essentially orthodox. But there is little evidence that the problem loomed large in the public consciousness. There were also periods in which the fear of Hussites grew intense, but the danger of Hussites within Germany was never so keenly feared as the incursions of militant Taborites from the east. In ordinary times the problem of heretics appears to have borne far less on the minds of contemporaries than, for example, that of Jews. Considered as a crime with religious overtones, heresy certainly ranked even below blasphemy as an object of public attention.[19] Despite one or two minor military "crusades" against German heretics, there was no parallel to the Albigensian Crusade in southern France. The problem in Germany was one of scattered heretics who for the most part remained effectively underground. There was no sense of urgency in their extermination; there were few spectacular gains to be made. In these circumstances it is not surprising that the papal inquisitors, subject to no institution, failed to attend even to those heretics who did exist, and either dissipated or misused their inquisitorial powers.

The situation in Germany was not altogether unique. The same pattern occurred in other areas where papal inquisitors had little real function. Several inquisitors appointed for the Iberian peninsula performed no recorded antiheretical work.[20] And in the second half of the fourteenth century, Nicholas Eymericus, eminent scholar though he may have been, spent most of his inquisitorial career in activities of dubious purpose. Around 1360 he consigned a relapsed heretic to the stake for claiming that his teacher was the son of God, that he was immortal, and that he would convert the world. In 1371 he silenced a Franciscan who taught that Christ departed from the eucharist if it fell into the mud, was gnawed by a mouse, or underwent other defilement. On another occasion he condemned Saint Vincent Ferrer for preaching that Judas had genuinely repented of his sins. In other episodes he proceeded against alleged devil-worshippers, the author of an apocalyptic treatise, and other eccentric but no doubt harmless souls. Not surprisingly, in the later part of the century the inquisitor himself was denounced by Juan I as an obstinate fool, and was exiled from the kingdom of Aragon.[21]

One might conclude that the significant factor, then, was merely whether heretics posed a conspicuous problem, and that institutional structure was irrelevant to whether inquisitors acted effectively. That this was not the case is suggested by a further consideration: even in Germany, where heresy was less threatening than in southern France, *episcopal* authorities proceeded against heretics in a relatively realistic fashion. It is true that German bishops and episcopal judges also tilted at occasional windmills, but they seem to have been less inclined to this sort of diversion than were papal inquisitors. More importantly, it was episcopal courts that were most keenly aware of those heresies that, allowed to spread, would genuinely have threatened the unity of the Church. As will be seen in following chapters, action against the clearly heretical communities, particularly Waldensians and Hussites, lay almost entirely in the hands of episcopal judges. Unlike papal inquisitors—who might be relegated to academic or administrative tasks, or might have contacts within only a single parish in a given city—the episcopal judge would usually be familiar with an entire city or diocese. The episcopal judge would have some acquaintance with the day-to-day lives of parishioners throughout the diocese, and would have routine contact with a broader range of diocesan clergy. Such familiarity might not have been required to discover beghards and beguines, whose presence was usually conspicuous. But the Waldensian and Hussite communities were more difficult to find, and an inquisitor who spent only a short time in any one community might readily overlook them—especially if he did not conduct a general inquisition, or a scrutiny of the entire vicinity.[22] In this respect the episcopal authorities had the advantage that even if they did not engage personally in routine parish work or regular visitations they had subordinates or colleagues who did maintain this kind of contact with lay religious life. Even their contact was no doubt haphazard; if it had been closer, prosecution of heretics would surely have been more constant than it in fact was.

The handicaps of papal inquisitors might have been offset by their maintenance of underlings, but there is little evidence that they did have staffs of any kind on a regular basis. The emperor Charles IV authorized them in 1396 to appoint notaries, and it is likely that they did so for specific trials, but nothing suggests that they had notaries permanently in their service.[23] In the mid-fourteenth century Pope Innocent VI made elaborate arrangements for the upkeep of the inquisitor John Schadeland and his associates, notaries, and other personnel.[24] Schadeland presumably did have such an entourage— though he is not known actually to have proceeded against a single heretic, and his costly retinue could have been a mere figment of his imagination. In any case, the example of a later inquisitor in Lübeck, who needed to use municipal functionaries to apprehend a heretic, appears to have been more typical.[25] The records have virtually nothing to say about these notaries, familiars, and agents of all kinds who accompanied inquisitors in areas of Europe where prosecution was more systematic.[26] Even the appointment of inquisitorial vicars seems to have been uncommon, though cases did occur.[27] The argument from silence is admittedly weak, but it is difficult to believe that inquisitors could have maintained extensive personnel without their being mentioned upon occasion in the extant documents. The most reasonable hypothesis is that papal inquisitors formed staffs only when these were required for specific proceedings. It is misleading, then, to speak of a papal Inquisition even for a specific city or diocese, just as it is a distortion to suggest a monolithic Inquisition spread throughout Europe.

In short, this study will attempt to show that there was indeed a serious weakness inherent in the machinery for repression of heresy in Germany, but that this weakness lay in institutional structure rather than in political circumstances. In certain situations, the lack of a well-developed institutional framework was not a debilitating handicap: in areas where heresy was a pressing and politically charged issue, repression could proceed apace. Furthermore, episcopal inquisitors did not need institutional support to be kept active and responsible in the prosecution of heretics, because they had the guidance and aid of their superiors and colleagues within the diocese. The lack of institutional sophistication most clearly affected the papal inquisitors in a country such as Germany, where they were allowed to dissipate their powers in inactivity or in arbitrary, dubious, or frivolous prosecution. And it was when such inquisitors proceeded in this fashion that they were likely to arouse opposition.

The chronological limits of this study are clearly determined by the events. Prosecution of heresy in Germany did not become even a sporadic concern of any significance until the eleventh century, and the Reformation placed the entire problem of orthodoxy and heterodoxy in a wholly new setting. Thus, the period under investigation will run from the eleventh century up to the year 1520—that is, to the end of the protracted trial of Reuchlin. Chapter 2 will deal with the long period, from the eleventh up to the early fourteenth century, which witnessed only occasional and for the most part unsystematic repression. The century of the greatest antiheretical efforts— roughly from the Council of Vienne (1311–12) to the Council of Constance (1414–18)—will be the subject of chapters 3 through 5. And chapter 6 will continue the discussion through the century that preceded the Reformation, on the whole a century of decline for the heresies and of relaxed vigilance for the Church.

The geographical limits are to some extent more arbitrary. It would be convenient if all the relevant geographical units—the linguistic areas, the political territories, the ecclesiastical provinces, and the provinces of the Dominican order—coincided with each other. Unfortunately they do not. The most clearly relevant units, though, are the ecclesiastical dioceses and provinces, which formed jurisdictional areas for all episcopal and most papal inquisitors.[28] Hence, those dioceses and provinces which can clearly be characterized as German will fall within the scope of this study: the provinces of Mainz, Cologne, Trier, Bremen, Magdeburg, Salzburg, and Riga, plus the dioceses of Bamberg, Camin, and Basel. Not coincidentally, it was for precisely these territories that papal inquisitors were delegated when they became established in Germany.[29] Bohemia will be included, but in a special category. Bohemia was an important part of the empire, and the homeland of certain of the late medieval emperors; Bohemian ecclesiastical affairs had great influence on those of Germany as a whole, especially in the fifteenth century. Yet antiheretical measures in Bohemia were in various ways different from those in other parts of the empire; inquisitors were delegated separately, and they had far more provocation to take action. Indeed, even the papacy viewed Bohemia as in a different category from the other imperial territories, as the grouping of inquisitors indicates. Thus, while it cannot be excluded from this study, it must be seen as a distinct case.

One more substantive question sheds some light on the general significance of this study: if it is misleading to speak of an Inquisition during the Middle Ages, why have generations of scholars, without exception, spoken as if there were such an institution? In part the reason may lie in the atypical use of the term "office of inquisition," which, as we have seen, occasionally suggests that contemporaries had an institution in mind. A more important factor no doubt was the rise of genuine institutions in the early modern period: the Spanish Inquisition and the Roman Inquisition. From the sixteenth century onward the term "office of inquisition" could realistically be applied in the sense of an agency, because institutional structures had by that time come into existence. It is at this point that the Latin phrase *officium inquisitionis* can appropriately be rendered as "office of the Inquisition." And there has no doubt been a tendency to interpret the term in its earlier employment as if it adumbrated the same kind of structure. In short, reference to a medieval Inquisition is largely an anachronism. But there is a third consideration that has also surely been significant. Those historians who have written about the general topic of medieval repression have inclined to focus particularly on the situation in southern Europe, where widespread and conspicuous heresy called for sustained and vigorous repression. As mentioned above, even in these areas there was no actual "Inquisition," but the continuity of prosecution in these regions easily leads to the false impression that such an agency existed. Hence, to rectify one's understanding of medieval repression it is perhaps necessary to turn away from those areas that have traditionally been seen as the heartland of heresy and antiheretical efforts—southern France and northern Italy—and to look at areas that are in many ways more typical. The following chapters will be a contribution toward this goal. The situation in Germany had its own peculiarities, and cannot claim to be representative in all respects of that throughout Europe. But in regard to those factors that we are now investigating, it was France and Italy that clearly were exceptional. By analyzing the repression of heresy in a country such as Germany one can hope at the very least to offset the imbalance created by undue attention to other lands.

2

Heresy and Repression in the High Middle Ages

While Germany was politically dominant during the high Middle Ages, it was not the center of cultural creativity or of religious innovation. Romanesque and Gothic styles were largely imported into Germany during this period from other areas of Europe, as were basic trends in literature. And during the same period, roughly the eleventh through the thirteenth century, heresy, too, entered German territories from lands to the south and west. Throughout this period, patterns of heresy in Germany seem to have paralleled those in other western European countries.

The first wave of heresy in high medieval Europe came in the first half of the eleventh century. The country most affected by this development was France, and within German territories the known incidents were confined mostly to the Rhineland, suggesting French influence.[1] Yet in 1051 a heretical community came to light as far to the east as Goslar, and showed its heterodoxy by its unwillingness to kill a chicken.[2] The sources reveal nothing more about the group's doctrine, but this ethical quirk was enough to convince the authorities that the heretics held unacceptable moral ideals, and that their presence would have a debilitating effect on Germany. Brought before the emperor, they were convicted and hanged. The reports from Germany, as from the rest of Europe, contain very little reliable information about the beliefs and practices of the heretics of this early period, and description and explanation of these movements rest largely on conjecture.[3]

For the rest of the eleventh century there was virtually no trace of heresy anywhere in western Europe. The usual assumption is that during this period dissident elements in the Church found an orthodox outlet for their reformist tendencies in the Gregorian reform movement.[4] But the eye of the hurricane soon passed, and in the early twelfth century a new wave of heretics arose, insistent on reforming the Church radically and stripping it of its superfluities. Again the main center of the turmoil was France, but various towns near the border between Germany and France, such as Liège and Trier, had their share of heretics.[5] The most important heretic during this period was Tanchelm, who operated in the diocese of Utrecht.[6] There is very little trustworthy information about his activities; for the most part one must rely on the attacks from his enemies, who charged him with blasphemies and inanities such as betrothing himself to a statue of the Virgin Mary and dispensing his bath water to his disciples as a relic. In all likelihood, he was a fervent but tactless reformer who aroused the animosity of the unreformed. After a stormy career and a period of imprisonment under the archbishop of Cologne, he was assassinated by a priest in 1115.

Apart from such sporadic incidents, heresy does not seem to have been an issue in Germany until the arrival of Cathars in the middle of the twelfth century.[7] Once again, Germany was not the primary field in which heresy developed; it was far more deeply entrenched in southern France and northern Italy. Imported from southeastern Europe, the Cathar religion was essentially a form of dualism, moral and metaphysical: moral in that the Cathar felt himself alien from the world about him, and sought to sever his connections with it and thus purify himself morally; metaphysical in that the Cathar explained the corruption of the world by a distinction between good and evil principles in the universe, that is, a good God, who had created the spiritual order, and an evil spirit, or Satan, who had created everything visible. For various reasons the Cathar religion was handicapped in its efforts to gain and preserve a following. Its doctrines were highly elaborate and speculative; its morality was rigid and demanding, at least for the leaders (or *perfecti*); and the sect was riddled with factions and rivalries, more than other medieval heresies. Yet in certain areas of Europe it flourished for a brief period, from the late twelfth through much of the thirteenth century.

In Germany, the Cathars appear to have gained a foothold only along the Rhine, and even there the heretics hardly flourished. Three of them were burned at Bonn in 1143 by the command of Count Otto of Rheineck, while suspects at nearby Cologne cleared themselves of charges by a judicial ordeal.[8] At about the same time, a group of Cathars in the vicinity of Cologne defended their heresy before an assembly of clergy, but the disputation was interrupted by certain overzealous people, who, despite the clergy's resistance, burned the heretics.[9] In 1163 Cologne was again the scene of executions, and not long afterward a Cathar community was discovered in the diocese of Mainz, where the heretics were revealed by a woman said to have been possessed by a demon. The Cathar bishop in this instance was converted, while other heretics were driven from the city.[10] In the long run, however, Catharism was unable to establish itself on German soil. There is no convincing evidence for the heresy's existence in Germany after the early thirteenth century.[11]

A more important sect in Germany, and in Europe generally, was that of the Waldensians.[12] Like the Cathars, whom they abhorred, the Waldensians grew into a well-developed sect, formally organized and intended to supplant the established Church. But neither their doctrine nor their moral code was so elaborate as those of the Cathars. Fundamentally, they believed that they alone represented the Church in its pure form, as it had come down from apostolic times, without the taint of superfluity and corruption. Founded in the late twelfth century by Waldo, a merchant of Lyon, the Waldensians had given new form to the evangelical movements of the high Middle Ages. Because of their vigorous missionary work in the thirteenth century, they spread throughout much of western Europe. By the end of that century they seem to have been established at least in the southern parts of Germany and in the eastern German territories, from Pomerania to Austria.[13] There are some indications that the German Waldensians formed a distinct organization, alongside corresponding organizations of French and Italian Waldensians.[14] The Austrian heretics maintained close relations with their Italian brethren; it is impossible to tell whether the Waldensians in other German territories allied themselves with the Italian group, or whether (as one historian suggests) the German branch was mixed in its doctrines and affiliations.[15] Whatever the case may be, this sect was far more cohesive than other heresies. Waldensian leaders, or masters, traveled about among their congregations, preaching, hearing confessions, collecting funds, and no doubt helping to maintain a degree of uniformity in Waldensian doctrine and practice. In later years, when they came under serious attack, Waldensian groups not uncommonly took in refugees from other Waldensian congregations. To be sure, the cohesion should not be exaggerated. There was considerable variation in doctrine, particularly among the Waldensians in remote areas of northeastern Germany.[16] Yet in contrast to other heretical groups, the Waldensians seem to have been tight knit.

Prior to the rise of the Waldensians, the Church in Germany had been relatively lenient with heretics, and when burnings occurred they usually were carried out at the instigation of secular authorities or of the people. In the late twelfth and early thirteenth centuries, however, popes began to encourage bishops throughout Europe to take more stringent measures against heretics.[17] These admonitions were not wholly without effect in Germany. The records tell of eighty heretics burned on one day in Strassburg, in 1211 or 1212.[18] Again in the following decade there were sporadic trials.[19] But the crucial step that resulted in zealous persecution through much of Europe was the initiation of inquisitorial proceedings under Gregory IX (1227–41). In the early 1230s, antiheretical measures began in various areas of Europe, notably France and Italy, when Gregory delegated special papal inquisitors to aid the bishops in their pursuit of heretics.[20] During the same period, antiheretical proceedings occurred in the German towns of Strassburg and Steding. In the latter, action against the allegedly heretical townsmen ended in a devastating crusade against them in 1234; the brutal repression appears to have been motivated entirely by a desire to keep the residents from asserting their independence of their lords.[21]

Th most zealous German inquisitor sanctioned by Gregory IX was the infamous Conrad of Marburg, who worked in the region of the Middle Rhine during the 1230s.[22] He is said to have accepted evidence from all sources, indiscriminately, without verification. When he summoned a person before his court, he peremptorily demanded that the accused confess his guilt, reveal his fellow heretics, and have his head shaved as a form of penance. Anyone who maintained his innocence was sent to the stake, with the meager comfort that if he really was innocent he would receive a martyr's crown in heaven. Conrad was supported in these efforts by the bishop of Hildesheim, who even solicited secular authorities to carry out a crusade against heretics. Despite the willingness of a handful of secular rulers to participate, the crusade never materialized. At length, members of the German hierarchy endeavored to end the carnage being carried out by Conrad himself. Although the archbishop of Mainz exhorted him to moderate his practice, Conrad proceeded to the dangerous step of accusing a nobleman, the count of Seyn, of heresy. Among other offenses against the faith, the count was supposed to have ridden on a crab, presumably in the course of some diabolical rite. Both Conrad and the court were called to a synod to determine the justice of the charges. The archbishop of Trier declared there that the accusations were groundless, and shortly afterward Conrad was assassinated, perhaps at the instigation of the count of Seyn. Later, certain associates of the inquisitor were likewise murdered.

The case of Conrad of Marburg is often cited as an example of how the Rhenish archbishops resisted the establishment of a papal Inquisition in Germany, since they protested against Conrad's methods, both to the inquisitor himself and to the pope, and they later worked to thwart Conrad's actions against the count of Seyn.[23] Yet the sources give no indication whatsoever that these archbishops were in principle opposed to inquisitorial prosecution of genuine heretics, or that they resented encroachment on their jurisdiction. Indeed, there is reason to believe that Conrad had a commission from the archbishop of Mainz to proceed against heretics even before he received letters from the pope recognizing his labors.[24] One historian who has analyzed Conrad's activities in detail concludes that the inquisitor cannot have held a papal commission, because he submitted ultimately to episcopal authority rather than claim independent judicial competence.[25] There is in fact no firm evidence that the pope did anything more than lend his support to Conrad's activities as an episcopal inquisitor. What is clear is that Conrad was a prototype of the inquisitor whose lack of discrimination led local authorities to curb his zeal. There is absolutely no evidence that Conrad's jurisdictional claims or his fundamental mission stirred the prelates' resentment. Instead, the sources suggest that the cause of offense was his arbitrary mode of procedure. In reacting against this arbitrariness, the hierarchy was not alone; the people at large, according to one of the chroniclers, supported Conrad in his work against heretics, though they resented his condemnation of faithful Catholics.[26]

During the same period, a similarly indiscriminate zealot, Robert le Bougre, was at work in France, and like Conrad of Marburg, he aroused enmity through his dubious procedures.[27] Robert clearly was a papal appointee. In his case, as in that of Conrad, the main complaint appears to have been that the inquisitor failed to distinguish between the genuinely heretical and those who had been accused falsely. Conrad is said to have demanded confession from all who were charged, no matter on what grounds, and is supposed to have had executed all those who maintained their innocence; similarly, Robert is said to have had a kind of magical card that he held over subjects to make them confess.[28] In both cases, the evident result was to bring disrepute to inquisitorial proceedings generally.

In Germany, as in France, the flurry of repressive activity in the

1230s was followed by a lull.[29] Proceedings in Germany were apparently resumed later than in France, in the 1260s, possibly on the initiative of Pope Urban IV, though the sources for this period are too scant to reconstruct the context of these inquisitorial efforts. There were especially vigorous measures against heretics in the southeastern territories.[30] After the 1260s there is little indication of prosecution for roughly half a century. In the meantime, one may assume that the Waldensians persisted, spread, and perhaps even flourished.

The role of emperors and kings in repression of German heresy during the high Middle Ages was apparently minimal. Unlike the French monarchs, the German rulers do not seem to have seen heresy as an excuse for crusades and confiscations.[31] As was mentioned already, Henry II was responsible for the execution of heretics at Goslar in the mid-eleventh century, but for motives that the sources do not disclose. In the later twelfth and thirteenth centuries, nearly every one of the German monarchs was concerned more with Italian than with German affairs, or at least was so much distracted with Italy that attention to Germany necessarily was reduced. Most of the Hohenstaufen emperors issued sporadic measures against heresy, and much of their legislation applied to Germany as well as to the southern parts of the empire. Yet the impulse to action came almost entirely from Italian circumstances, and the legislation was clearly directed primarily against Italian heretics. Furthermore, as Hermann Köhler argued persuasively many years ago, none of these rulers proceeded of his own accord against heretics. To the extent that they joined in the struggle against heresy, they did so to win the support of the popes, or to placate the Curia; and when political circumstances did not call for an alliance with the papacy, the emperors almost never took antiheretical measures.[32]

Frederick Barbarossa exemplifies this pattern nicely.[33] In 1153, when Frederick sought the imperial crown from the pope, he received a promise that he would obtain this dignity only on the condition that he aid the pope against the demagogic and allegedly heretical Arnold of Brescia. And it was only after Arnold's execution that Pope Hadrian crowned Frederick as emperor. For several years thereafter, however, Frederick did nothing against heretics. On numerous occasions he issued constitutions and decrees for the northern Italian cities, which were notorious as centers of heresy, but he consistently refrained from requiring that they uproot their heretical populations. In his negotiations with Venice in 1154, he made provisions for dealing with crimes of all sorts, but did not mention heresy. In the provincial councils of Montpellier in 1162 and Tours in 1163, Alexander III fostered the repression of heresy. But by this time Frederick himself was in conflict with the pope, and at the latter council was excommunicated. When the third Lateran Council declared new sanctions against heresy in 1179, Frederick made no response. It was only in 1184 that the pope finally induced Frederick to lend his support to the battle against heretics. In that year Lucius III issued three edicts against heresy at Verona, and Frederick not only declared his consent to these measures but proclaimed an imperial law by which heretics were subject to ban and outlawry. The motives for this cooperation with Lucius are transparent. At precisely this time Frederick was attempting to secure imperial control over the long-disputed inheritance of Matilda of Tuscany; he was striving to obtain the consecration of the Hohenstaufen candidate for the archbishopric of Salzburg; and he needed papal consent to elevate Henry VI to the rank of emperor. For support in all these projects he was willing to make concessions to the pope. Under papal pressure he agreed to allow Duke Henry the Lion to return from exile; he pledged that the next year he would undertake a crusade; and in the same context he declared his support for the effort against heresy. But although he did in fact recall Duke Henry from exile, and he did go on crusade, there is no evidence whatsoever that he actually enforced the measures against heresy. And the same pattern recurred, *mutatis mutandis*, with almost all of Frederick's successors.

The only significant exception to this general Hohenstaufen policy was the thirteenth-century monarch Henry VII.[34] Until his rebellion against his father, Frederick II, Henry served as king of Germany; while his father devoted his attention primarily to the southern part of the empire, Henry ruled in the north. But unlike his father—who, when it was politically expedient, did a great deal toward the repression of heretics—Henry appears to have been reluctant to join the antiheretical action of his contemporaries. True, in legislation of 1224 he did provide that heretics, like sorcerers, should be burned at the stake. But when Gregory IX admonished him in 1231 to make himself pleasing to God by extirpating heretics in Germany, he evidently did not respond to the plea. And when the newly appointed inquisitors proposed that the property of condemned heretics be shared among the inquisitors themselves and the king, bishop, and municipal authorities, Henry refused to accept this arrangement; instead, he provided that the heretics' inheritance should go to their rightful heirs, and their feudal holdings and moveable property to their lords. Again, in 1233, Gregory exhorted

the king to take up arms against the enemies of the faith, but Henry
did nothing of the sort. Instead, he did his best to thwart the fanatical
zeal of Conrad of Marburg and the bishop of Hildesheim. In cooperation with the German episcopacy generally, Henry terminated the
proceedings of Conrad against the count of Seyn, and nipped in the
bud the plans for a crusade against heretics. By the time he took
these measures, Henry had already decided to rebel against his father,
and his recalcitrance spoiled any chance that he might have had of
papal support for his rebellion; Gregory IX wrote explicitly to members of the German hierarchy to indicate his displeasure with Henry's
position. Perhaps, as Hermann Köhler suggests, Henry had already
realized that he could not obtain such an alliance, and sought instead
to solidify his position with the German bishops, who were resisting
arbitrary inquisitorial proceedings. Yet it does not follow, as Köhler
proceeds to argue, that Henry was protecting the jurisdictional interests or the national pride of the episcopacy.[35] Indeed, there is direct
evidence that Henry, like other secular and ecclesiastical authorities
in Germany, was willing to support (or at least allow) judicially
proper action against genuine heretics. Early in 1234, shortly after he
had impeded Conrad of Marburg and the bishop of Hildesheim, Henry
issued a declaration encouraging all those who were so authorized to
work diligently against heresy, but admonishing them to uphold
justice in their prosecution.[36]

In summation, the high Middle Ages witnessed the arrival of
organized heresy in Germany, the short-lived movement toward
Catharism, and the implantation of Waldensianism. None of the
sources indicates how widespread these heresies became during this
era; the question can better be dealt with in the context of later trials,
which do furnish at least rough and partial statistics. Whatever the
extent of the heretical population, heresy does not appear to have
been perceived as a major problem, and efforts to extirpate it were
sporadic and halfhearted. Even at this early date, arbitrary inquisitorial measures provoked opposition, and the flurry of indiscriminate
trials in the 1230s was followed by a sort of moratorium. It was only
in the fourteenth century that systematic antiheretical efforts got
under way. And when vigorous prosecution began, it was at first
directed not so much against the classic sects of the high Middle
Ages as against a new species of heresy—that of the Free Spirit, or of
the so-called beghards and beguines.

3

The War Against
Beghards and Beguines

A papal bull from the late fourteenth century indicated that over the course of that century scarcely a year had passed without the burning of beghards and beguines somewhere in Germany.[1] An overstatement, no doubt, but nonetheless a poignant reminder of passions and conflicts that did indeed stir the ecclesiastical life of fourteenth-century Germany. Between the ecumenical Council of Vienne in the early fourteenth century and that of Constance in the early fifteenth, the German Church carried on what one might refer to, with only minimal risk of exaggeration, as a hundred years' war against beghards and beguines. In France or Italy, the action against these groups might seem less significant, but in Germany this kind of prosecution was exceptional.

BEGHARDS, BEGUINES, AND FREE SPIRITS

Oddly, there was confusion at the time about which of two groups was the genuine object of attack—the beghards and beguines, or the heretics of the Free Spirit. In retrospect it is clear that these two groups overlapped but were by no means identical. To contemporaries, however, the distinction was a difficult one to keep in mind.

Unlike Waldensianism, the heresy of the Free Spirit was not the doctrine of a fixed and more or less coordinated sect, but simply a type of radical mysticism that developed and spread by personal

contacts and by the dissemination of literature.² These heretics held
that it was possible for them to become perfect while still on earth—
the logical consequence being that after attaining perfection they no
longer needed the Church as a mediator between themselves and
God. The heresy's origins are obscure: it developed in Germany
sometime in the later thirteenth century, and spread particularly
among the semireligious communities of beghards and beguines.

The terms "beghard" and "beguine" apply to communities of men
and women, respectively, who lived religious lives without taking
vows that bound them to the rules of an order. The words also refer,
especially in the case of men, to isolated individuals who went about
begging and leading (or claiming to lead) religious lives. In either
event, the movement of beghards and beguines constituted an interesting experiment. Its roots can be traced back to the movement of
the "apostolic life," which, as early as the twelfth century, had inspired men and women throughout western Europe to renounce their
property, to live off alms, and frequently to wander about preaching.³
Most of the important religious developments of the later Middle
Ages, whether heretical or orthodox, owed something to this apostolic
or evangelical revival: the Waldensians, the mendicant orders, and
even the Rhenish mystics of the fourteenth century. The distinctive
feature of the beghards and beguines, however, is that they sought
to carry out this kind of apostolic life by adopting a role that was
half religious and half lay: religious because of the abandonment of
ordinary means of sustenance, the adherence to communal life, and
the adoption of special habits, and lay because the adherents took no
vows. It was a bold experiment; not surprisingly, the Church had
difficulty accepting it. It violated a provision of the fourth Lateran
Council (1215), which had proscribed new *religiones*, or forms of
religious community. Furthermore, it gave a religious role to laymen
without full assurance that they would be controlled adequately.
And there was the inevitable protest that those beghards and beguines
who went about begging were competing with those who actually
needed to beg for sustenance. In the long run, however, the surprising
fact is not so much the bias against the movement and the resultant
persecution of the fourteenth century, but rather the eventual victory
that the beghards and beguines and their supporters won. While the
late medieval Church may in some respects have been a bastion of
closed-mindedness, it is worth bearing in mind that in the course of
time it went beyond the fourth Lateran Council in accepting innovations that made for greater diversity in religious life.⁴

The reasons for the conflict during the fourteenth century were complex. As already mentioned, there was ample reason for the Church to be suspicious of beghards and beguines as such, but to compound the difficulty these groups became hopelessly confused with the heretics of the Free Spirit. Being vernacular and nontechnical terms, "beghard" and "beguine" came to be used in an extremely broad variety of senses, for various forms of community, for itinerant beggars, and in general for religious enthusiasts of all kinds. When the Council of Vienne condemned the heresy of the Free Spirit, however, it used the same terms for adherents of the heresy, as if beghards and beguines were by definition heretical. Doubtless many beghards and beguines did incline toward some variety of radical mysticism, but the council's use of the terms was flagrantly misleading. In legal and inquisitorial usage, therefore, the words acquired a highly specific meaning: a beghard or beguine was someone who subscribed to a specified set of heterodox principles. The result of this ambiguity was disastrous, for anyone who could be labeled a beghard or beguine in the loose sense might become suspect of being a beghard or beguine in the excessively strict sense, and hence would be subject to inquisitorial proceedings. This confusion has obvious implications for the historian: though it is reasonably easy to trace the history of prosecutions directed against beghards and beguines, it is difficult in the extreme to extrapolate from this a history of the actual heresy of the Free Spirit.

The decrees of condemnation formulated at the Council of Vienne have been analyzed in detail elsewhere, and need not be discussed here extensively, but they are too important for the present study to neglect them entirely.[5] The first document, *Cum de quibusdam*, was directed primarily against the communities of beguines, which were viewed as irregular religious groups, founded in violation of the norms set down by the fourth Lateran Council. Consequently, the offending houses were to be dissolved. The decree also accused the beguines of entertaining heresies, but reported their heretical doctrines only vaguely. The second decree, *Ad nostrum*, was more specific in its allegations of heresy. It accused both the beghards and the beguines of holding that they could attain a state of perfection in this life, and that once they had done so they no longer were bound to the Church's authority or to moral norms.

Historians have disagreed about the extent to which these heretics challenged conventional morality and threatened the ecclesiastical order.[6] There clearly were mystics who felt that union with God would liberate them from moral law, but in the Pauline sense: a soul that had become essentially holy had no need of artificial commandments and regulations because it was not included toward sin.[7] There may have been some who took the further step of claiming that even if they performed objectively immoral acts they would not be committing sin. At least one beghard enunciated such doctrines in an extreme form under interrogation. He went so far as to claim that fornication on the part of a beghard, far from being sinful, had the power to restore a girl's virginity.[8] Whether the heretics actually engaged in libertine behavior, however, is an entirely different question. It would be hazardous to give a universal negative answer, but one must emphasize that no truly convincing evidence exists for antinomianism among the beghards and beguines, and that antinomian principles were surely not an integral element of their doctrine.

In any case, one cannot claim that beghards and beguines presented a threat to the late medieval Church as great as that of the Waldensians. Heretics of the Free Spirit were even more of an elite than Cathars; their mysticism was obscure and lacking in broad, popular appeal, and by some accounts they underwent long and arduous periods as novices before they received full partnership in the heresy.[9] Furthermore, the heresy appears to have been exclusively an urban phenomenon, as was the movement of beguines among whom this doctrine tended to spread. Beghards and beguines may have posed a threat to the organization of the Church even when they were orthodox, since the Church's control over their lives was at most a loose one and their form of community was not fully accepted. Yet this threat did not typically extend to matters of doctrine; the extraregular communities do not seem to have developed commonly into genuine centers of resistance to the Church. Whereas the Waldensians challenged the Church as such, beghards and beguines usually challenged only a decree of the fourth Lateran Council. Even if they flirted occasionally with radical mysticism, their potential for posing a serious challenge to doctrine and authority was not equal to that of the Waldensians.

THE COURSE OF PROSECUTION

During the early years of the fourteenth century, there was synodal legislation against beghards and beguines in several Rhineland cities.[10] When actual prosecution began, it centered for some time in the Rhenish ecclesiastical provinces, and remained in the hands of the episcopacy. Between 1317 and 1319, the archbishop of Strassburg proceeded against beguines and especially beghards, forcing many either to flee from the town or to abjure, while many others went to the stake. Even at this early date, extreme tension between the secular clergy and the mendicant orders led to the widespread opinion that the teritaries (groups of men or, more often, women associated with the mendicants) should be classed as beguines and forced to disband.[11] Other Rhenish cities witnessed similar measures in the early part of the century.[12] The trial of Meister Eckhart, which began at Cologne in 1326 and ended posthumously three years later, must also be seen in the context of these measures against radical mysticism, though the connections between this Dominican mystic and the others suspected of heresy appear tenuous.[13] To some degree the antiheretical momentum spread eastward; in 1318 the bishop of Regensburg dissolved a community of beghards which had been established in a nearby forest, and heretics prosecuted in Austria during this era may have included beghards and beguines.[14] The concern with these groups persisted over the next few decades in a series of sporadic and more or less unconnected trials, directed occasionally against communities of beguines, but more often against individual male subjects, who apparently did not belong to religious communities, but who seem to have been viewed as beghards in some sense of the term.[15] The records from these early years are not always as explicit as one might wish about the character of the heresies. For example, reports of a trial at Cologne tell more about the heretics' nocturnal orgies in subterranean chambers than about their doctrines, though it is likely that the subjects were beghards and beguines.[16]

Perhaps the most significant result of this concern about beghards and beguines is that it led to the establishment of papal inquisitors. Until the middle of the fourteenth century, virtually all heresy trials in Germany were conducted either by secular authorities or by episcopal courts. Only three inquisitors in Germany definitely held papal commissions, all of them in the far eastern territories, while Conrad of Marburg received some papal sanction, and two other inquisitors may have been thus empowered.[17] In these early years there was no regularity whatsoever in appointment. In 1348 another inquisitor was delegated—John Schadeland, who clearly held a papal commission. But although he demonstrated great zeal in collecting the funds needed for his office, there is no record of what measures, if any, he took against heretics.[18]

The significant dates, then, in the establishment of papal inquisitors for Germany fall in the later fourteenth century. In 1364 Pope Urban V appointed four Dominicans as German inquisitors, and exhorted the native authorities to support them.[19] Five years later the emperor, Charles IV, issued a series of edicts taking these inquisitors under his protection and assigning them various tasks and privileges. The emperor appointed commissions of aristocratic guardians to protect the inquisitors, and laid down fines that were to be levied for violations. To aid in their labors, he empowered the inquisitors to appoint notaries, and made specific provisions for the houses that they confiscated from beghard and beguine communities. Furthermore, he encouraged them to devote themselves to the task of removing from circulation certain pernicious vernacular tracts—"vicious, erroneous, and infected with the leprosy of heresy"—which laymen were reading out of an inordinate desire for knowledge.[20] The last of these directives is important in the history of censorship, serving as it did as recent precedent for the control over printed materials when printing became widespread roughly a century later. These measures not only assured imperial support for the inquisitors; because the proceeds from the sale of beguines' houses were to go partly to the municipal governments, the aid of local authorities in prosecution of these groups was in effect solicited.

The most essential step came in 1372, when Gregory XI assured continuity of inquisitorial personnel by entrusting the routine appointment of five inquisitors to the Dominican master and provincial for southern Germany.[21] This measure was revised in 1399, perhaps because of factional conflicts among the south German Dominicans; authority to appoint inquisitors was now transferred to the provincial for northern Germany.[22] From the late fourteenth century on, inquisitors were in fact delegated with regularity, well into the Counter Reformation. Appointments were soon being issued not by the German Dominican authorities, but by the Dominican general in Rome, though the choice of inquisitors was still no doubt guided by the counsel of German superiors.[23] In addition, there were some non-Dominicans who on rare occasions obtained papal commissions as inquisitors in Germany, though for purposes of this study the role of such agents is negligible.[24] In any case, there were papal inquisitors regularly present in most if not all regions of Germany during the century and a half before the Reformation.

Soon after the delegation of papal inquisitors, certain of these men began an intense and widespread campaign against beghards and beguines that lasted from 1366 to 1375. Most of the trials in this campaign were the work of one particularly energetic papal inquisitor, Walter Kerlinger, who operated in the northeastern part of Germany: Thuringia, Saxony, and adjacent areas.[25] Between 1367 and 1370,

Kerlinger and his subordinates pursued heretics in Erfurt, Mühl-hausen, Misenach, Magdeburg, Nordhausen, Lüneburg, Rostock, probably Bremen, and no doubt numerous other cities. The emperor himself credited Kerlinger with successfully exterminating beghards and beguines in the provinces of Magdeburg and Bremen, and in the territories of Thuringia, Saxony, and Hesse, as well as certain other parts of Germany.[26] From the evidence that remans, one may tenta-tively conclude that the proceedings during these years were largely confined to the northeastern territories. It is possible that inquisitorial work in the province of Cologne was similarly vigorous; one Domini-can chronicler remarked that, according to inquisitorial records, heresy trials were centered in both Cologne and Erfurt.[27] Yet the preponder-ance of extant documents pertain to Kerlinger's work in the north-east, while only fragmentary records survive from the northwestern and southwestern parts of Germany, and none at all from the south-east.[28] It is not surprising, then, that after Kerlinger's death in 1373 that was little further action against heretics. The demise of this important inquisitor was, to be sure, not the only reason for the slackening of zeal. The Franciscans at Strassburg, whose tertiaries came under attack in the course of prosecutions against the beguines, appealed the matter to Rome, and soon afterward, in 1374, the pope issued a bull urging caution and discrimination in the prosecution of religious communities.[29] The campaign had been directed primarily against communities of females, whether beguines or mendicant tertiaries, and in many instances it was no doubt difficult to determine whether such groups had violated disciplinary regulations or doctrinal norms; in neither discipline nor doctrine were the bounds of accep-tability altogether clear. The pope's bull of 1374, then, evidently served to cool the fervor of inquisitors who, in compliance with earlier papal decrees, had exercised their rigor against any communi-ties whose practice or doctrine seemed questionable.

The reaction against this campaign appears to have been firm. One trial in 1375 at Bern involved only a single beghard, and the court in this case was not papal but episcopal.[30] There were a few sporadic cases in following years: an episcopal trial of a single beghard at Eichstätt in 1381, and the trial of another beghard in the same year by the municipal council at Augsburg.[31] It seems to have been typical that major campaigns centered on conventual beguines, perhaps be-cause they were readily ascertainable and thus served as easy game for itinerant inquisitors, but that during times of lessened zeal the authorities' attention was more commonly aroused by isolated beg-hards. Apart from such minor incidents, the beghards and beguines appear to have enjoyed a respite for the eighteen years following the bull of 1374. Granted, a papal bull from the end of the century suggests that prosecution had been consistently vigorous; yet this is surely a broad overstatement.[32] Unless the pattern of extant records is wholly misleading, inquisitorial vigor seems to have abated until the end of the century.

Prosecution revived during the papacy of Boniface IX (1389–1404). This pontiff's own attitude toward beghards and beguines was constantly in flux; though suspicious of their orthodoxy, he was easily swayed by the reports of their supporters and detractors. Depending on which of these groups had most recently communicated with him, he would either distinguish carefully between "good" and "bad" beguines or castigate them all without evident discrimination.[33] There is some reason to think that papal inquisitors played a major role in trials at this time. Though sources are fragmentary, it is likely that certain little-known papal delegates were involved in trials during the 1390s in Rostock, Austria, and Cologne.[34] Yet the only papal inquisitor whose activity can be traced in any detail during this period is Eylard Schoneveld. This inquisitor began his career in the 1390s in the diocese of Utrecht, and at the turn of the century conducted an inquisitorial tour of several Baltic towns before returning to the Low Countries.[35] Once again, as during the campaign of 1366–75, initiative appears to have lain primarily with a single zealot. Yet none of the papal inquisitors at this time matched Walter Kerlinger in energy, and in virtually every case they proceeded against individual beghards rather than groups.

In the meantime, however, a regional campaign against conventual beguines was developing in the southwest. In various ways it differed from the cases prosecuted under Boniface IX. First, while the action against beghards and beguines under Boniface IX generally took place on the initiative of papal inquisitors, the series of trials that began slightly later in the southwestern territories was primarily the work of bishops and their agents. Second, the subjects in the earlier wave of prosecution were more often than not individual beghards, whereas the judges in the southwest directed their efforts primarily against communities of beguines. Third, the trials in the former campaign ended most commonly with condemnation and execution, while the goal sought in the southwest was dissolution of the irregular religious communities. Fourth, the charges raised in the earlier campaign were almost invariably those of heresy in a strict sense, specifically the heresy of the Free Spirit, while the heresy charge was less dominant in the cases in the southwestern territories.

An understanding of the situation in the southwest requires some background information.[36] In general, the conventual beguines in the later fourteenth century seem to have been immune to prosecution, largely because during that period (especially, no doubt, after the action of 1366–75) many of them became Franciscan or Dominican tertiaries. The protection they obtained was twofold. First, by accepting a rule approved by the Church, these groups cleared themselves of the disciplinary charge that their communities were established in violation of ecclesiastical law. Second, by placing themselves under the supervision and patronage of Franciscans or Dominicans, they reduced the chances that they would become suspect of heresy. The safeguard, however, did not always work. Particularly when the Franciscans themselves fell into disfavor in a diocese or community, their tertiaries were easy targets for attack. Thus, in the late fourteenth and early fifteenth centuries, a movement to abolish the beguines' houses began in and around Basel, with attention directed mainly against the tertiaries.

The first indications of conflict came in the diocese of Constance, in 1396, where several times the Franciscan tertiaries came under attack from those who did not differentiate between them and the reprobate beguines.[37] In Basel, the prelude to battle occurred in 1400, when two members of the clergy began to preach against beguines.[38] After these early rumblings, the storm broke in 1405, when the beguines' enemies accused them of heresy, and the bishop undertook an inquisition to investigate the charge. Fortunes shifted frequently in the course of the struggle, and at one point the beguines attained victory, when the Franciscan pope Alexander V was elected in 1409 and took them under his protection. In the following year, though, Alexander died, an antibeguine faction seized municipal power, and a series of scandals in Basel diminished popular esteem for the Franciscans. Powerless to resist the attacks, the Franciscans no longer tried to defend their former associates. Soon afterward the beguines were forced to leave the town, and their property was confiscated. Many of them fled to nearby towns, where they received little welcome. In places such as Strassburg and Mainz, there was further prosecution, based either on the practices or on the beliefs of the beguines.[39]

Within a few years, however, the basic charges against beghards and beguines were for the most part put to rest, when it became clear that one needed to distinguish between those communities that were orthodox and under proper control and those that lacked such qualifications. The issue came before the Council of Constance, which after debate gave its sanction to the notion of semireligious houses.[40] The council did not, of course, lend its approval to the heresy of the Free Spirit, but by this time there seems to have been little conviction that beghards and beguines were in fact generally heretical. By putting an end to the remaining accusation—the charge of religious irregularity that had loomed so large during the crisis of the southwest—the Church introduced an era of toleration for conventual beghards and beguines. Prosecution of isolated beghards and beguines continued in sporadic fashion throughout the fifteenth century, but it becomes increasingly difficult to ascertain the sense in which the subjects were in fact "beghards" or "beguines."[41] Neither frequent nor momentous, the later trials demonstrate that after the Council of Constance the heresy of the Free Spirit and the issue of beghards and beguines had become very much incidental concerns.[42]

Is it correct to speak of inquisitorial campaigns during these years directed specifically against the beghards and beguines? Or were these groups merely one target of attack, alongside other heretics? As following chapters will indicate, there were other heretics who came under attack during the fourteenth century, but, with only two possible exceptions, the inquisitors in these instances were different from those who prosecuted beghards and beguines.[43] In other words, there were other campaigns that occurred alongside those against beghards and beguines, distinct from these latter campaigns. It is clear that the popes intended repressive efforts expressly against beghards and beguines; virtually all papal and imperial documents of this time singled out these groups as special objects for investigation.[44] To be sure, these documents are in part stereotyped. Innocent VI's bull of 1353 lamented that "this pestiferous madness of those who are called beghards is said to have arisen in parts of Germany, at the devil's instigation," and this wording recurred in 1368 and 1396.[45] Yet standard rhetoric of this sort is not the only indication that beghards and beguines stood in the forefront of attention. References to the decrees of Vienne, and to the customs and habits of these communities, make the intention of these edicts clear.[46] It is only rarely that other heresies entered into the question, and the only other major heresy in Germany at this time, Waldensianism, was never explicitly mentioned in any surviving papal or imperial document. Granted, once inquisitors were delegated they could proceed against any kind of heretic. There is evidence that on certain occasions Walter Kerlinger was directed to work against flagellants, to investigate a bishop who was preaching fatalistic doctrines, and even to condemn certain "heresies" in the North German law code, the

Sachsenspiegel.[47] But there is no record of his having complied with these directions, and even if he did, the campaigns were only incidental diversions from his work against beghards and beguines.[48] Or at least against persons he thought of as beghards and beguines; one cannot conclude that only genuine beghards and beguines, in any strict sense of the terms, were swept up in the inquisitorial net. Some of the victims may have been merely religious eccentrics, labeled beghards because of inquisitorial prejudices and methods of inquiry.[49] Others may have been members of other sects, though there is no concrete evidence of this suspicion. The essential point is that the inquisitorial net was lowered mainly to capture one species of heretic.

It is furthermore interesting to observe the connection between the character of these campaigns and the lack of a genuine institutional Inquisition. For lack of institutional restraints, the individual inquisitors were left more or less free to decide for themselves precisely what constituted a beghard or beguine, and which members of these classes were culpable. The confusion that ensued is reflected in the vacillation of the popes during this period. The pattern seen in the pontificate or Boniface IX seems to have been typical: popes appear to have been swayed continually by the conflicting reports they received from north of the Alps. Upon hearing of the dangers of beghards and beguines, presumably from inquisitors, the popes would issue directives urging their elimination. Other Germans would then send protests, assuring the popes that innocent groups of pious women were suffering repression, whereupon the pontiffs would advise greater discretion in the pursuit of justice. The papal inquisitors were by no means alone in the attack on beghards and beguines, but after their establishment in Germany they do seem to have carried out the majority of trials, and while bishops occasionally indulged in repression, one also finds cases in which the bishops served as restraining forces.[50] Perhaps the perplexity would have occurred even if there had been an institution, but it is at least conceivable that a tight-knit and firmly directed Inquisition could have acted with greater consistency, and perhaps even with more realism.

PROCEDURES

For an understanding of how inquisitors succeeded in representing beghards, beguines, and other persons as Free Spirits, it is necessary to examine certain aspects of inquisitorial procedure. When inquisitors examined suspects, they did not simply ask whatever questions came to mind, but would rely on a standard inquisitorial formulary, or interrogatory.[51] Inquisitors' handbooks usually supplied such interrogatories, along with relevant bulls and canons, treatises on the powers of inquisitors, descriptions of heresies, and instructions for conducting trials.[52] There was nothing unusual about the use of an interrogatory; during the period under consideration such forms were commonly employed in both secular and ecclesiastical courts, and were adhered to with some degree of strictness.[53] When the questions concerned matters of faith, however, there was a special danger that the interrogatories might serve as means for stereotyping the accused, particularly when the matters in question were subtle or obscure.

One of the decrees of the Council of Vienne, the canon *Ad nostrum*, commonly served as such an interrogatory in fourteenth- and fifteenth-century Germany. Used in this way, the decree furnished a Procrustean bed on which heretics and eccentrics were fitted to the description of heretics condemned at Vienne. For example, the eight articles of this decree were incorporated in an interrogatory used in 1374 at Strassburg in an endeavor to portray conventual beguines as heretics.[54] At Basel, in 1405, one beguine was accused of adherence to the "eight articles," but she denied that she knew anything about them.[55] Even when they did not rely heavily on the articles of *Ad nostrum*, inquisitors sometimes showed familiarity with the decree. For instance, during the interrogation of Constantine of Arnhem in 1350, the examiners asked him about the "grace and perfection" that he claimed for himself as the basis of his power to absolve others from sin, but they did not probe further along these lines.[56] In one instance an inquisitor drew an item from this decree even in a trial for Waldensianism: after questioning his subject at great length about Waldensian doctrines, the inquisitor posed a question drawn directly from *Ad nostrum*—"whether a person in this life can attain such a degree of perfection that he is no longer able to sin." The subject's answer was in no way heretical, though it might be construed as nonsensical: "He responded that he believed that even if a person were perfect he would still be able to sin and to commit sins." Unless the inquisitor had simply turned to the wrong page of his manual, he must have thought it possible that a Waldensian might fall into the wholly different heresy of the Free Spirit, but his subject bungled his way out of this suspicion.[57]

Much more typical was the use of *Ad nostrum* in three trials of individual beghards: the case of Berthold of Rohrbach at Speyer, that of John Hartmann at Erfurt, and that of Conrad Kannler at Eichstätt. Berthold of Rohrbach had already appeared before a tribunal at Würzburg in the mid-fourteenth century, and had abjured certain errors: that Christ doubted on the cross whether he was saved, and uttered curses on his own mother and on the ground that soaked up his blood.[58] After his abjuration Berthold was released, and fled to Speyer, where he again proclaimed these heresies. Supposedly he added three more doctrines to his repertoire before falling prey to an inquisitor at Speyer. The three new doctrines were entirely different in character from those he is supposed to have abjured earlier. The previous tenets were no doubt eccentric and blasphemous, and could easily suggest heretical implications, but had nothing to do with any of the standard heresies of the time. The new doctrines, on the other hand, savored more distinctly of heresy. Berthold supposedly claimed now that man can reach such a degree of perfection in this life that he need not fast or pray—a clear conflation of the first two articles in *Ad nostrum*. In addition, the inquisitor charged Berthold with certain standard anticlerical and antiecclesiastical doctrines. Berthold may have joined a group of radical beghards after his abjuration in Würzburg and adopted their doctrines. It is far more likely, however, that the inquisitor in Speyer drew the new doctrines from a formulary, and imputed them to his subject.

The inquisitor who interrogated John Hartmann was Walter Kerlinger, who made more extensive and more explicit use of *Ad nostrum*.[59] The inquisitor asked his subject about each of the articles in this decree, and in each case Hartmann affirmed his belief in the article, expressing himself (as the protocol would have us believe) in the exact words of *Ad nostrum*. As Robert Lerner has remarked, it would be interesting to know whether the heretic could have listed these articles if the inquisitor had not supplied them.[60] Although the decree furnished the basic framework for interrogation, the heretic in this instance refused to be bound to it, and discoursed extemporaneously at great length on the wonders of life as a Free Spirit. He suggested that the inquisitor should be grateful for the chance to hear a person who was truly free in spirit, for only such a person could reveal all the truths he had to offer. In response, Kerlinger asked if the heretic was demented. (The insanity plea could be used to avoid capital punishment, and in at least one other trial the judges offered this escape.)[61] With the greatest relish Hartmann elaborated on the forms of immorality that would be allowed to a Free Spirit; neither murder nor incest was forbidden to such a person in the pursuit of his inclinations. The inquisitor seems to have encouraged Hartmann to expand upon the sexual content of his heresy. At one point he asked what would happen if two Free Spirits lusted at the same time after the same woman. In another passage he asked whether Christ and Mary Magdalene had sexual relations after the resurrection; while Hartmann claimed to know the answer, he refused to divulge it. Toward the end of the trial, Hartmann expressed his belief that it was permissible to lie in order to save one's life, and to abjure one's beliefs in court without truly rejecting them. He, however, disdained to use such devices, and remained gloriously impenitent.

The case of Conrad Kannler is more complex, since the doctrines ascribed to this heretic were drawn from two sources: the bull *Ad nostrum* and the trial of John Hartmann, who had been dealt with fourteen years earlier.[62] The reliance on *Ad nostrum* is obvious from the format of the protocol; having established that Kannler was "free in spirit," the inquisitor asked a series of questions drawn explicitly from the list of heretical doctrines given in the bull. The answer to each of these questions was a mixture of phrases drawn from each of the two sources, with certain original phrases—presumably reflecting Kannler's actual response to the questions—inserted among the borrowings. In other words, what the inquisitor did was to ask Kannler whether he held a certain heretical doctrine, which he would then read to the accused. Kannler affirmed in each case that he did believe the doctrine, and might or might not add further comment or qualification. His own statement might be taken into account when the protocol was drawn up, but only incidentally; the formulation of the protocol derived primarily from the articles drawn up in advance. An inquisitor who used such procedures did not need to be greatly concerned about whether his subject was in fact a heretic of the Free Spirit, since it was a simple matter to transform him into one, at least for the sake of the records.

REASONS FOR PROSECUTION

The use of such elaborate techniques to incriminate subjects raises an important question: did the inquisitors, or those who supported the inquisitors, have ulterior motives for seeking condemnations? More specifically, there are three questions that come to mind. Did the emperor, Charles IV, have political motives for the aid that he lent to inquisitors? Did the churchmen who sought to repress beghards and beguines do so because of animosities rooted in ecclesiastical politics? And were the authorities responsible for repression swayed by a desire to obtain revenues through fines or confiscations?

That Charles IV played a significant role in fostering the repression of heresy in Germany is suggested by the contrast between him and his predecessor, Louis the Bavarian. Historians have suggested that Louis actively impeded the establishment of papal inquisitors in the early fourteenth century.[63] Indeed, he was long involved in a legal and political battle with the papacy regarding his rights to the throne; he had been excommunicated, and harbored at his court Marsilius of Padua and others whom the popes had condemned as heretics.[64] It was hardly likely, therefore, that he would cooperate with the papacy in any project, and particularly in the repression of heresy. By the end of his life, the enmity between him and the papacy had developed to such a feverish peak that Pope Clement VI fostered the scheme that put Charles IV in power. The contrast between the two kings has long fascinated historians: the obstinate and uncompromising Louis, determined to assert his rights despite papal repudiation, and the shrewd and flexible Charles, whose initial claim to the throne was based in large part on his recognition by the papacy, and who might be relied upon to aid the Curia in establishing control over the German Church.[65] It is probably not coincidental, therefore, that Pope Clement appointed John Schadeland in 1348, roughly half a year after Louis had died.[66] The accession of a more sympathetic king no doubt seemed auspicious for the establishment of papal inquisitors. On the other hand, one must not make too much of this contrast. In the first place, there is no reason to think that Louis was averse in principle to repressive activity. On the contrary, when the bishop of Regensburg suppressed a house of beghards north of the episcopal city in 1318, Louis confirmed the bishop's provisions three months later in his capacity as duke of Bavaria.[67] Despite his break with the papacy, one need not suppose that he grew more tolerant of beghards and beguines in his later years, since his opposition to Rome was based solely on political and legal grounds, and had no intrinsic religious implications. There is no evidence that Louis did anything to hinder inquisitors in any direct way, or even any indication that his lenience in this regard was seriously tested. If his rule was inauspicious for the establishment of papal inquisitors, it was probably so only in the sense that he could not be counted or to act in their support. Perhaps for that reason the Curia may have felt it preferable to leave the pursuit of heretics in the hands of the local hierarchy. Nor was there anything exceptional in this policy; the repression of heresy was primarily a concern of the local clergy in most parts of Europe, and the fact that this was so in Germany is not a matter of special note.

Furthermore, it would be misleading to see a dramatic reversal in the papal policy in 1348 with the appointment of John Schadeland, since this inquisitor was evidently the only papal delegate in Germany at the time, and his zeal in pursuit of heretics seems to have been less than overwhelming. The real breakthrough in curial policy came only in 1364, when not one but four inquisitors were named, and in the years immediately following, when these inquisitors were given continued support by both pope and emperor. It is the political background for the developments of the 1360s, therefore, which most deserves scrutiny.

H. C. Lea's view on this subject (which have been echoed in the historical literature for a century) are summarized nicely in his comment on the imperial decrees of 1369: "It was rare indeed for an emperor to have the cordial support of the papacy, and we may reasonably assume that Charles was made to see that through their union the Inquisition might be rendered serviceable to both in breaking down the independence of the great prince-bishops."[68] Presumably Lea meant that the pope and emperor were conspiring to limit the bishops' jurisdiction. There are three problems with this interpretation. First, as will be argued in the following section, there is absolutely no indication that bishops and papal inquisitors viewed themselves as competing with each other for jurisdictional rights. On the contrary, they seem to have cooperated with each other on the best of terms, except when papal inquisitors used procedures that were flagrantly arbitrary. Second, the ascription of ulterior motives to Charles and the pope is evidently based on a questionable conception of what a "papal" inquisitor represented (quite apart from the dubious reference to an "Inquisition"). Installment of papal inquisitors was not a measure for the direct augmentation of papal control over local affairs. Popes might provide general guidelines for inquisitorial activity, but they rarely gave specific directions. They seldom seem even to have maintained close contact with the inquisitors, though in this respect there were clear exceptions.[69] More often than not, they even left the appointment of inquisitors to the superiors in the Dominican order—a provision that would have been odd if the popes had wished to create inquisitors as agents of direct papal authority. It is thus only in a formal sense that the appointment of papal inquisitors contributed toward what some historians have called the "judiciarization" of the Curia.[70] Third, Lea's reconstruction of imperial

policy seems inconsistent with the emperor's general political program. From Charles's viewpoint, an alliance with the pope against
the bishops would have been inconsistent, because the key to
Charles's control of Germany was an alliance with the higher nobility, including the Rhenish bishops and archbishops. In some ways
this alliance was directed *against* the papacy. Though the cismontane
element was not so explicit that one can speak of Charles as fundamentally antipapal, he did allow for considerable augmentation of
the princes' and prelates' independence.[71] And even if Charles had
wanted to ally himself with the pope against the bishops, establishment of papal inquisitors would not directly have furthered imperial
purposes, since the jurisdictional rights that the bishops were supposedly being forced to relinquish were exclusively ecclesiastical
rights, which could not have accrued to the emperor, and which had
never been used by local authorities against the ruler.

There are some respects in which Charles's activity no doubt was
political. There is a sense in which any exercise of authority by a
political figure is a political act. In supporting papal inquisitors, the
emperor was *inter alia* asserting his right to protect agents of the
Church, and to lay down penalties for those who violated his sanctions. As medieval rulers long before the Investiture Controversy
were well aware, the right to protect an organ of the Church could
easily be extended to include the right of control over that organ.
It may even have been the case that Charles acted in part on the
advice of clerics at his court who desired action against beghards and
beguines because of their antipathy toward the mendicant orders;
again, the support that Charles lent inquisitors would in this case
have been politically inspired.[72] Charles himself can only have bene-
fited from supporting a papal project that cost him nothing. The
leading inquisitor of the era, Walter Kerlinger, was an associate of
his.[73] It is further worth noting that one of the edicts of 1369
allocated to the imperial coffers part of the fines obtained from
inquisitors' opponents. On the other hand, one can scarcely question
Charles's devotion to the conventional, orthodox piety of his era.
As a child of his time he practiced the standard devotions, and went
to the trouble of acquiring important relics for his capital city of
Prague; included in his substantial collection were a flask of the
Virgin's milk, one of the nails used on Calvary, and one of the
diapers that adorned the infant Jesus.[74] He wrote religious works,
such as a life of Saint Wenceslas. He obtained papal approval to
carry a portable altar everywhere he went, so that he could hear
mass even in places that lay under interdict.[75] Examples of his con-

ventional piety could easily be multiplied. It was no doubt because of his commitment to this orthodox piety that he took stringent anti-heretical measures in his kingdom of Bohemia, especially in his proposal for a national law code, the *Majestas Carolina*.[76] Thus, even if his support for inquisitors in the 1360s incidentally profited him as emperor, there is little reason to think that his zeal was motivated exclusively or even primarily by self-interest.

One might also question the significance that Charles's support had for inquisitorial proceedings. His decrees of 1369 were promulgated in the midst of the antibeghard campaign of 1366–75. But most of the trials in this campaign took place before the edicts were set forth. The most vigorous of papal inquisitors at this time, Walter Kerlinger, began his involvement as early as 1367, armed with a routine imperial decree of assistance, but without the sweeping concessions of 1369.[77] Nor is there any cogent evidence that the death of Charles was responsible for the waning of inquisitorial fervor. So far as the records indicate, there were two main reasons for the termination of the campaign against beghards and beguines around 1374: the death in 1373 of Walter Kerlinger, and the papal bull of 1374 admonishing greater caution in proceeding against the religious communities in question. By the time Charles died in 1378, the inquisitorial campaign had already ended.[78] While it lasted, his aid may have been influential in winning the support of municipal authorities for inquisitors. But as other repressive campaigns (especially that against Waldensians, to be discussed in the following chapter) were to prove, imperial consent was neither a necessary nor a sufficient condition for the success of antiheretical efforts.

If it is impossible to give a simpler answer to the question whether Charles IV had political motives for aiding repression, it is perhaps somewhat easier to assess the motives of other authorities who became involved. It would surely be misleading to seek specific political plans in the directives issued from the Curia, since these directives seem to have been inspired for the most part by pleas and appeals that came from Germany. One may meaningfully ask, however, whether the native German cleargy had political reasons for attacking beghards and beguines. In one sense, the answer must self-evidently be affirmative. It is particularly clear in the trials at Strassburg and Basel that the conflicts were first and foremost battles between mendicant and diocesan clergy—that conventual beguines who had become mendicant tertiaries or otherwise placed themselves under the auspices of the mendicant orders become objects of attack by the mendicants' rivals. More fundamentally, the Church's repudiation of beghards and beguines was in a sense inherently political. In such cases one need not seek ulterior political motives; even the ostensible reason for prosecution, that is, the belief that beghards and beguines represented an irregular mode of religious life, was political at least in the sense that it pertained to a matter of ecclesiastical polity. This political dimension is not so clear when the trials lay in the hands of papal inquisitors alone, or when the initiative was primarily theirs, as when bishops took the lead. One would not expect prima facie that mendicant inquisitors would be eager to assail beguines allied with the mendicants. In some instances these trials were no doubt manifestations of rivalry between Dominicans and Franciscans, with inquisitors from the former order and beguines from the latter.[79] In all too many cases, however, the sources do not indicate the allegiance of the subjects of prosecution, and the political implications are uncertain. Further complications arise in those cases in which inquisitors proceeded not against conventual beghards and beguines but against isolated individuals; trials of this sort can only with difficulty be ascribed to political motives. Nonetheless, the campaigns against beghards and beguines surely did arise in large part out of the concerns of ecclesiastical politics, even if these considerations cannot explain every single trial that occurred. And the political factor in these campaigns may help to explain why papal inquisitors took a leading role in them, as they never again were to do in major campaigns. As in other parts of Europe, so also in Germany, it was relatively easy for papal inquisitors to immerse themselves in antiheretical action when their zeal was augmented by political pressure.

To some extent, action against conventual beghards and beguines may have been motivated by monetary considerations also. The last of the edicts of Charles IV in 1369 extended the practice of confiscation. Normally used only for heretics who had been condemned to death, it now became standard in the case of beghard or beguine communities that had been dissolved and forced to abandon their houses.[80] The houses in which beghards had lived were to be converted into inquisitorial prisons. The beguines' houses, on the other hand, were to be sold, and the proceeds were allocated in equal shares to charitable purposes, the inquisitors, and the towns where the houses lay. The gift to the towns was ostensibly a compensation for the harm done them by the presence of heretics, but it was earmarked for the restoration of the towns and the repair of public roads—purposes that had little connection with the stigma of having harbored heretics. In effect, what Charles did was to solicit the cooperation of town governments in the repression of heretics, and evidently the plan had the desired effect. There are at least two cases in which inquisitors brought this edict to the attention of municipal authorities; at least once, and perhaps routinely, the inquisitors had it inscribed in the official records of the town governments.[81]

Inquisitors themselves, on the other hand, do not seem to have availed themselves of the opportunity to enrich themselves or their orders. The only exception even suggested by the sources is Walter Kerlinger, who managed to amass 1,500 gold florins, which before his death he deposited with the town council of Erfurt.[82] When he died the Curia made claim to this sum. The funds may have had some connection with Kerlinger's duties as Dominican provincial, but the Curia's claim suggests that the money represented his share of the money obtained from confiscations. If one were predisposed to believe the worst of him, one might suspect that his extraordinary zeal was based on mere avarice. If there were further evidence (for example, complaints about his behavior from defenders of beghards or beguines), this judgment might be justified. With the evidence at hand, however, there is no solid ground for concluding that enrichment was in itself a motive for Kerlinger's action, and there is no indication that he used his funds for illicit personal purposes.[83]

The trial of Meister Eckhart illustrates fully the complexity of the factors that could bear upon prosecution.[84] This trial was begun on the initiative of the archbishop of Cologne, who entrusted the investigation to a commission on which the Franciscan order was represented, but not Eckhart's own Dominican order. Two key witnesses against Eckhart were fellow Dominicans. On the whole, though, his colleagues within the order supported him and testified to his innocence of heresy; indeed, an earlier inquiry within the order had already ascertained that his teaching was orthodox. Protesting that the accusations arose from envy and that the archiepiscopal commission was improperly constituted, Eckhart appealed the case to the papal court at Avignon; and when he himself went to Avignon in 1327, the documents of the archiepiscopal commission were forwarded there for new proceedings. Eckhart died before the end of the trial, but in 1329 Pope John XXII condemned twenty-eight articles from his writings as either heretical or dangerous. The condemnation applied only to Eckhart's teachings and not to him personally; according to the papal document, Eckhart had remained a faithful servant of the Church, and before his death he had recanted all those oral and written teachings of his that could be taken as heretical, and had submitted his statement to papal judgment.[85]

What were the factors that led to these proceedings? One possible answer is that Eckhart was accused of heresy, and his teachings condemned as such, because his utterances were in fact heretical.[86] This is not an appropriate context for examination of the theological issues, but most recent scholarship has clearly exonerated Eckhart of the charge.[87] He delighted in using bold and paradoxical language that could easily lead to suspicion of heresy. (One of the passages from his writings that gave rise to the accusation read in part: "A humble man does not need to ask God: he can command God. A humble man has power over God as he, God, has power over himself. If that man were in hell, God would have to come to hell, and hell would have to be the Kingdom of Heaven. . . .")[88] Yet when his statements are read sympathetically, in the total context of his corpus and in the context of medieval spiritual writings, an orthodox meaning is virtually always apparent.

How, then, does one explain the trial and the condemnation? Some scholars have seen these developments as the product of enmity between the archbishop and the Dominican order.[89] Essentially, the argument is that the Dominicans had received special exemption from archiepiscopal jurisdiction, and the archbishop wished to assert his judicial rights over the order. Eckhart, as a target who could plausibly be accused of heresy, thus served as a test case for the archbishop's authority. Another explanation has it that Eckhart was a victim of dissension within the Dominican order.[90] As already mentioned, two chief witnesses against him were fellow Dominicans, and a letter from one of Eckhart's defenders assails these witnesses as immoral and intriguing; one of them is dismissed in this letter as an excommunicated monk, an unjust judge, and the author of defamatory writings.[91] Indeed, Eckhart himself protested against the ill-willed and slanderous members of his own order who had maligned him.[92] Yet a third interpretation sees the trial as resulting from conflicts between the Dominicans and the Franciscans.[93] Quite apart from the natural competition and rivalry between two orders that had been founded to serve similar congregations, these groups were divided on matters of politics and principle. While the Dominicans were generally loyal to the pope in his conflicts with the German monarchy, the Franciscans, having quarreled with successive popes over the question of Franciscan poverty, generally sided with the king.[94] Furthermore, there were philosophical and theological conflicts between the orders; Eckhart himself had disputed with a noted Franciscan theologian at Paris.[95] Thomas Aquinas, the primary source of Dominican teaching, had been canonized in 1322, and now (it is argued) the Franciscans saw their opportunity to retaliate. The argument receives some of its force from the inclusion of Franciscans on the archiepiscopal commission that originally tried Eckhart.

While none of these factors can be ruled out of consideration, it would surely be pressing the argument too far to take any of them as decisive. After all, Eckhart's teachings were condemned at Avignon in proceedings that were in principle independent of those in Cologne.[96] The archbishop is known to have maintained an interest in the affair even after the appeal, and the Franciscans and dissident Dominicans no doubt exerted whatever influence they could. But Eckhart's supporters, who stood generally in the good graces of the papacy, surely applied their influence as well. Under these circumstances, it is reasonable to assume that the papal commission that condemned Eckhart did so in good conscience and with full conviction that his teachings were heretical. In short, Eckhart was apparently the victim not of a single political factor, but of a coincidence of circumstances that brought about a kind of coalition against him. And even those who had one or another political reason to oppose him could undoubtedly persuade themselves that he was in fact heretical.

The abundance of records in Eckhart's case allows us to perceive something of the complexity of pertinent influences. Thus, this case serves as a warning never to oversimplify in those instances where the extant documents furnish fewer insights. Yet to insist upon specific speculative reasons (such as Lea's) for the general establishment of papal inquisitors would be equally misleading.

REASONS FOR RESISTANCE

H. C. Lea and others have argued that there were political reasons not only for the establishment of papal inquisitors, but also for resistance to those agents. According to this interpretation, the political rivals of papacy and empire—that is, princes, magistrates, and especially Rhenish prelates—resisted the encroachment of papal judges and did everything in their power to thwart the success of these inquisitors. On analysis, however, the very idea that there was widespread resistance breaks down. Both secular and ecclesiastical authorities did oppose inquisitors whose proceedings struck them as arbitrary or whose judgments seemed biased or clearly incorrect, as they had done in the case of Conrad of Marburg. But there is no foundation whatsoever for the thesis that papal inquisitors and native authorities in the fourteenth century were engaged in politically motivated conflict.

The idea that the native hierarchy resented the jurisdictional rivalry of papal inquisitors rests in large part on mere supposition, and even overt error. For example, Ernest McDonnell in his discussion of this matter quotes the title of a canon set forth in 1338 by a synod at Trier: "Lest anyone involve himself in episcopal cases."[97] McDonnell suggests that this canon was the assertion of episcopal rights in response to the claims of papal inquisitors.[98] But as the text of the canon makes entirely clear, the reference is not to papal inquisitors at all, but rather to priests who exceeded their powers in the confessional, absolving penitents of sins reserved for episcopal absolution. In another passage McDonnell cites the trial at Strassburg in 1366, in which the papal inquisitor Henry of Agro acted in conjunction with an episcopal vicar.[99] McDonnell argues that the bishop of Strassburg "had gratified episcopal jealousy by not allowing [Henry of Agro] to perform his office independently, but had supplemented his work with a vicar, Tristram, who conducted himself in the matter not simply as a representative of the bishop in the sentence, but as co-inquisitor."[100] Yet the vicar's precise role in the trial is not ascertainable from the sole surviving document. Canon law required that bishops and papal inquisitors work in cooperation with each other, as a safeguard against procedural irregularity.[101] This requirement was by no means regularly observed, but the cases where it was followed cannot count as evidence of jurisdictional conflict. It is more probable that the bishop in this instance merely wanted to ensure that the inquisition proceed effectively. It was evidently toward this end that he allowed the inquisitor to use the episcopal court for the proceedings. Thus, this case might be taken far more plausibly as an example of outstanding cordiality between bishop and inquisitor. As will be seen in later chapters, there are other trials in which papal inquisitors and bishops seem to have interacted cordially, and there are a few instances in which bishops resisted arbitrary proceedings, but there is *no* known case in which bishops and inquisitors disputed over jurisdiction. Alexander Patschovsky has recently shown that, contrary to often-repeated claims, harmony prevailed in Bohemia between papal inquisitors and bishops; the point applies just as well to other parts of the empire.[102]

Is it inherently likely that the German hierarchy would have resisted encroachment on its jurisdiction? Jurisdictional rivalry had for centuries been a dominant motif in the institutional history of many European towns. In Germany and elsewhere, there had in particular been attempts on the part of episcopal towns to restrict the rights that bishops exercised over the population, including rights of jurisdiction. The conflicts were in part over finances; jurisdiction could in some circumstances be lucrative, provided the courts that administered justice consumed less money than they obtained in fines and confiscations. Perhaps a more fundamental issue, though, was one of power: along with military force, jurisdiction was a basic means for wielding authority in the most diverse matters. Yet there have been historians in recent years who have emphasized that, despite the proclivity of early European courts to enter into conflict, there was a high degree of cooperation between them in their efforts to suppress crime.[103] The citizens of a town might seek to wrest jurisdictional rights from a bishop's control, but so long as these rights remained in the bishop's hands the townsmen would generally prefer episcopal justice to no justice. Furthermore, the concurrence of two different jurisdictions—episcopal and municipal, episcopal and papal—did not in itself arouse conflict. It was only when jurisdiction was perceived as an instrument of political power that such controversy ensued. If papal inquisitors in Germany had been more vigorous and systematic, or if they had used their offices for purposes that were not in the bishops' interest, or if there had been an Inquisition in the later sense of the term, it is conceivable that jurisdictional conflicts might have occurred. This situation, however, does not seem to have come about. Neither examination of the sources nor consideration of the issues at stake lends credibility to the established view of this matter.

The relations between inquisitors and bishops in other countries were essentially the same as in Germany. In southern France, for example, it was not uncommon for the bishops to aid inquisitors in the thirteenth century.[104] The Council of Vienne did, it is true, curb inquisitorial autonomy by requiring inquisitors to work in conjunction with bishops, but thre is no reason to think that this measure arose from jurisdictional rivalry. In the first place, if the bishops who attended the council had sought to protect their own jurisdictional powers, it is unlikely that they would have supported the provisions of Vienne, which prohibited independent action on the part of either inquisitors or bishops. Second, the papal commission that preceded the inquisitorial reforms was clearly concerned with procedural abuses rather than with matters of jurisdiction.[105] Here too, therefore, there is no evidence of conflict in principle between papal and episcopal authorities.

The secular powers do not seem to have been any more averse to the activity of papal inquisitors than were the bishops. Once again, however, there was resistance to arbitrary procedure or misdirected zeal. The best example is a case at Cologne in 1374, in which a Dominican inquisitor harassed the local beghards and beguines.[106] Early in the following year the town council sent a letter to the pope protesting against the inquisitorial proceedings. The council assured the pontiff that the inquisitor's subjects were orthodox, and that they were held in esteem by their fellow citizens.[107] To establish the truth of the matter, the council had called an assembly of all the clergy throughout the city in whose parishes these groups lived. Asked to give their impressions of the beghards and beguines, the clerics had given the unanimous opinion, "not induced by any inappropriate interest, money, reward, or favor, but in the expression of plain truth," that the beghards and beguines were good and orthodox Christians. The council carefully explained to the pope that it did not wish to impede or trouble the inquisitor in any way, and it promised that if any heretical beliefs came to its attention it would bring the matter before the inquisitors. The present inquisitor, though, had set questions of faith before illiterate laymen that were so difficult that even a great theologian could scarcely answer them without ponderous deliberation and consultation of books. The procedure seemed most unreasonable. Hence, the council asked the pope to issue a letter to this inquisitor ordering that he cease molesting such persons. Once again, at the end of the letter, the council offered its support to this or any future inquisitor whose services were required against real heretics.

Why was the council so eager in this case to protect the communities? Conceivably it was because the groups under attack had members related to the patriciate. At least some of the beguines' houses in Cologne had the patronage of patrician families, and these may have been the ones afflicted.[108] On the other hand, the town council does not seem to have been antecedently convinced that the groups in question were orthodox, since it called in the parish clergy to determine that this was the case. Unless this consultation was carried out only *pro forma*, with the foregone conclusion that the beghards and beguines would prove themselves orthodox, one must suppose that the concern for matters of faith was genuine. Furthermore, the letter speaks almost disparagingly of the illiterate laymen who went before the inquisitor.[109] While members of the patriciate might be illiterate, the wording suggests that the lower classes formed at least part of the group under attack. The sources do not permit firm conclusions, or even specify which houses were suspected of heresy. For lack of further information, though, one cannot conclude that either familial interest or jurisdictional concern had any part in the council's action. The municipal authorities are likely to have defended the beghards and beguines not because they had a personal or political interest in the affair, but because they sincerely believed the afflicted persons were innocent.

An even more difficult case to unravel is the prosecution in the Rhineland in the late fourteenth century. Around 1398 an episcopal inquisitor in Mainz, John Wasmod, wrote a treatise against beghards and beguines. In it he alluded to inquisitions against these groups in which he had evidently had some role, probably as judge.[110] He conceded the distinction between good and bad (that is, orthodox and heretical) beguines, yet he complained that even the latter received protection from the patricians and magistrates in certain Rhenish towns, which made it impossible for inquisitors to deal properly with the heretics. His report is tantalizingly brief. Presuming that Mainz was one of the Rhenish cities Wasmod was referring to, one might conjecture that the patricians were acting out of familial loyalty, since many of the beguines in that town came from upper-class families.[111] Perhaps, then, this is an exceptional instance in which townsmen did sympathize with heretical communities and put personal interests above religious concerns. Yet this is the case only if Wasmod was correct in his distinction between heretical and orthodox beguines, and if the particular houses that received patrician support were in fact clearly heretical. The alternative possibilities are numerous. Perhaps the most plausible suggestion is that in certain convents, which housed well-educated beguines from the upper classes, some of the residents began reading the mystical literature that was current at the time: literature that often expressed radical ideas, and sometimes crossed the vaguely defined border between orthodox and heterodox mysticism. The inquisitor might insist that these beguines were heretics. But the criteria would be no means be clear-cut, and the families of these beguines, even if they were fervently orthodox, might be inclined to give them the benefit of the doubt. It is one thing to support the victims of an inquisition with full confidence that they are innocent; it is quite another to encourage known heretics. In any event, it would be pure speculation to suggest that jurisdictional conflict underlay the controversy here. And if one could demonstrate that the inquisitor met opposition on jurisdictional grounds, this would be an instance of rivalry between secular leaders and episcopal, rather than papal, authorities.

Municipal governments may in some cases have resisted the confiscation of beghards' and beguines' houses, though once again the evidence is unclear. On one occasion Walter Kerlinger requested and obtained papal confirmation for the imperial edict specifying the uses to which such confiscations should be put.[112] It is impossible to say precisely why he needed this confirmation. Perhaps he had encountered difficulties in his efforts to confiscate the houses, but it is at least as likely that the allocation of this property was disputed. Alternatively, it is possible that the inquisitor had met opposition from persons who remained unconvinced of the beghards' and beguines' guilt, and who hoped to reinstate these groups in their houses when the wave of prosecution had passed. The matter does not, in any event, demonstrate resistance in principle to the prosecution of known heretics. Nor does an obscure case at Lüneburg in 1370, in which an inquisitor had the local bishop and burgomasters sell the houses of allegedly heretical beghards and beguines.[113] A prominent member of the community bought both houses involved; both the bishop and the town council drew up documents regarding the sale. It has been claimed that the beguines in this instance had the support of the town government, and later retrieved their house; yet the evidence even for this meager information is unconvincing, and there is no clue at all to the motives for whatever took place.[114]

Papal inquisitors may in fact have anticipated opposition, and when they were first appointed the pope and emperor may have shared their apprehension. In his decrees of 1369, Charles IV established two dukes, two counts, and two lords as guardians and defenders of the inquisitors. Whoever violated their privileges was subject to a fine of a hundred gold marks, half of which would go to the imperial treasury, while the rest remained for the inquisitors' purposes.[115] There is no record that inquisitors ever invoked these strictures or called upon their guardians for protection, or that they needed to do so. Possibly the threat of such severe punishments sufficed to deter offenders. It is not even clear, though, that the inquisitors had any foes (other than alleged heretics) who needed to be deterred. Perhaps the pope suggested these measures to Charles to avert the sort of dangers that inquisitors had met in other countries.[116] In any event, one cannot conclude from this edict that the papal delegates in Germany were beset with immediate opposition. Even if one could show this much, it would require further evidence to prove that this resistance arose from jurisdictional concerns or sympathy toward clearly recognized heretics. And this kind of evidence is precisely what is lacking.

One region where inquisitors did meet considerable resistance from diverse quarters was Bohemia. The proceedings there (which may have been on Charles IV's mind when he issued his measures against disruption in the decrees of 1369) have been examined carefully by Alexander Patschovsky.[117] In some instances it is reasonably clear that controversy arose in Bohemia because of irregularities in prosecution. Thus, the parish clergy in and around Pisek refused to acknowledge the authority of papal inquisitors when they were summoned on the charge of heresy, although they were willing "to obey their own prelates and superiors." Yet the conflict appears to have been not between rival jurisdictions but between secular and mendicant clergy. The inquisitors, as mendicants, were seeking to use their power against the diocesan cleargy in the course of traditional rivalry between the two.[118] Somewhat more obscure is the incident in which the papal inquisitor John Schwenkenfeld was assassinated.[119] He had entered into a controversy of long standing between the bishop of Breslau and the city of Breslau, in which the king of Bohemia stood on the side of the city. In league with the bishop, Schwenkenfeld proceeded against a renegade Cistercian of dubious orthodoxy who, as a radical reformer, had aroused the sympathies of the town authorities. In the course of the struggle, in 1341, the king of Bohemia summoned both sides to Prague, where the inquisitor was assassinated. The incident may have involved jurisdictional conflict, but once again, it is most likely that the townspeople were merely defending a figure whom they judged innocent.

There were, however, other cases in which cities (and sometimes also local clergy) resisted papal inquisitors, in Prague, Budweis, and elsewhere.[120] In some instances the municipal authorities forcibly released incarcerated suspects, and even imprisoned inquisitorial personnel. Patschovsky explains these measures as attempts to preserve the judicial autonomy of the towns. But is it really likely that civil authorities would have asserted autonomy in a clearly ecclesiastical matter? There is no firm evidence for this conclusion; the interpretation is entirely speculative.[121] The facts at hand, meager as they are, can be explained at least as readily by the supposition that, once again, the inquisitors' opponents viewed the defendants as innocent. Patschovsky cites as support for his interpretation a line from one inquisitor's correspondence with the clergy of Prague: "Nor should any of you presume, as has elsewhere rashly been done, to discuss the motives or causes of our trials, and of their development [aggra-

vacionis ac innovacionis eorundem] . . . seeing that none of you is entrusted with knowledge of the cause of their affairs, but that you are entrusted with the simple execution of the mandate, to obey simply whatever is ordered you on apostolic authority."[122] If the parties addressed were inclined to dispute the inquisitor's jurisdiction, it is unlikely that they would be discussing the "motives and causes" for the specific trials; the phrase surely suggests that native Bohemians questioned the justice of the accusations. Patschovsky also refers to events in the town of Saaz. In 1337 the municipal judge accused certain townspeople of heresy, and the accused themselves retaliated by murdering the judge and his son; the assumption of jurisdictional rivalry would certainly be superfluous in this case.[123] More importantly, around 1348 a papal inquisitor ordered the burgomaster and jurors of Saaz to deliver to him the property of four women who had been burned as heretics; when the civil authorities failed to carry out these instructions, the inquisitor threatened interdict.[124] In this instance the town government may have been resisting encroachment on its own right of confiscation, as Patschovsky suggests. In 1348 Charles IV gave the town of Saaz the right to confiscate the property of criminals, and the town may have been defending this right.[125] But this issue is very different from that of the inquisitors' right to try heretics in the first place, which does not appear to have been questioned.

There may have been cases outside Germany in which civil authorities either resisted encroachment on native jursdiction or sought to protect known heretics. But in virtually every case, the powers in question claimed that they were merely defending the innocent, and this claim can seldom be disproven altogether.

For the sake of comparison, it may be useful to investigate an example of how secular authorities resisted inquisitors in other countries. One interesting incident that particularly merits attention for comparative purposes is the trial at Narbonne in the 1230s. The episode has been examined in detail by Richard Emery, whose account remains definitive.[126] The inquisition here was the Dominican Friar Ferrier, who began as an archiepiscopal delegate. Though in the course of proceedings he gained papal authority for antiheretical action, he always worked in close conjunction with the archbishop of Narbonne. In 1234 Ferrier captured an allegedly heretical preacher from the bourg of Narbonne, and initiated further inquiry into heresy there. The citizens gathered and forced him to release one prisoner. Eventually the archbishop laid the bourg under interdict and excommunicated the leaders of the resistance, to which the citizens replied by seizing the archbishop's property and revenues, and later attempting an attack on the archbishop himself. Attempts at negotiation proved fruitless. When Ferrier attempted further proceedings, the consuls of the bourg went so far as to forbid townspeople to go to him for confession. The inquisitor openly accused the bourg as a whole of heresy, provoking an attack on the Dominican convent. The case continued for roughly two years, with further recrimination between the bourg on the one hand and the archbishop and the city proper on the other. In the end, the affair was settled only by outside arbitration and elaborate provisions for redress of grievances on both sides.

For an understanding of the issues involved in this case, one may turn to a protest submitted by the leaders of the bourg to external authorities.[127] In the first place, they denied that there was heresy in the bourg, and recalled that its citizens had been loyal to the Church, and during the recent Albigensian Crusade had supported the orthodox forces in their attack on heretics. No doubt the majority of residents in the bourg were indeed faithful Catholics, though there is evidence that there were heretics both in the bourg and in the city proper. Second, the authorities of the bourg charged that the bishop was seeking to destroy its emergent consulate. It was precisely during this era that the institution of the consulate was arising, in Narbonne and in other southern French towns, in opposition to seigneurial control. The archbishop of Narbonne was one of three lords who held jurisdictional rights in the town. The citizens maintained whatever liberties they had largely by playing off one lord against another; it is thus not surprising that in their conflict with the archbishop the citizens of the bourg apparently sought support from another of these lords, the viscount Aymery III, among others. The bishop denied that he was seeking to overthrow the bourg's consulate, and insisted that he merely wanted the dissolution of that *conjuratio* that lay behind the resistance to antiheretical measures. The citizens replied that there was no *conjuratio* other than the consulate itself, and they persisted in their suspicion (which was probably correct) that the consulate was the real target of the archbishop's attack.[128] The third part of the citizens' protest dealt with inquisitorial procedure. According to the customs of Narbonne, citizens were entitled to various judicial rights—for example, the right to choose which court one would be tried in, the right to trial by prud'hommes, and the immunity of heirs from punishment—which inquisitorial procedure violated. Furthermore, the citizens charged that the inquisitor was infringing ordinary standards of justice, imprisoning suspects without condemnation, confiscating their goods before trial, and trapping the unsophisticated with overly subtle questions. For example, the inquisitor would ask whether four hosts consecrated simultaneously each became the body of God; if the suspect answered in the affirmative, he was charged with believing in four Gods.

The proceedings at Narbonne represent political conflict in its clearest (though certainly not its simplest!) form. Even if one grants that the archbishop and inquisitor sincerely sought to eradicate heresy and that the authorities of the bourg genuinely felt that their citizens were being subjected to injustice, the political implications of the case are transparent. Jurisdictional and procedural matters were both central issues in the controversy. But can one take his case in Narbonne and use it as a model for interpretation of proceedings in German towns? In various respects the analogy seems inappropriate. Both in German towns and in Narbonne, the claim was made that inquisitors were proceeding against innocent persons. But beyond this factor the similarities cease. In Narbonne the conflict arose because a previously established political figure was using inquisitorial proceedings as a tool for specific political purposes. Significantly, the citizens of the bourg resisted Ferrier not in his capacity as papal delegate, but as an agent of the archbishop. In Germany, too, it was the bishops who had jurisdictional rights in various towns, and if jurisdictional conflict was to erupt, one would expect that the townspeople's attacks would be directed not against the papal inquisitors, but against the episcopal judges. It was the bishops, after all, who could use their jurisdiction to augment their power within the towns. The papal inquisitors merely claimed authority over heresy and related offenses. While it was conceivable that they could use their authority to gain power of a broader sort in the political affairs of a city, there is no evidence that they sought to do so, or that anyone suspected them of such attempts. And yet it was the papal and not the episcopal inquisitors who aroused protest. That the opposition was based on jurisdictional considerations analogous to those at Narbonne is scarcely credible. Perhaps there is better ground for analogy in the complaints at Narbonne about inquisitorial procedure. In Germany, too, there was occasional complaint about the inquisitors' devices; the authorities at Cologne, for instance, protested against their technique of confounding illiterate laymen with subtle theological puzzles. But in this respect also there is an important difference. The citizens in the bourg of Narbone appear to have taken offense not only at abuses of inquisitorial procedure, but at the essential features of that procedure, which violated their accustomed judicial liberties.

There is not a single case in which German authorities objected to inquisitorial procedure as such. Even in the affair of Conrad of Marburg, when inquisitorial procedure was first being introduced into German lands, there is no evidence for opposition to basic inquisitorial practices: accusation and judgment by the same person, withholding of the names of accusers, allowance of testimony inadmissible in ordinary courts, and so forth.[129] By the later fourteenth century practices of this kind, along with the use of torture, were being adopted even by many municipal governments throughout Germany.[130] To be sure, the subjects themselves may have resented the application of such procedures. But there is no reason whatsoever to assume that the civil authorities repudiated procedures that they themselves quickly began to adopt.

There are two exceptional instances in which a secular authority in Germany did indeed grant asylum to "heretics," and while these cases do not shed light on ordinary circumstances, they must be examined precisely as atypical and extreme cases. On two important occasions, Louis the Bavarian took under his protection theoreticians who shared with him a bitter animosity toward the papacy and curial power: Marsilius of Padua and William of Ockham. Marsilius had resided for some time at Paris, where in 1324 he completed his antipapal treatise, *Defensor pacis*.[131] In this work he argued that the papacy is an institution of human rather than divine origin, and that the entire hierarchy derives its authority not from God but from the "whole body of the faithful." When his authorship of this work was revealed in 1326, he fled in haste from Paris, and in the following year joined Louis the Bavarian during this ruler's expedition to Italy. He spent his remaining years in Louis's court at Munich, serving as a propagandist. By 1343 he was dead; in that year Pope Clement VI condemned 240 heretical propositions extracted from *Defensor pacis*, which he referred to as the most heretical work he had ever read. The instance of William of Ockham was in some respects similar.[132] Accused of heresy by a colleague at Oxford, he was summoned to the papal court at Avignon in 1323 for examination. In his case the allegations of heresy arose from logical, ontological, and eucharistic disputes rather than from a political conflict. It was only after he had fled from Avignon in 1328 (along with his fellow Franciscans Michael of Cesena and Bonagratia of Bergamo, "heretics" in their own right by virtue of their stance on Franciscan poverty), been excommuncated by the pope, and taken refuge with Louis the Bavarian that he became seriously involved in antipapal propaganda.

These cases are atypical in two ways. First, the subjects were academicians, whose alleged heresies arose in university circles and found expression in formal academic treatises. There had been similar trials outside of Germany for generations, but Germany had not been the scene of such affairs for the simple reason that most Germans who received university education did so outside their native land. It was not until the Great Schism that universities proliferated in Germany, and in their early years these institutions were staffed very largely by loyal partisans of Rome, who more often attacked than disseminated heresy. Second, in these two cases the alleged heretics were guarded by Louis the Bavarian—who clearly did not view them as heretical—against any possible papal action. Though the heretics themselves were imported into Germany, these affairs were not German in origin, and they are relevant to the present inquiry only as exceptions to the rule.

In those typical cases of local resistance to prosecution in Germany, it is important to note that the subjects of prosecution were almost invariably beghards and beguines.[133] This phenomenon is readily comprehensible; it was these groups, which so often lay near the border between orthodoxy and heresy, that were most likely to occasion dispute between accusers and defenders. When we turn now to the trials of Waldensians, who were usually more clear-cut in their deviance, we will find a very different situation. With only the rarest exceptions, the episcopal authorities who proceeded against Waldensians were convinced that their subjects were guilty; in virtually all cases this judgment seems to have been correct. Hence, trials of the Waldensians show more clearly than those of beghards and beguines the unanimity with which authorities at various levels were willing to repress genuine heretics.

4

The Crisis of the Waldensians

The period between the two councils was very much dominated by the issue of beghards and beguines, but not to the total exclusion of concern about other heretics. Apart from the doctrine of the Free Spirit, the only significant heresy in Germany during the fourteenth century was that of the Waldensians. Presumably they had been among the persons tried during the high Middle Ages. But for generations they had remarkable success in concealing their presence, largely through a practice that would later be known as occasional conformity: to avoid detection, they would go through the motions of compliance with Catholic ritual.[1] When apprehended they were usually eager to abjure their heresy; but when danger signals had passed, many of them would resume their old ways.[2] Through such means they persisted more effectively than other medieval sects. In various areas of Europe there were substantial numbers of Waldensians remaining to merge with Protestantism in the sixteenth century, while other have maintained their separate identity into the twentieth century.[3]

THE COURSE OF PROSECUTION

For the greater part of the fourteenth century, while beghards and beguines remained the center of attention, the Waldensians seem to have gone all but unnoticed. Between 1311 and 1315, and then again

53

between 1327 and 1341, there was prosecution of heretics in and around Austria.[4] The sources, which are almost exclusively chronicles, give hardly any reliable information about these groups, though they do give stereotypical accounts of the heretics' debauchery. Perhaps the most bizarre account from this period tells how the heretics gathered to hear their leader preach heretical sermons, whereupon a king entered in splendid array, accompanied by torchbearers and a bodyguard, and proclaimed that he was king of heaven. A grasshopper then jumped on the mouths of those in attendance, inducing a state of ecstasy in which they gave themselves over to their libidinous inclinations.[5] After reading fables of this sort, the historian can find redeeming merit in those further sources which, while relating little substantive information, at least do not lead one astray. Historians have long disputed the identity of the sect or sects in question.[6] Judging by later discoveries in the same region, however, it seems reasonable to conjecture that many of the heretics were Waldensians.

During the 1360s and 1370s the Waldensians underwent apparently minor trials in various parts of Germany, and it may have been Waldensians who were tried repeatedly in Nürnberg over the course of the century.[7] But even as late as the 1380s, the German Waldensians enjoyed generally placid conditions. Around 1380 or 1381, and again slightly later, an inquisitor worked at Regensburg, but there is no suggestion of continuous, systematic operation.[8] The heretics in Pomerania likewise underwent sporadic repression, though the halfhearted measures there merely demonstrate the laxity of antiheretical efforts: apart from a few excommunications in 1382, there seems to have been action only in 1384, when five Waldensians, evidently prominent members of the sect, came under suspicion of heresy.[9] The authorities took them first to Kolberg, where a canon threatened to burn them unless they gave him three marks, though in the end they appeased him with merely one mark. He then sent the accused to the episcopal official at Stettin, where on examination they denied all charges, and the official sent them home with an exhortation to be good. Soon they again fell under suspicion, and were sent first to Camin, then to Gramzow, and then to Prenzlau, where they were charged with venerating the devil. At first they were found guilty and banished from the city, but then they purged themselves of the charges on oath. The mere fact that these heretics were shuffled about so much, and received such inconsistent treatment, seems to indicate that no one took the problem of heresy altogether seriously. It is likely that Waldensians in other parts of Germany underwent similar harassment during these early years. But there were complaints from orthodox contemporaries that some bishops were lax in their defense of the faith.[10] These charges may in exceptional cases have stimulated action, but the general antiheretical momentum was as yet weak.[11]

The clouds were nonetheless building, and in the last years of the century the storm broke. Within slightly more than a decade, from 1389 to 1401, prosecution occurred in numerous towns of southern and eastern Germany, in one of the most important repressive endeavors of fourteenth-century Europe, and surely one of the most vigorous antiheretical campaigns of all medieval Germany. In one important respect, the organizational basis for this campaign was distinctive. Of all the known inquisitions that made up this series, roughly two-thirds were conducted by three itinerant inquisitors, none of whom was a Dominican, and none of whom (with one possible exception) held a papal commission for work in Germany.[12] Information for one of them, Martin of Amberg, comes from diverse sources, most of them disappointingly fragmentary.[13] Still, even his itinerary gives some notion of the sweeping character of his anti-Waldensian effort. By 1391 he had acquired a reputation for knowledge of heretics, based on his familiarity with them in various regions; in the same year he appeared in Würzburg (one chronicler tells that he arrived there after an excursion through Swabia) and in Erfurt; in 1396 he was in Prague, probably at work against heretics; between 1399 and 1401 he engaged once more in a flurry of activity in Franconia, Styria, and even the western part of Hungary. Peter Zwicker, who in many cases acted together with Martin, was even more wide-ranging in his activity.[14] He proceeded alongside Martin in Erfurt in 1391 and in Styria and Hungary at the turn of the century; in between, however, he carried out extensive inquisitions at Stettin (where he tried more than four hundred heretics), in Upper Austria, and possibly also in Vienna. The third of these itinerant episcopal inquisitors, Henry Angermeier, was neither so ambitious nor so important as the first two, but his pattern of activity appears to have been much the same, as he proceeded through Franconia, Swabia, and Switzerland.[15] Apart from the cities visited by these three men, episcopal inquisitors are known to have proceeded against Waldensians in numerous other cities of southern Germany.[16]

The causes of this extraordinary campaign are obscure, but two factors appear to have been significant: the zeal of individual inquisitors, and internal developments within the Waldensians. The role of the inquisitors was clearly paramount. During the 1360s and 1370s Walter Kerlinger had shown the importance of personal dedication to the *negotium fidei*, though it might be argued that he succeeded in his work largely because of the support he had from ecclesiastical and secular authorities. The itinerant inquisitors in the campaign against Waldensians had no highly placed authorities to lend their weight to the antiheretical effort. Neither pope nor emperor seems to have shown any interest at all in the campaign against Waldensians. If the campaign had been the work of papal inquisitors, one might expect curial directives to have underlain their work, but the standing Dominican inquisitors with papal commissions were almost entirely uninvolved in these proceedings. Indeed, not a single papal document that survives shows awareness that there were Waldensians in Germany. Not even the city governments seem to have worked with the inquisitors to any appreciable degree in the proceedings.[17] Although the burgrave of Steyr cooperated on occasion with Peter Zwicker, the German nobility did not play a major role in the trials.[18] The dukes of Austria issued an antiheretical decree, but the connections between this document and Peter Zwicker's work are at best obscure.[19]

So far as the sources reveal, these inquisitors acted primarily on their own initiative. The archbishop of Prague may have sent Martin of Amberg into the diocese of Regensburg, but it is difficult to believe that the bishops of Würzburg, Mainz, Bamberg, Raab, and Salzburg each summoned the inquisitor into their dioceses specifically to uproot heresies.[20] In other periods, bishops throughout Germany were content to entrust repressive measures to ecclesiastical judges who belonged to the diocesan hierarchy. For lack of evidence to support the hypothesis, it would be gratuitous to assume that all these bishops went out of their way to summon an inquisitor from outside diocesan bounds. Similarly, there is no reliable evidence that any local authorities ever called on Zwicker's services, and a joint summons from the bishops of Brandenburg, Camin, and Lebus (all of whom authorized proceedings at Stettin) to an inquisitor from much farther south would be most unlikely.[21] Zwicker, like Martin of Amberg, seems to have requested episcopal authorization wherever he knew there were heretics to stand trial. This pattern is especially clear in the case of Henry Angermeier, who according to the explicit comment of a chronicler solicited the bishop's authority for work in Augsburg, and who acted on his own at Rothenburg despite episcopal skepticism about his accusations.[22] It is perhaps natural for historians to suspect that initiative proceeds from higher ruling circles downward, but this model most clearly does not apply in the present instance. The ferment aroused by the three itinerant inquisitors may even have produced the information necessary for trials in Mainz,

Regensburg, Eichstätt, Bern, and Fribourg, where local authorities in-stigated the proceedings.[23] In any event, since most of the trials during this time arose from the work of the three special inquisitors, there is little difficulty in accounting for the spread of antiheretical fervor; the inquisitors carried this zeal along with them.

Is it purely fortuitous, however, that these itinerant inquisitors began the same sort of careers at the same time, while there is no group quite parallel to this in any other campaign? One might argue that it was easy for such individuals to take matters into their own hands during the Great Schism, which was a time of ecclesiastical disorder.[24] But it is far from clear that the conflicts during the schism caused a breakdown of judicial machinery within particular dioceses, or incapacitated even the papal inquisitors. In other words, there is no real basis for the suggestion that these wandering inquisitors were filling a vacuum left by the displacement of ordinary tribunals. The causes of this inquisitorial campaign, and also of its special character, may more plausibly be sought in events within the Waldensian sect—events that are known only in obscure outline.

The tight organization of the Waldensians was both a safeguard and a liability. At times it enabled the sect to take systematic pre-cautions to conceal its identity; it also provided a unified, cohesive body that, when necessary, could rally to its own defense by violent means.[25] When their solidarity broke down, however, the Walden-sians were more vulnerable to attack than other heretics. Because they formed close-knit communities, any member of the sect was likely to know the names of other members, and in interrogation the inquisitors could readily obtain names of fellow Waldensians from those being questioned. Because the Waldensians lived in such readily ascertainable communities, they were usually prosecuted en masse. Whereas beghards often went individually before an inquisi-tor, there are only a few cases in which individual Waldensians were tried.[26] One more frequently reads that thirty, forty, or fifty members of the sect were brought before an inquisition, and there is unimpeachable evidence that hundreds of suspects were brought to trial on one occasion. This kind of massive attack would scarcely have been possible without reliance on informers. In some instances the inquisitors could obtain from their subjects information about fellow Waldensians even in other cities.[27]

An inquisitor might find the most helpful information of this sort from a converted master of the sect. It was probably such a source that led to the extensive trials that Peter Zwicker conducted at Stettin. Around 1391 a Waldensian master who had just been in the region of Stettin converted to Catholicism at Prague, and apparently divulged considerable information about his former flock.[28] Authorities at Regensburg consulted with converted masters when charges were pressed against an alleged heretic in that city.[29] In the later part of the fourteenth century, several Waldensian masters converted to Catholicism. Such conversions occurred as early as the 1360s; further conversions took place around 1374 and again in the 1390s.[30] The most important source of information for these conversions is a list of twenty Waldensian masters, all but one of whom had converted to Catholicism by the late fourteenth century.[31] Five of these converts became priests, and one entered a monastery. In at least two cases the converts were given missionary assignments among their former coreligionists, though predictably they had little success.[32] The Waldensians who remained in the sect recognized that these conversions placed them in jeopardy, and in at least a few instances they retaliated by killing the renegade masters. Four of the masters on the above-mentioned list are supposed to have been assassinated.[33] Likewise, heretics in Strassburg agreed to pay three disciples fifty pounds for murdering a departed leader. These three men met their victim one evening outside the town walls, and stabbed him. Two servants came running when they heard the master's dying screams; they were apprehended as the murderers, and confessed to the deed under torture. The real perpetrators received their money from the heretical community, and the heretics later took up a collection that served as monetary "penance" for the misdeed.[34]

To pursue the matter further: it is clear that all these masters left the sect, but why? There are various conceivable answers. Possibly the masters were afraid of being detected; perhaps many of them were captured at once and made to abjure; or disillusionment may have resulted from friction and dissension within the sect.[35] The only one of these hypotheses that can be confirmed by hard evidence is that of internal dissension, which did indeed occur, at least among the Waldensians in Strassburg.[36] It is unclear whether it existed before the prosecutions began, yet this is entirely possible, and it may have been especially keen among the masters. The hypothesis of doctrinal or organizational dispute is also best compatible with the fact that the defections took place over a period of time, rather than on one particular occasion. But for lack of sufficient evidence, it is impossible to distinguish with certainty which of these causes, if any, underlay the inquisitorial campaign.

For whatever reason, the Waldensians were undergoing a crisis that was at least partly responsible for both the defections and the trials. Once the inquisitorial campaign got under way, the crisis itself grew all the more intense. The most evident effect of prosecution was flight to avoid detection.[37] The hardships imposed on the heretics, and the mingling of Waldensians who may have had slightly differing beliefs and practices, must have intensified the effects of the previously existing tension and crisis. With their confidence broken, deserted by many of their leaders, the Waldensians must surely have been in a mood to abjure their faith on the slightest provocation, and to furnish information about other Waldensians. In later and safer times, to be sure, they might revert to their heresy; there is abundant evidence that they did so in many instances.[38] But in the meantime, entire congregations might be affected. Particularly when inquisitors obtained information from the heretics' own leaders, it is likely that entire heretical populations in certain towns came under accusation.

A situation of this sort must have been especially favorable to the operation of itinerant inquisitors. In other periods an inquisitor in one city might obtain only isolated items of information about heretics elsewhere—not enough, perhaps, to warrant his traveling halfway across Germany to attempt trials. But during this campaign, when the sect was conspicuously vulnerable, the inquisitors must have sensed that they had an ideal opportunity to track down the heretics wherever they were to be found. One should not imagine that these inquisitors began with the intention of conducting such extensive operations. Rather, they seem to have begun by proceeding against heretics in restricted areas. Yet one trial led to another, if this interpretation is correct, and the result was one of the bitterest religious encounters in pre-Reformation Germany.

In view of the wide-ranging and thoroughgoing character of this repressive campaign, it is of the utmost significance that the papal inquisitors in Germany played virtually no role whatsoever in it. Only in Strassburg did the Dominicans, who were routinely delegated as papal inquisitors, participate in the anti-Waldensian campaign, and even there their involvement does not appear to have been wholly enthusiastic.[39] The Dominican John Arnoldi had received a commission as inquisitor for the province of Mainz, probably sometime in the early 1380s.[40] Sometime in or shortly before 1390, he undertook what seem to have been halfhearted efforts against the Waldensians in Strassburg.[41] These heretics had shown in earlier years that they could use violence to protect themselves.[42] Thus, when Arnoldi began his proceedings, the heretic John Blumenstein approached him in the confessional, and instead of confessing his sins, warned the inquisitor that unless he abandoned his task the Waldensians would kill him.[43]

On 4 April 1390, the general of the Dominican order released Arnoldi from his inquisitorial functions, at the inquisitor's own request.[44] Six days later, the Dominican general appointed Nicholas Böckeler as Arnoldi's successor, and sometimes around the middle of the 1390s, Böckeler conducted an extensive inquisition against the Waldensian community.[45] This, then, is the only known case in which a papal inquisitor in the ordinary succession of such delegates took part in the entire complex of trials. And even Böckeler seems to have devoted more energy to the purely political trial of John Malkaw (an adherent of the Roman papacy who sought to dissuade Rhenish townspeople from supporting the Avignonese pope) than he gave to his prosecution of Waldensians.[46]

The noninvolvement of papal inquisitors may in part be the result of geographical factors: the most active of the papal inquisitors seem to have been assigned to those dioceses of northern Germany where Waldensians were virtually unknown. One of the most zealous papal inquisitors of the fourteenth century, Walter Kerlinger, might have been expected to find Waldensians when he worked at Erfurt; they were found there roughly twenty years after he held trials against beghards and beguines.[47] But in most of the cities where he labored, there do not appear to have been Waldensian communities. The southern parts of Germany, where most of the Waldensian groups came to light, were entrusted in the later fourteenth century to two papal inquisitors who seem to have been more or less consistently inactive: Henry of Agro, who is known to have sentenced only one heretic, and John of Moneta, who is not recorded as having done anything to repress heresy.[48] Yet the failure of papal inquisitors to involve themselves in this campaign was totally characteristic of these men, and cannot be explained entirely on geographical grounds. What one encounters in this instance is a typical example of how papal inquisitors operated, or rather failed to operate. For lack of institutional guidance to direct them toward Waldensians, they preferred this period and in others either to remain inactive or to expend their efforts on easier prey.

There are no doubt further alternatives that might be explored. It might be argued, for example, that the Dominican order suffered such a decline in the quality and quantity of its membership as a result of the Black Death that it was no longer capable of exerting itself vigorously against deeply entrenched heresy. Yet the pattern shown here was a general one for papal inquisitors, before and after the Black Death, in Germany, and elsewhere. And it is difficult to believe that the Dominicans suffered that much more than the diocesan clergy. An explanation of the patterns of antiheretical action must take into account both sides of the phenomenon: the tendency of the papal inquisitors to dissipate or abuse their authority, and the relatively effective work of the episcopal inquisitors.

It should be noted that the itinerant episcopal inquisitors of the late fourteenth century were by no means typical episcopal agents, and one might wonder whether they confirm or disconfirm the thesis that diocesan personnel were relatively attentive to the danger of real heresy. This thesis would admittedly be weak if it were based exclusively or primarily on such atypical examples. Even so, the trials in question do show that, in the absence of a genuine Inquisition, judicial action was largely the work of individuals, who, once aware of heretics' presence, needed to obtain authorization for action from the local bishop. One should also remember in this connection that the bishops themselves proved far more vigilant than papal inquisitors in this anti-Waldensian campaign, and in several cities they proceeded without the aid of the itinerant inquisitors.

THE STRENGTH OF THE WALDENSIANS

The records scarcely permit even a rough conjecture of how many heretics there were, but it seems unlikely that heresy was an endemic in Germany as it was in southern France or northern Italy.

Minimum statistics are available for a few towns; for example, in the last years of the fourteenth century, authorities prosecuted more than 130 Waldensians at Bern, 53 at Fribourg, 36 at Bingen, about 34 at Augsburg, 32 at Strassburg, and lesser numbers in other towns.[49] There is no way of even guessing the number of heretics who evaded the authorities. In many of these trials, however, the inquisitors seem to have had detailed information about the members of the sect, which they had obtained from renegade Waldensian masters; it is thus possible that some of these figures approximate the total Waldensian populations in the towns in question. During this period, most of the towns concerned probably had populations of no more than five to ten thousand, but still the heretical element does not seem to have been a large percentage.

In some rural areas it may have been a different matter, at least in the remote areas of the east. Sources from Brandenburg and Austria, for example, sometimes suggest that very large numbers, perhaps even entire villages, belonged to the Waldensian sect.[50] Yet even so, the evidence is by no means conclusive. Peter Zwicker tried at least 443 Waldensians from the lower Oder, but they came from more than 120 towns and villages.[51] And a treatise written in the late fourteenth century spoke of more than a thousand converts from Waldensianism within two years, but these came from a very widespread area: Thuringia, Brandenburg, Bohemia, and Moravia.[52] Even agrarian areas, then, may not have been as prone to heresy as were lands in southern Europe.

As was mentioned before, contemporaries' perceptions are more important for present purposes than actual numbers. But there is reason to think that contemporaries' complacency may have been grounded in a real paucity of heretics.

PROCEDURES

For several trials in this campaign there are especially extensive records, which furnish insight into inquisitorial procedures. Although procedures are not of primary interest in a study that is attempting to isolate the specific dynamics of prosecution in a single country, it may prove useful to sketch the course of action in a few cases to give some idea of how the momentum for antiheretical work was put into effect in concrete terms. Three cases that are especially revealing are Peter Zwicker's trials in Stettin, Zwicker's work in Upper Austria, and a series of connected trials in Eichstätt and Regensburg. There are extended documents from other places, such as Strassburg, but in many such cases there are obscurities that reduce the value of the information for present purposes.

When Zwicker set to work at Stettin in 1392, he gathered about himself a vast number of assistants.[53] Apart from the inquisitor himself, there was an inquisitorial subdelegate, who occasionally took Zwicker's place. And during the course of the trial almost a hundred persons participated as notaries, assessors, and witnesses, some of them from outside the diocese. Of the suspects, some were summoned individually, while the inquisitor also issued general citations for any heretics who might be resident in certain communities. Some of the heretics even appeared of their own accord, or on the advice of other persons. More than 120 towns are mentioned as origins or domiciles of the accused, or as places where the bones of deceased heretics lay, awaiting disinterment and burning. Apart from some Pomeranian towns to the east, the centers of the heresy were concentrated near the northern part of the Oder River.

Large parts of the original records have survived. Unlike the shorter protocols that notaries often drew up to summarize the findings of an inquisition, these records give the statements of all persons tried, in the order in which they made their confessions. These records reveal a number of details regarding the lives and beliefs of the Waldensians, and show that their religion was in some ways remarkably unsophisticated.[54] They believed that their masters made periodic trips to paradise, and one woman held that they preceded this journey with a visit to hell. Most of them held it senseless to pray for the dead, and they gave the standard Waldensian explanation that after death there are only two paths, that to heaven and that to hell. One member with especially strong feelings declared that praying for the deceased is like feeding oats to a dead horse. Still, there were others who prayed out of habit, conviction, or affection for those who had died. The heretics on the whole subscribed to standard Waldensian tenets, but the members of the sect could not always dispense with the orthodox devotions that strict Waldensians abhorred; some even paid veneration to the Virgin Mary. The inquisitor tested their observance of popular religious customs by asking them whether they, like most Catholics of the day, had chosen their own special apostles to whom they prayed. Some of them either had no such apostle or could not recall his name, but one woman said she venerated Saint Bartholomew, and another heretic blithely claimed the archangel Michael as his patron apostle. Another subject confessed that he had gone once to a Waldensian master and confessed his sins, but had not gone a second time, since he preferred going off to drink beer.

The protocols shed light on the order of inquiry for each heretic. After administering an oath, the inquisitor drew questions from an extensive formulary. The questions fell into three sections. The inquisitor first asked about the subject's personal background—his parents, place of birth, and so forth. Second, he asked about the subject's relations with the sect—how long he had belonged, whether he had confessed his sins to the masters or heard their sermons, given them food or money, escorted them anywhere, etc. Finally, he asked about their beliefs, and in most of the interrogations this third part was the most extensive.[55] Following this systematic inquiry, the inquisitor asked the subject if he wished to abjure his heresy. All the heretics in this inquisition seem to have consented, so the inquisitor then absolved them and imposed a penance, usually penitential crosses or private devotions. (These were the almost universal punishments in Germany for heretics who repented—though in one case a chronicler mistook the cloth crosses attached to the penitent's clothes for a crusader's cross.)[56] In two cases, when persons admitted contact with Waldensians but denied that they themselves belonged to the sect, the inquisitor had them undergo canonical purgation, and granted them conditional absolution.[57]

Some of the heretics resisted the proceedings.[58] Two persons are said to have been brought out of prison for their interrogation, which may be an indication that they had in some way tried to resist; it seems unlikely that all the subjects in so extensive an inquisition would have been imprisoned before their hearings. One woman tried at first to deny her membership in the sect, and so she was questioned two more times; another woman is said to have been interrogated several times. In one instance the inquisitor needed to extort information from a subject, but neither in this trial nor in others does torture appear to have been used commonly; and when it was employed, it was intended more to obtain information (for example, names of other heretics) than to induce confession.[59] In the towns of Gross-Wubiser and Klein-Wubiser, some Waldensians refused to go to the inquisitor for penance, in some cases taking flight to avoid prosecution. Certain residents of these towns even took to calling the inquisitor a forerunner of Antichrist and a devil. But the inquisitor's lenience encouraged the rest of the heretics to cooperate.

When the same inquisitor operated in Upper Austria, however, both he and his subjects resorted to more violent measures.[60] Whereas Zwicker is not known to have sent any heretics to the stake at Stettin, he had many executed in Austria. And while the heretics in the northeastern territories resisted passively at most, Zwicker's inquisitions in Austria provoked active opposition. In both instances, the difference can perhaps be explained by the length of the inquisitor's stay. In his more extended proceedings in Austria, Zwicker had occasion to detect the relapse of many heretics, and his persistence in that region may have driven the Waldensian communities to desperate measures. The first certain indication of his activity in Austria is a report that he drew up in 1395, describing the errors and atrocities of the Waldensians and calling urgently for aid in their extirpation.[61] According to this report, the Waldensians in the town of Steyr had recently burned the barn of a parish priest who had harbored an inquisitor (probably Zwicker himself); they had also affixed a charred block and a bloody knife to the town gates as a symbolic warning of their power to resist. Appended to the manuscript of this report is a brief record of two similar incidents in a nearby town. In 1393 the heretics there had set fire to the home of the vicar, burning him and his household, and in the following year they had unsuccessfully attempted the same with his successor.[62]

More important for present purposes are three series of protocols dealing with Zwicker's inquisitions. The first series is undated, but refers to trials from before 1398.[63] Among the heretics were two widows who had received absolution earlier but had continued in their heresy. One of them was sentenced to wear penitential crosses for the rest of her life; for seven consecutive Sundays she was to go to the local church and receive public penance and a beating from the parish priest; and before and after mass she was to lie down at the threshold of the church and allow the congregation to trample on her. The other woman was to wear the crosses for twenty years, and receive public penance on one occasion. Penitential crosses and various other penances, in one case a pilgrimage to Rome, were assigned to three other persons, who were abjuring their heresy for the first time. Although these sentences were all technically imposed by the inquisitor himself, they seem to have been given only in his name, by a commissary appointed to act in his absence. This circumstance perhaps explains why the relapsed heretics were merely given penances, whereas technically they should have been executed.[64]

When Zwicker returned, treatment of relapsed heretics was evidently more rigorous, as one can see in the second series of protocols, from 1398.[65] One of the persons mentioned in these documents is the widow who had abjured twice earlier and received the penitential crosses to wear for the remainder of her life; another of these heretics had abjured before Zwicker in 1395; a third had been absolved twice before; and a fourth was unwilling to take the required oath, despite the inquisitor's repeated persuasions. All four were released to the secular authorities and presumably burned. The fifth protocol refers to a heretic who had earlier denied his membership in the sect, but who now confessed after lengthy interrogation, and was sentenced to public penance for seven consecutive Sundays and holy days. While performing his penance, he was to wear a cap with a picture of a devil pulling out a peasant's tongue—a memento of his earlier perjury. The records also tell that the inquisitor had previously condemned to the stake at least seven heretics from nearby villages or towns.

The remaining series of protocols, which cannot be dated, deals with three clerics.[66] One priest of the diocese of Passau had himself been a Waldensian from youth and had renounced his heresy before a previous inquisitor. Nonetheless, Zwicker was lenient; he imposed only private penances on the priest when he abjured the second time. In the next case, a priest had been excommunicated for refusing to obey the inquisitor's summons, but on presenting himself before the inquisitor he received absolution from censures. It is not clear whether he was himself suspect of heresy or whether he had been cited as a witness. Another cleric, a canon, had been excommunicated for vaguely specified offenses, and on intervention of an episcopal commissary was released from this excommunication.

Zwicker's career illustrates one way in which the campaign against Waldensians spread over such a wide area—that is, through the efforts of an individual inquisitor, evidently armed with information about heretics in diverse regions. The trials in Eichstätt and Regensburg exemplify the interlinking of trials that could occur even without such an itinerant inquisitor.[67] The initial subject in this instance was John Oertel, a Waldensian who had fled from Donauwörth to avoid prosecution late in the year 1393. Oertel went to Regensburg, where he made contact with a man he had known for several years, the former Waldensian Conrad Huter, who had probably abjured his heresy before Martin of Amberg in the early 1380s.[68] Huter was conspicuously inhospitable to Oertel. He refused to speak to him face to face, and when Oertel told of the hardships he had undergone, Huter replied that he, too, had suffered much because of his heresy in Regensburg. Eventually Oertel left Regensburg, perhaps in hopes that the situation in Donauwörth had improved. By the spring of 1395, however, he found himself in the hands of the bishop of Eichstätt, whose diocese he must have passed through en route to his home. He abjured his heresy, and at the same time gave a strong suggestion, perhaps in revenge, that Huter and his wife still belonged to the Waldensian sect.

Four months passed, in which time the authorities in Eichstätt notified those in Regensburg of these allegations. Then, in September of the same year, Oertel was again interrogated in Eichstätt; this time the vicar Albert Staufer, from the diocese of Regensburg, was present. At this second examination, Oertel was questioned in greater detail about Huter and Huter's relatives (some of whom had gone to the stake as relapsed heretics in Oertel's home town of Donauwörth). Oertel told of a visit that Huter had made to Donauwörth in 1391, in which he had enjoyed the company of certain Waldensians. According to Oertel, he had understood at this meeting that Huter was still a Waldensian.

Within a week, the vicar from Regensburg was back in that city, where he attended hearings against Huter. The episcopal inquisitor, Frederick Süssner, examined Huter twice, and then questioned his wife and his niece. Huter and his wife admitted that they had earlier been heretics, but said that they had abjured and had not relapsed into heresy. Huter repeatedly denied any acquaintance with Oertel, and though he admitted that he had been in Donauwörth, he claimed that he had thought the heretics there were sincerely converted to Catholicism. Both of these subjects were able to recite the basic Catholic prayers (the Pater Noster, Ave Maria, and creed); and though they made errors in their recitation, they agreed to accept any corrections the inquisitor might suggest. Süssner questioned them at length about points of disagreement between Catholicism and Waldensianism; their answers were thoroughly orthodox. Perhaps bearing in mind that Waldensians were often deceitful under interrogation, he asked them whether anyone had advised them how to answer his questions, and they replied that no one had done so.[69]

Rather than act precipitously, the inquisitor or the bishop forwarded the records of the proceedings (apparently both those from Eichstätt and those from Regensburg) to Martin of Amberg, who had originally absolved Huter and his wife. The suspects evidently waited in a municipal jail while Martin scrutinized their records. Only in May of the following year did he write back from Prague that he found no reason for punishing the accused, and that a check among recently converted Waldensian masters had produced no evidence of their continued membership in the sect. As soon as this letter reached the bishop of Regensburg he had the suspects released, though only after they had taken a standard oath that they would not take vengeance for the measures against them.

The affair was not quite over. Six months later, Huter became embroiled in a quarrel with an acquaintance, Frederick Goldner, who, while slightly intoxicated, had interpreted an offhand remark by Huter as an offense against the faith. Although Goldner and others later teased Huter about the affair, when they took the matter to the inquisitor they evidently had no substantial charges to press. The incident thus illustrates little more than the widespread antiheretical sentiments among Germans of the late Middle Ages.

REASONS FOR PROSECUTION

In investigating the motives for this inquisitorial campaign, one must first and foremost take into account the widely shared antipathy toward religious deviants in German society. To be sure, there may have been incidental ulterior motives in specific trials, but the campaign as a whole can best be explain on what one might term socio-religious grounds.

By the late fourteenth century, the era of lynch justice against heretics had long passed. The Church had established more or less regular norms for prosecution, and it was no longer necessary for the people at large to give vent to their sentiments through violent action. But evidence for continued antiheretical attitudes is not altogether lacking. A man tried at Stettin in 1393 told how he had left the Waldensians because of popular aversion to the sect.[70] In the same year heretics in Augsburg paid a substantial amount of money to avoid the opprobrium of public penance, thus suggesting that their fellow townspeople would have taken their heretical associations amiss.[71] A few years later the town council of Strassburg banished a group of erstwhile Waldensians because they had brought dishonor to the city; while the banishment was strictly a governmental action, the implication was that the presence of heretics would be interpreted widely as a disgrace.[72] In 1435 a widow in Augsburg suffered abuse from other townspeople, who charged that her husband had been among the Waldensians tried forty-two years earlier. She was sufficiently concerned about the allegation to go to the trouble of procuring a letter from the town government certifying that her husband had not been a member of the sect.[73] In short, Waldensians (like beghards and beguines) were commonly viewed as deviants, and despised as such by large segments of society.[74] No doubt there were also many persons who remained indifferent to matters of heresy and orthodoxy, but there is sufficient evidence, at least from cities and towns, that antiheretical sentiments were widespread. Thus, it is not surprising that popular dialect in parts of southern Germany placed heresy and unnatural sexuality on the same level, as perversions of Christian decency: the term *Ketzerei* could mean either "heresy" or "sodomy."[75]

Wilhelm Wattenbach suggested that the popular aversion to heretics may have been provoked by the heretics' own hostility toward orthodox Christians and their feeling that they alone were saved.[76] This factor may well have been vital. The Church provided a sense of moral security, which surely fulfilled an important psychological function. Those who abided by its regulations and received its sacraments did so because they felt that they were thus attaining salvation, and any questioning of the Church's efficacy was a challenge to their own religious hopes. The "churchliness" that Bernd Moeller cites as the dominant feature of pre-Reformation German piety was an intense commitment to the established Church and its means of salvation.[77] Though Moeller gives evidence for this sentiment only from the half century or so before the Reformation, its roots surely went back much earlier. Such an attitude would carry as a logical corollary an antipathy toward heretics. But closely linked with these religious considerations there was assuredly a social factor: in medieval Germany, as in any society, deviance from a commonly accepted tradition marked a person as an outsider.

This widely shared animosity toward heretics goes a long way toward explaining why genuine heretics were repressed, and why there was general support for repression, with little if any resistance except from the heretics. But it is reasonable to ask what further, ulterior motives there were—whether political or monetary—for attacks on heretics.

Occasionally there is a hint of a political factor in the prosecution of Waldensians, though it does not appear to have been of primary significance. For example, a group of fifty-three suspects was brought to trial at Fribourg in 1399, though eventually they were acquitted.[78] Many of those accused of heresy belonged to what one historian has called the rising "new bourgeoisie," whereas the municipal authorities who called for repression represented the older bourgeoisie.[79] Conceivably the incentive for prosecution in this instance was political—the older bourgeoisie may have thought of a heresy trial as a convenient way to attack their new rivals for social and economic standing in the town. But it is dangerous to use the social backgrounds of the heretics and their adversaries as keys to the motives for prosecution. The new bourgeoisie, being engaged in commerce, would have more opportunity for contact with other cities, and for exposure to Waldensian ideas; the older bourgeoisie, which had control of the city's government, might act out of a sense of public responsibility even if it did not desire conviction of the Waldensians for ulterior motives. The only thing that seems clear is that the charges were not contrived; later proceedings demonstrated that there was indeed a substantial Waldensian community in Fribourg, to which the subjects in 1399 quite probably did belong.[80] Thus, the charges were not unfounded, even if the trial did prove politically advantageous to the accusers.

Another trial that may possibly have given vent to political animosity was the prosecution of Waldensians at Augsburg in 1393.[81] Most of the heretics in this town accepted public penance and at least ostensibly returned to orthodoxy. Fourteen of them, however, attempted shortly afterward to relieve themselves of the penitential crosses. They went to the bishop and offered him seventy guldens in exchange for his permission to dispense with this penance. The citizens and town council took this transaction amiss; they burned

five of the fourteen, and required the others to resume their penitential crosses. Commutation of the punishment was unquestionably
within the bishop's legal rights; the inquisitor had acted as a delegate
of the bishop, and in inquisitorial proceedings the right was routinely
reserved for the judge (or a fortiori his source of authority) to com-
mute or mitigate the punishment. The citizenry and council, however, seem not to have thought of the affair in such legal terms, but
viewed the case as a sign of relapse on the part of the heretics, and
probably of venality on the bishop's part. The antipathy to the
bishop, if such was involved, is readily comprehensible, since the
bishop and the town had long been bitterly at odds with each other.[82]
It is furthermore possible that the town council had political reasons
for acting harshly toward the heretics. One of the chroniclers mentions that all of the heretics in Augsburg were weavers, and that
"very few of them belonged to other crafts"; the same chronicler,
however, states that some of these men were wealthy and reputable
members of the community.[83] Not all members of the weavers' guild
necessarily practiced weaving as a trade, and even those who did
might be men of respectable means if they had attained the status of
masters. There is reason to believe that at least one of the heretics
who was burned was a leading member of the weavers' guild, and
represented this guild in the town government.[84] Yet this guild was
never especially powerful in municipal affairs at Augsburg, and it is
possible that its representatives were at odds with the ruling powers
in the town.[85] It is also conceivable that the weavers' political opponents were responsible for the execution of the five "relapsed"
heretics. If this conjecture has any substance, this episode exemplifies
the sort of political influence that probably entered repressive under-
takings on more than one occasion: political motives were not responsible for the inquisition itself; but once the trial occurred, it may
have become partly a tool for political ends.

The mere fact that most repression occurred in campaigns makes
it difficult to believe that extraneous or ulterior motives were essential in the instigation of proceedings. To account for the campaign
against Waldensians during the years from 1389 to 1401 by reference
to such extraneous considerations, for example, one would have to
hypothesize a peculiar coincidence of personal or political circumstances that gave rise to trials in a wide variety of towns at roughly
the same time. The occurrence of a campaign against heretics is
explicable in terms of the contagion of genuine antiheretical sentiment; it is much less comprehensible as the product of particular,
local circumstances in a wide variety of places.

Closely analogous to political motives were monetary considerations. As was already mentioned, jurisdiction could be made profitable, and even if rival jurisdictions did not contend with each other for the spoils, the opportunities for revenue may have been important to certain inquisitors. In the first place, heretics could be burdened with fines as a form of penance when they abjured their doctrines. When more than 130 Waldensians recanted at Bern in 1399, the inquisitor made them pay fines of various amounts, totaling more than three thousand guldens.[86] Likewise, inquisitors at Strassburg imposed fines on penitent Waldensians; the inquisitor assigned a pilgrimage to one man, but because this penitent's feet hurt, he arranged that the inquisitor himself should undertake the pilgrimage in exchange for three guldens.[87] Second, there was the possibility of bribery, though the only recorded example of this is the case of the canon at Kolberg who threatened to burn a group of Waldensians unless they paid him three marks.[88] The main difference between a judicial fine and bribery was that the bribe did not require either conviction or penitence. Third, and perhaps most importantly, there were confiscations of the goods and houses of condemned heretics. For example, the bishop of Augsburg enriched himself with the property of heretics convicted at Donauwörth. If the story of one chronicler can be taken as fact, the episcopal inquisitor in this case released the poor heretics and had the rich ones executed, as a means of obtaining revenue.[89] There is nothing inherently implausible in this allegation. At least some of the heretics in Donauwörth were propertied, since a house donated in 1438 to the town hospital reportedly had been owned in earlier years by heretics.[90] In short, wealthy persons were apparently included in the inquisition, if not singled out as its special targets. It may be too much to agree with the cynical comment of a chronicler regarding this and other inquisitions of the same year: "I believe that the principal cause was wicked [that is, mercenary]."[91] There is abundant evidence that there actually were heretics in Donauwörth, so one need not conclude that the charges were contrived or insincere.[92] Probably the fairest conclusion is that the inquisition was undertaken with a sincere desire to restore the community to religious orthodoxy, but that once under way the trial was used for purposes other than those of principle.

One inquisitor who plainly was not seeking enrichment was the one who worked at Nürnberg in 1332, in all likelihood against Waldensians.[93] This inquisitor focused his attack on the poorer members of the sect. Indeed, the municipal authorities became concerned that by singling out only the lower classes for prosecution, the inquisitor might give rise to protest. Hence, they sent a liaison to direct the inquisitor's attention against those rich persons who were also suspect. Two of these wealthy individuals even came forth and asked for an examination to prove their innocence, but the inquisitor inexplicably refused the offer. Apparently it was only after considerable pressure from the local authorities that the inquisitor acceded to the demand for an impartial inquiry. When he finally produced a list of ninety-one or more heretics, it included the names of certain citizens from wealthy families, though the greater number were still from the lower classes. Perhaps this inquisitor was atypical, but there is little evidence that his colleagues habitually sought opportunities for gain.[94]

If there is little indication of politically or financially motivated action against Waldensians, there is absolutely no sign whatsoever of politically inspired *resistance* to prosecution. When the bishop of Strassburg established a commission in 1392 to seek out heretics, particularly Waldensians, he instructed the members to act in cooperation with the papal inquisitor in the diocese, who at that time was Nicholas Böckeler.[95] Contrary to what H. C. Lea suggests, the bishop does not seem to have made any deliberate effort to keep the proceedings "in his own hands."[96] If Böckeler did not yet act against Waldensians, and if other papal inquisitors throughout Germany failed to act against that sect, it was not because the bishops prevented such action. Instead, it was clearly because the papal inquisitors lacked interest in such measures, and had little occasion to develop such interest.

There was one instance of opposition to repression during this campaign (apart from several cases of resistance by the heretics themselves). It involved one of the itinerant episcopal inquisitors, rather than a papal inquisitor. But once again it illustrates the need for constant checks on the power of individuals to avoid arbitrary proceedings. In 1394 the wandering heresy hunter Henry Angermeier arrived in Rothenburg ob der Tauber to press charges of heresy against one John Wern.[97] The suspect was a prominent member of the community, who had served as member of the town council. His accuser seems to have lived outside the town, and in any case did not appear in Rothenburg for the trial. Angermeier himself did not act in this case as judge, but merely as "denunciator" of the accused, though he still styled himself an inquisitor. The judge was Walter Schubel, vicar general for the diocese of Würzburg, though it is not evident precisely how he became involved in the affair.[98] In view of Angermeier's procedure in other cities, it is unlikely that he intended

merely to denounce Wern before an episcopal judge. Most probably
he appealed to the bishop of Würzburg for authority as inquisitor,
but the bishop preferred to assign the case to a person more familiar
to him, and perhaps more reliable. In any event, the episcopal vicar
went to Rothenburg and examined the accused, but could only conclude that Wern was in all respects "a good Christian and true
Catholic." Although Angermeier presented certain letters and documents testifying against Wern, Schubel did not accept these as
establishing his guilt, or even as ground for suspicion. Even at a
later hearing, Angermeier was unable to present incriminating evidence or witnesses. The vicar then undertook a formal inquisition
against Wern—that is, an examination of other townspeople to ascertain whether there were grounds for questioning his orthodoxy. Examination of both clerics and laity merely confirmed Wern's good
repute. As a final assurance of orthodoxy, Schubel suggested that
Wern might purge himself of the charges on oath, with the assistance
of five, seven, or more cojurators. On the day appointed, Wern appeared with roughly ten times as many cojurators as the vicar had
proposed. Thus, Schubel issued a formal acquittal, effectively vitiating
Angermeier's attempt at conviction. Still, it would not be accurate to
characterize this case as one in which rival jurisdictions contended
for power. The difference of opinion was clearly substantive rather
than political; the vicar saw no validity in Angermeier's evidence,
and apparently feared that if Angermeier were in charge of the investigation he would convict the subject on invalid grounds.

The reasons for prosecution of the Waldensians were undoubtedly
complex, and it would be difficult to gauge the relative importance
of the various factors responsible for their repression. It is probably
safe to say, however, that the fact that they were authentically heretical probably counted for less than the public perception of them as
deviants, and thus as a threat to the social order. Indeed, it was quite
possible for groups that were less clearly heretical to serve as the
focus of judicial action if they could be portrayed as similarly deviant,
as the next chapter will endeavor to show.

5

Heresy As Civil Disorder

In the last two chapters we have seen that papal inquisitors focused their energies during the fourteenth century primarily on conventual beguines and to some extent on beghards, while episcopal authorities labored against both beghards and beguines on the one hand and Waldensians on the other. We have also seen how the secular authorities occasionally became involved in the proceedings; at times they sought to restrain arbitrary prosecution, while on other occasions they aided both papal and episcopal agents in their efforts against heretics. To complete the story of repression during this tumultuous century, we should now note that secular authorities, princely and especially municipal, at times took matters into their own hands. Sometimes they seem to have taken autonomous action against Waldensians, as was perhaps the case in Nürnberg.[1] More often than not, however, their subjects were not members of identifiable sects, but merely isolated religious eccentrics, even if sometimes they were labeled "beghards" or "beguines." It may not be altogether accidental that the known instances of municipal involvement in prosecution for heresy occurred almost entirely in southern German cities—Augsburg and Nürnberg in particular—for it was predominantly in Upper Germany that municipal courts were beginning at this time to assume competence over religious and semireligious offenses of other kinds, such as blasphemy and sorcery.[2]

In two respects the heresy trials in municipal courts differed from ecclesiastical inquisitions. First, these courts used nonecclesiastical forms of interrogation. Secular authorities evidently did not concern themselves with the precise character of a heretic's doctrine. The extant records, at any rate, merely specify that a person was a heretic, or perhaps a "beghard," without enumerating his heresies. For instance, the town council at Augsburg banished two men in 1353 "because they were seen to be heretics."[3] In the previous year it had banished three beguines and a beghard, who apparently were non-conventual, but whose status otherwise remains obscure—though the court record notes that the beguines were "bad women."[4] With information as meager as this, municipal records are virtually worthless for the history of medieval heresies, though they occasionally furnish interesting materials for the study of repressive measures.

Second, the punishments that town governments inflicted were usually distinctive. City courts never imposed penitential practices on heretics, and seldom sentenced obdurate heretics to death.[5] Instead, they commonly banished the heterodox from the cities. If the culprit returned within a certain radius of the city before his period of banishment expired, he was to suffer a specified punishment. The relative infrequency of death sentences, though, is not necessarily a sign that municipal governments were in principle more lenient than the Church. Rather, the form of punishment reflected the special purposes of the secular courts. The Church had prescribed exile for heretics in earlier centuries, but exile and banishment did not further the ends that the Church desired: cleansing of Christendom as a whole from corrupting influence, and conversion of persons who had fallen from the faith.[6] Indeed, banishment was more likely to defeat these purposes, since heretics who wandered to distant places carried their doctrines with them, and might give rise to new heretical communities. Banishment did, however, serve the ends of urban authorities, who generally concerned themselves with the more limited task of ridding their own localities of heretics and other criminals. One may even take it as reasonable basis for conjecture, whenever one finds that heretics were banished from a city, that the municipal authorities had a hand in determining the sentence, even if they did not initiate the proceedings.[7] The best examples are three trials in Nürnberg, in which the heretics may well have been Waldensians.[8] Eighteen men and five women convicted of heresy in 1354 were banished from the city for five years, on threat of being hanged. The impetus for this inquisition came from the clergy, and whatever role the town government had is unclear. But both the banishment and the threat of hanging (rather than burning) suggest that the government had a hand in the proceedings. This impression is corroborated by the fact that the case appears in municipal records rather than ecclesiastical documents.[9] Again, in 1362, eight male and seven female heretics were banished for life. Some of these latter heretics had been among those banished in 1354, and according to canon law should have been burned as relapsed heretics. That they escaped burning is no absolute proof that their tribunal was secular, but the suggestion is strong that this was the case.[10] Less clear than these two instances is one in 1379, in which many heretics who came to trial, and several who had fled prosecution, were declared banished from the town. In all other respects the trial was clearly ecclesiastical, but evidently the municipal authorities offered their own proposal for the specified groups. An ecclesiastical court might have excommunicated fugitive heretics after a certain period (usually a year), but it is difficult to imagine that it would have banished them from a city.[11]

Why did municipal courts concern themselves with heresy? At times it is clear that the municipal governments took action against heretics specifically in periods of political turmoil. Thus, the town of Nürnberg found itself in a state of chaos in 1348. The guilds had overthrown the existing government and expelled the patriciate from the town.[12] The patricians received the armed support of Charles IV, and soon regained control. But during the brief period when it was in power, the guild government was singularly incapable of maintaining order within the city, and encountered a plethora of disruptions. A secular priest named Hartman Graser, who had "preached against the Christian faith," was evidently considered among those responsible for the disorder in the town, and thus was banished for a period of a hundred years.[13] Analogously, the town of Augsburg seems to have been especially sensitive to religious disorder in 1381, when war broke out between the Swabian towns, including Augsburg, and the Swabian lords, including the bishop of that town.[14] The dangers of internal dissension during such a crisis could hardly have escaped the council's notice, and in fact the town government took a series of antiheretical measures during this year. A vagabond named Brother Hans, afflicted with a disease that the chronicler called gout, settled in a chapel in the town churchyard. He quickly attracted roughly fifty other persons suffering from the same disease. Presumably they sought to cure the illness by collective prayer, but the burgomasters, seeing their devotion as a form of fanaticism, closed the chapel. Eventually Brother Hans went to the stake as a heretic, along with four associates, while his wife was banished for life.[15] During the same year, the council banished two other persons for religious offenses: one Ruff der Sturme, who in addition to engaging in ribald and lecherous behavior had gone about as a "beg-hard"; and a cobbler who had preached in front of churches as though he were a priest.[16]

It remains obscure how town governments could claim jurisdiction in cases of heresy. Offenses against the faith were strictly matters for ecclesiastical courts, and certain secular law codes, including the law book for Augsburg, explicitly recognized the Church's competence in these cases.[17] Town councils might claim that they were concerned about heretics not as offenders against the faith, but as potential sources of civic disruption, and perhaps as causes of dishonor for the city. Nonetheless, the Church could have insisted on its right, according to canon law, of determining whether an alleged heretic actually subscribed to heterodox doctrine. From the Church's viewpoint, this right was important not only because it took a man with theological training to decide what was heresy, but also because a heretic was primarily a sinner needing to be converted, rather than a criminal subject to punishment.[18] The peculiarity is that the Church does not seem to have protested against the usurpation of its jurisdiction by city governments. The most plausible explanation for the cities' action, and for the Church's acceptance of it, is that the terms "heretic" and "beghard" were applied so loosely that the charge of doctrinal heterodoxy became incidental. When a town council banished a person as a "heretic" or "beghard," it was probably a matter of indifference whether the accused actually subscribed to heterodox beliefs, and the municipal authorities were not claiming to pass judgment on this question. What mattered to the towns was that these persons held, and doubtless also preached, religious principles that might cause disturbances within the cities.

Were the town governments seeking to exclude ecclesiastical judges from such cases? There is absolutely no ground for such speculation. In at least one case the authorities at Nürnberg banished a "heretic" with the threat that if he returned to the town he would be turned over to the bishop of Bamberg.[19] In this case it is entirely clear that the city claimed concurrent jurisdiction over heretics when they threatened civil order. There is no indication whatsoever that any city government anywhere in Germany ever claimed exclusive jurisdiction over heretics. Nor is there reason to imagine that the claim of concurrent jurisdiction was a political device intended to wrest power from the clergy. If this had been the case, one would surely expect indications that the Church resisted such secular intervention, but there is not a single case in which churchmen are known to have protested. Secular action against heretics cannot plausibly be seen as a manifestation of Church-state conflict; rather, it shows the essential harmony of secular and ecclesiastical authorities in their reaction against religious deviance.

Apart from instances in which cities tried persons for heresy, one should take note of certain cases in which the municipal authorities tried heretics, or religious enthusiasts designated as beghards, on charges other than heresy. While these latter trials do not strictly fall within the purview of this study, they shed light on the general relations between town governments and religious dissenters. A series of such trials occurred in Augsburg in mid-century. The council banished a beghard in 1347 along with other persons included in a list of blasphemers, and in the following year it banished a man designated as a beghard because he had practiced deception.[20] The only hint of heresy in the latter case is the cryptic statement attributed to the beghard that "the higher spirit has arisen, and the lower spirit should also arise."[21] Once again, in 1349, a beghard was banished on the charge of being a deceiver.[22] All three of these cases occur in "Saint Gall Day" lists of socially undesirable persons, all of whom suffered banishment from the town for three years.[23] No further cases of this sort arise until 1364, when a *Grüblinsmann* was banished for a year on the charge of leading respectable townsmen's children and servants into a brick shed and taking their money by gambling. The term *Grüblinsmann* seems to have been used at a later date for Waldensians; though the behavior of the present offender seems singularly un-Waldensian, he may have been some sort of heretic or religious enthusiast.[24] Records for other towns are generally less complete than those for Augsburg, but one does occasionally find relevant cases elsewhere; thus, a beghard was banished from Rostock in 1353 on the charge of murder.[25] What these cases suggest is that words such as "heretic" and especially "beghard" were used in a highly undifferentiated sense, even for persons who can scarcely be considered religious. These designations were perhaps used to add force to other charges; conversely, the charges may have arisen because of antecedent suspicion and animosity toward these people.

A special case of a religious threat to civil order came in 1348–49, when the Black Death gave rise to the penitential exercises of the flagellants.[26] Wandering from town to town, without clerical supervision, the flagellants would strip themselves virtually naked and proceed to whip themselves, inducing profuse bloodshed. Wherever they went they heightened emotions, and when they preceded the plague in a given town they seem to have aroused feverish anxiety regarding the disease. Occasionally they stimulated violence among the townspeople; though there is no convincing evidence that the flagellants themselves indulged in widespread violent action, they at least served as the occasion for assaults on both Jews and clergy. In view of these dangers, it was convenient to call these groups heretical because the term provided an excuse for their suppression. The term "heretic" was highly flexible and connotative, and suggested that the persons in question might be not only anticlerical but perhaps anti-social as well. Possibly at times the flagellants did adhere to heretical doctrine, but more commonly the term was a mere label used to justify their condemnation.

Action against the movement took various forms, ranging from mere prohibition of entry into a city all the way to execution. Both ecclesiastical and secular authorities became involved in such action. Late in the year 1348, the flagellants entered the city of Prague, but the archbishop and clergy "forced them to depart from Bohemia," through means that the chronicler unfortunately does not specify.[27] The bishop of Breslau at first tolerated and even approved the move-ment, but later revoked the approval, and according to one source even released a leader of the flagellants to the secular court for burn-ing.[28] The processions appeared outside Lübeck in the following spring, and the leaders appealed to the town government for permis-sion to enter. But upon consultation with the bishop, members of the clergy, and certain monks in the city, the authorities decided that they should exclude the movement from the town. The town council was particularly apprehensive that the flagellants might lead townspeople into their "heresy," though the chronicle gives no specific information about heterodox dogmas. Some of the group's members succeeded in entering the city, where the officials took them prisoner; their ulti-mate fate is unknown.[29] Probably about the same time, the town council at Erfurt refused to allow the processions within that city.[30] And in Aachen, the council issued an edict against alleged carriers of the plague, with a clause forbidding flagellants to enter the city. If any were caught within the town walls, they were to be turned over to the municipal judge.[31]

Prior to the autumn of 1349, reaction against the flagellants was mainly local. The question whether the flagellants should be allowed to continue, however, eventually received attention in broader cir-cles. It became such an issue in the Low Countries and in northern France that the theological faculty of the University of Paris received a request to pass judgment on the movement.[32] This faculty decided to refer the matter to Avignon, and sent a preacher to give a sermon in Pope Clement's presence regarding the flagellants.[33] After an elaborate—and flattering—demonstration of the need for referring weighty questions to the pontiff, the sermon proceeded in three sections. In the first, the preacher argued that the flagellants drew their members for the most part from "the people," whom one could not expect to act rationally. In the second, he recounted how the movement had spread throughout Christendom, gaining uncountable followers, and how its very size was one reason why some rulers feared to take action against it. In the third part, he detailed certain of the new and vain customs elaborated by the flagellants, particularly the alleged attacks on the Jews (whom the flagellants and others accused of inducing the plague by poisoning the wells). In all three sections of the sermon, though particularly in the first and second, the preacher emphasized the flagellants' civic disruption rather than their supposed heresy. This sermon was not Pope Clement's only source of information regarding the movement, for a group of penitents left Basel, probably in the early autumn, and went to Avignon to perform their rites before the pope. The pontiff at first gave thought to imprisoning them, but was dissuaded by certain cardinals who took a more indulgent view of their ceremonies.[34]

In October Clement issued a bull calling for the suppression of the movement by ecclesiastical and secular authorities.[35] Many of his charges, including that of attacks on the Jews, may have derived from the above-mentioned sermon. He indicated that certain religious had abused their function of caring for souls, and had joined the flagellants. These offenders, he alleged, were primarily Franciscans—members of the order among whom antipapal attitudes had become common because of the conflict between the papacy and the Spiritual Franciscans.[36] One may take this accusation with a grain of salt, for while there is no evidence supporting the pope's charge against the Franciscans, there is directly contrary evidence from Tournai, where it was the Franciscans who aroused the enmity of the flagellants, and a certain Dominican who supported them.[37] Toward the end of his bull, Clement specified that his prohibitions did not apply to those penitents who practiced their devotions in their own homes, without joining the "superstitious congregations, societies, and conventicles aforementioned."[38] This qualification lends an important clue to the pope's motives in condemning the processions: it was not the act of penance that he found reprehensible, but the public and organized character of the movement, which made it threatening to both the religious and the civil order.

The effects of this bull were most evident in France and in Flanders, where royal and municipal authorities lent their weight to its enforcement.[39] There were apparently only scattered efforts to restrain the movement in Germany during the next few years. The bishops of Magdeburg and Regensburg forbade public flagellation.[40] The town council of Nürnberg condemned a leader of the flagellants in mid-1350 and banished him from the city, threatening to drown him if he should return.[41] In the diocese of Cologne and in that of Utrecht, the "sect" survived until later in the decade, and required the attention of local synods.[42] The most remarkable incident (if indeed our source is at all reliable) occurred at Herrieden, in the diocese of Eichstätt, where a large number of flagellants are supposed to have been slaughtered, whereupon their bodies "were cast into the flames of vengeance."[43]

The flagellant movement survived into the fifteenth century, especially in and around Thuringia, where in some respects it appears to have become radicalized. To some degree it took on millenarian doctrine; for the most part, however, its only point of divergence from the established Church seems to have been its repudiation of the sacraments.[44] Apart from rare instances of repression, it evidently remained an essentially underground movement until its uncovering in the early fifteenth century.[45] As such, it lost much of its potential for civil disturbance.

The "heretics" dealt with in this chapter are of only passing significance in the history of medieval spirituality, but the repression that they underwent reveals a great deal about the attitudes of authorities during the late Middle Ages. Whether genuinely heretical or not, religious deviants were seen as a threat to society. During the fourteenth century, a period of social upheaval, there were numerous religious eccentrics who posed only minimal threat to either Church or secular affairs. In a minor way, however, these "heretics" set the stage for the radicals of the following century, who integrated a more radical religious challenge with a far more serious affront to the secular order.

6

Orthodox Reaction in an Age of Revolution

Between the Council of Constance and the Reformation there were perhaps half as many heresy trials as there had been in the preceding century. There are two obvious explanations for the decline: that there were fewer heretics, and that the Church was less apprehensive about heresy. Both explanations are probably correct, and they are perhaps interrelated, in the sense that the dwindling of heretics left churchmen with less occasion for anxiety about those heretics who remained. Still, the instances of repression that occurred during this century tended to be more spectacular than those of the fourteenth century—not surprisingly, since the heretics themselves tended in many cases to be more radical than their predecessors.

THE HUSSITE REVOLUTION

Unquestionably the most important radical movement of the period was the Hussite movement in Bohemia.[1] As Howard Kaminsky has persuasively argued, "the Hussite movement was both a reformation and a revolution, in fact *the* revolution of the late Middle Ages, the history of which period cannot be properly understood if the Hussites are left out."[2] Not only did the Hussites take control of Bohemia itself, but they had some success in spreading their doctrine to other countries, especially to German-speaking lands. In an effort to under-

stand their impact, we shall look first at the situation in Bohemia and
then at the Hussite infiltration of Germany.

Bohemia had long had a reputation as a breeding ground for
heresy. While the identity of the Bohemian heretics remains a controversial topic, the rural setting of most inquisitions points more
toward a simple and evangelical form of heresy than toward a radical
form of mysticism; it is surely safe to conclude that many, though not
all, of the heretics in question were Waldensians.[3] In any case, the
prevalence of heresy in Bohemia resulted in the routine appointment
of inquisitors for that country considerably before any such development in German-speaking territories. Two Franciscans were appointed
for this task in 1257 and were apparently active heretic hunters.[4] A
synod of 1301 advised that heresy should be reported to episcopal
inquisitors, and episcopal inquisitors took charge of a trial around
1315 or 1316.[5] From 1318 until at least 1348 there was a series of
papal inquisitors, and an effort seems to have been made to find
eminent and highly respected Dominicans for these positions.[6] These
papal delegates worked in close conjunction with the episcopal authorities, and in later years certain of them were called back into
service with episcopal commissions.[7] Inquisitors remained at least
intermittently active as the century proceeded, and at the end of the
century Bohemia was one of the lands in which Waldensians suffered
vigorous attack.[8] The need for such antiheretical measures became
especially clear in 1339, when one of the papal inquisitors went to
Avignon along with a local lord, and returned to find that a group
of relapsed heretics had plundered ecclesiastical property and burned
the lord's castle plus a number of villages. In retaliation, the lord
secured papal approval for a "crusade" against the heretics.[9] But
drastic as that measure may have seemed, it did not solve the problem of Bohemian heresy. It would thus perhaps be an understatement
to say that by the early fifteenth century the ground was well prepared for the Hussite movement.

The movement named after John Hus can in a sense be explained
as a merger of two previous movements. The Hussites borrowed
some of their reformist piety from earlier reformers in Bohemia, such
as their insistence on religious literature in the vernacular, their strict
morality, and their devotion to the eucharist. And they took a great
deal of their specific doctrine—for example, their concept of the
Church—from the English Wyclifites, even if they transformed this
doctrine in important ways and reduced its heretical content.[10] Still,
one cannot reduce the Hussite movement to merely a convergence
of these two streams. There were new doctrinal motifs that arose

spontaneously. Largely because the early Church had given the eucharist under both species, and because the Hussites viewed the apostolic practice as normative, they adopted the principle of utra-quism (the doctrine that communion must be administered under both species to the laity as well as the clergy) as their special concern.[11] More importantly, the dynamism that underlay the movement was distinctive and complex. From its origins in the early fifteenth century, Hussitism involved both urban and agrarian unrest and served as a focal point for Bohemian resentment of German control over Bohemia. It would be an oversimplification to say that the Hussite movement was merely a protest by native Bohemians against a Church that lay largely in the hands of Germans, but the anti-German aspect of the movement was pronounced.

In the early stages of the movement, the orthodox authorities attempted to control the Hussites through traditional measures directed against individuals. Thus, in 1412 three men who, under Hus's influence, had protested against the sale of indulgences were arrested and executed.[12] Hus himself fled from Prague to avoid a similar fate, but both he and his follower Jerome of Prague were burned as heretics at the Council of Constance, in 1415 and 1416 respectively, even though Hus had traveled to the council with a safe-conduct from the emperor.[13] The execution of these heresiarchs intensified national sentiment within Bohemia and lent further impetus to the spread of nationalist ideology and Hussite doctrine within that country. The Bohemians, holding the emperor Sigismund largely responsible for these executions, refused to recognize him as king of Bohemia when he inherited that throne in 1419. By that time the country had become for all intents a Hussite nation; whether out of sincere conviction or as a pretext for plundering Church property, the ruling powers generally accepted Hussite principles. And while there was factionalism within the Hussites, they reached agreement on the four Articles of Prague, which called for unrestricted preaching of God's word, administration of the eucharist under both species, punishment of mortal sins, and restoration of the Church to its apostolic poverty. Those within Bohemia who deviated from this program were liable to prosecution and burning; in the early 1420s, numerous radicals were burned for disbelief in the eucharist and for other teachings or practices recognized by the Hussites as heretical. Yet there was clearly no more chance for traditional antiheretical measures against the Hussites themselves within Bohemia.

The first alternative to standard remedies was a crusade. This was a device that had been used before against heretics—against the

Albigensians in southern France, and on a smaller scale in parts of Germany and even Bohemia. The difference in this case is that the crusading armies, gathered together under imperial auspices, were repeatedly and resoundingly defeated. Between 1421 and 1431, imperial forces carried out a series of crusades against Bohemia, but they proved painfully abortive. Using innovative formations of battle wagons for defense, and intimidating the crusaders with their martial hymns, the Bohemians repulsed successive attacks and won substantial booty from the fleeing troops. The radical Taborite branch of the Hussites, which was largely responsible for the successful defense of the country, demonstrated its prowess in offensive action as well as it swept through parts of Germany, depopulating towns and ravaging the countryside.[14]

One of the proponents of the crusades, Giuliano Cardinal Cesarini, suffered personal disgrace in the general rout that terminated the crusade of 1431. Deprived of his clothes (including his cardinal's hat) and possessions, he rode unceremoniously from the battlefield in his underwear. Thus, when the Council of Basel began in the same year, it was Cesarini who convinced his fellow churchmen that they should abandon the idea of a crusade and undertake negotiations with the Bohemians.[15] The Hussites, after conferring among themselves, agreed to the negotiations on specified terms: they were to meet with the council fathers as equals, the discussion was to focus on the Articles of Prague, and both sides would recognize Scripture and its interpretation as the ultimate authority. The Bohemians did in fact travel to Basel, where they were met with excitement and some measure of hospitality, but the negotiations accomplished nothing. It was agreed that discussions would resume in Prague. When the conciliar envoys went to Prague in 1433, they succeeded in dividing the moderate Hussites from the radicals; they persuaded the university masters, and through them the burghers of Prague and the nobles, to settle for the largely symbolic concession of communion under both species. In the following year, the moderate and orthodox forces decisively defeated the weary and impoverished radicals in the battle of Lipany. And by 1436, the same year in which Sigismund was recognized as king of Bohemia, the Council of Basel had made a formal agreement with the Bohemians (later repudiated by the pope), in which they were allowed to take communion under the species of bread and wine. The radicals survived as the Unity of the Brethren, but the Hussite movement was no longer a vital force or a national cause within Bohemia.

The history of the Hussite revolution contributes little to an understanding of the judicial apparatus used against heresy, simply because it became clear at an early stage that the ordinary procedures would be of little use in this instance. But the affair is nonetheless of considerable relevance to this study in two ways. First, it demonstrates the kind of extraordinary measures that the Church was forced to take in extreme circumstances. (And for orthodox churchmen to negotiate as equals with heretics, on the subject of their heresy, was indeed extraordinary!) Second, the Hussite revolution set the stage for German reaction to heresy for the remainder of the fifteenth century. Despite the anti-German tendencies in the Hussite movement, the Hussites attempted on numerous occasions to disseminate their doctrine outside Bohemia, and especially in Germany.[16] They sent manifestos to foreign countries in an effort to win support for the Articles of Prague; they combined military excursions with propaganda during the 1420s and 1430s, attempting with some measure of success to win over dissident elements within German society; and Hussite missionaries went about preaching their doctrine. Not surprisingly, Germans feared that the Hussite heresy might take hold in German territories, where its adherents could serve as a sort of religious and political fifth column, opening the way for both spiritual and temporal disruption. Just as the beghards and beguines dominated most of the period between the councils of Vienne and Constance, the Hussites were the main object of concern during the century that followed the Council of Constance. The extent to which Hussitism dominated the consciousness of inquisitors during this period can be gauged from the fact that during the trial of John of Wesel in 1479, one judge questioned him about his relations with a religious leader from Bohemia.[17] Though John was patently not himself a Hussite, the association with this Bohemian figure was enough to render him suspect, even at that late a date. Indeed, as late as 1515, long after there was any realistic danger of Hussite encroachment, Jacob Wimpfeling suggested that widespread popular resentment of papal extortion and control over German affairs made conditions right for the spread of Hussitism: "It would not take much for the Bohemian poison to penetrate our German lands."[18] The fear was no doubt exaggerated, but to a German aware of recent history it did not appear to lack substance. Indeed, one of the arguments with which Cardinal Cesarini induced fellow churchmen to undertake negotiations with the Hussites was the danger of German conversion to Hussitism. In correspondence with the pope, Cesarini expressed fear that Germans might be convinced by Hussite propaganda. Already, he said, townspeople in Magdeburg and Passau (towns close to Bohemia) had been roused to rebellion, and alliance between such towns and Bohemia could be catastrophic.[19]

One may entertain doubt whether the citizens of Magdeburg and Passau had much understanding of the doctrinal issues at stake, but Hussite doctrine did enter Germany, in two distinct waves—first during the early fifteenth century, and then again toward the middle of the century.[20] In the early years of the Hussite movement there were Germans who had personal and academic contact with Hussite theoreticians. One of the most important leaders of the movement at Prague was a German named Nicholas of Dresden, who instilled in his followers a radical form of Hussitism, alloyed with Waldensian teachings.[21] When these Germans returned to their homeland, they frequently went about seeking converts.

The first wave of prosecutions came only in the 1420s, the decade of wars between Germany and Bohemia. Tension regarding the Hussites was greatest in towns nearest to Bohemia. It was in these places especially that the military threat was combined with an abiding fear that German townspeople might collaborate with the enemy, and might even be converted to his doctrine. An imperial edict of 1421 recommended that the citizens of each town be given an oath affirming their orthodoxy, and the episcopal towns of Regensburg and Bamberg are known to have issued orders to this effect.[22] In accordance with papal instructions, town governments commonly prohibited trade with Bohemia.[23] Under such circumstances, the Hussites were objects of hatred for two reasons; not only did they accept a despised doctrine, but they represented a religion associated with the military foe.

Meanwhile, many of the Germans who had absorbed Hussite doctrine in Prague returned home. When they arrived in Germany, they brought with them doctrines typical of the early Hussite movement. They did not commonly encourage the formation of distinct sects, and might not even consider themselves members of a distinctively Hussite religion. The most important of their teachings were the principle of utraquism and the insistence that the Church should be stripped of secular power and non-Biblical ritual excrescences. The diocese of Regensburg, whose priests often studied at the nearby University of Prague, became infested with the heresy earlier than most places, and in the years from 1420 to 23 the bishop there sent two Hussites to the stake.[24] At the same time, a heretic in Magdeburg protested that he would defend his beliefs even to his death, and the opportunity was not denied him.[25] There were similar incidents in Nürnberg, Worms, and elsewhere.[26] The case at Worms reveals something of the hysteria that the Hussite problem aroused: evidently the greatest cause of concern on the part of the judges was the fact that the suspect had been in Bohemia, and largely for that reason they interrogated him at length on such matters as the legitimacy of oaths, which Hussites called into question.[27] (It was only in passing that the judges charged this subject with having uttered certain oddly anti-clerical remarks to the general effect that priests pay homage to the devil and perform magical acts with diabolical aid, and that the eucharist really consists of snakes, toads, and other poisonous creatures.)[28]

The same anxiety underlay the prosecution of three heretics in 1425 at the hands of the bishops of Worms and Speyer.[29] The dominant figure here, John Drändorf, had been ordained at Prague, where he was introduced to Hussite doctrine. In the mid-1420s he set out on a missionary journey through Germany and even into Brabant. In the course of this trip he found that the bishop of Worms had for political reasons imposed ecclesiastical sanctions on certain cities, particularly Weinsberg; he denied the legitimacy of these sanctions, and encouraged the citizens to resist the bishop. Before long the bishop had him captured and subjected him to an inquisition. At the beginning of the first hearing, Drändorf took the fatal step of refusing on principle to take the preliminary oath, thus marking himself as a heretic. In the ensuing inquiry, the judges asked him repeatedly about matters that the Waldensians, Wyclif, and Hus had called into question: the Church's authority to impose canonical sanctions and to condemn heretics (specifically, Hus and Jerome of Prague), the form under which the eucharist should be administered, the Church's right to hold temporal jurisdiction, and so forth. He replied to questions arrogantly, sometimes sarcastically, and with consistent self-assurance. At one point he remarked that he could afford to pay the tribunal 300 gulden, if it would save his life, but he knew the judges wanted his life more than his money. Asked whether the emperor Constantine had acted rightly in bestowing half his empire on the Church, Drändorf commented that if he had been a bit more generous and given the other half as well, he might be venerated as a saint.[30] Under torture, he referred vaguely to certain acquaintances, all clerics, who shared his beliefs. Refusing several pleas to recant, he was degraded solemnly from orders (he was dressed in clerical garb specifically for this purpose, and degraded by the removal of these garments) and released to the secular authorities for burning. Two of Drändorf's attendants had been captured along with him. One of them, Martin Borchard, began bravely by refusing to take the oath at the outset of his inquisition, but after sitting in jail for almost a month he confessed and abjured his heresy. The other, Peter Turnau, a trained jurist, answered the judges' questions with subtle distinctions, so that they had to remind him repeatedly to give straightforward responses. He was not above sarcasm and rebuke; at one point he admonished his judges not to waste time with trivial questions. Neither Borchard nor Turnau was the sort of zealously disruptive figure that Drändorf had shown himself to be, and whereas the judges had been eager to consign Drändorf to the stake within a few days, they gave his associates several weeks in which to convert. Yet Turnau used this time only to attempt an escape, and in the end he went to the stake.

Opportunities for personal and academic exposure to Hussite doctrine became drastically reduced for most Germans when hostilities broke out between Bohemia and Germany. And those Hussites who returned to Germany in the 1420s appear to have been dealt with in one way or another without much delay. Consequently, there is no further evidence of trials against German Hussites for twenty-one years after 1425.[31] In the meantime, however, Hussitism became firmly established within Bohemia, and Hussite preachers again entered Germany and made converts.[32] One of these, Frederick Müller, made numerous converts in Middle Franconia; another, Frederick Reiser, had connections in places as far apart as Strassburg and Brandenburg. In many cases they seem to have gone to previously existing Waldensian communities, since the doctrines of Waldensianism and Hussitism were closely analogous. Even in the early part of the century, Nicholas of Dresden had taught an amalgam of the two heresies. Consequently, many heretical congregations were found in the 1440s and 1450s that held fundamentally Waldensian doctrines, but maintained relations with the Bohemian church, and administered the eucharist under both species. Such groups came under investigation particularly in southern Germany. Roughly 130 of these heretics abjured their heresy in Würzburg; 27 were reconciled to the Church in the diocese of Eichstätt; and a substantial number came to light in Strassburg, where the itinerant preacher Frederick Reiser suffered execution.[33] Northeastern Germany also had its share of trials: inquisitors uncovered large numbers of heretics in Brandenburg and Misnia, where members of the sect kept emerging sporadically throughout the century.[34] There were further, isolated cases at Walkenried and Vienna.[35] In most of these instances the followers were more inclined to recant than were the leaders, several of whom went to the stake.

By the later years of the century, Waldensians in Brandenburg had established contact with the Bohemian Brethren, an offshoot of the Hussite movement. Many of the German heretics fled to Bohemia, where they merged with the doctrinally similar sect in that land.[36] One record of this contact is a poignant letter written in 1480 to the Bohemian Brethren, recounting the prosecution to which the Waldensians in Brandenburg had been subjected in the preceding two years.[37] This letter is an exceptional document in that it gives an extended narration of events from the heretics' own perspective. It thus deserves examination in some detail, even though it is just as much a partisan statement as are ecclesiastical records. The member of the sect who wrote this letter told how certain priests of the region had approached the margrave, Albert Achilles, and asked his permission to condemn "the brethren" (the author's designation for the members of the sect). The margrave answered that they should investigate the suspects, who should be reprimanded if they deviated from the truth, but otherwise should be left in peace until further information was available. Distorting the margrave's instructions, these priests claimed that he had given them authority to capture the "brethren." They went to two cities and asked the burgomasters to have the suspects apprehended, but evidently the burgomasters did not believe the charges and refused to accede to the priests' demand. The priests then threatened one of the burgomasters that they would denounce him, too, to the margrave as a heretic; the burgomaster himself went to speak with the margrave, but by this time the margrave had left the region. In the meantime, the priests summoned some of the "brethren" and, seeking incriminating testimony, interrogated them about their views on immoral priests. To protect themselves, a few of the "brethren" went to the younger margrave, John Cicero, who gave them a letter ordering the clergy to leave the suspects alone until he arrived in the region.[38] Upon reading this letter, the priests were all the more enraged against the "brethren"; they took some captive, while other suspects fled.

Soon afterward, the heretics of Brandenburg received a letter from the Bohemian Brethren dealing with matters of faith. The bearer of this letter admonished the recipients to be careful lest it fall into the hands of "priests or unreasonable persons." The "brethren" showed it to a certain lord, presumably one of the margraves, who found it edifying, and is supposed to have exclaimed that the "brethren" had found "the true foundation of the first Christians." But then the council of an unspecified city asked to see the letter and entrusted it to a clerical scribe for copying. The scribe secretly released it to

the priests of the area, who falsified it (according to the possibly
biased version) and showed it to the bishop. The bishop in turn trans-
mitted the letter to one of the margraves, who, despite the earlier
sympathy both margraves had shown the heretics, now seems to have
been persuaded that the "brethren" really were heretical, and ac-
cordingly allowed them to be tortured. One morning a group of
heretics was apprehended; six men and four women were burned.
The priests also seized a leader of the sect named Peter Weber.[39]
Though he appealed to one of the margraves, they did not let him go
to this lord, and whenever a lord intervened in favor of the "brethren," the priests assured that lord that the "brethren" were heretics.
They then turned Peter over to a "monk" (presumably a Dominican)
who was a doctor of liberal arts, and who apparently lost little time
in condemning the heretic. In a sermon before the people and one of
the margraves, this inquisitor related that Peter had erred against
the Church, the priests, and the sacraments. The priests offered to
release him if he would recant and go to the members of his sect to
convert them to Catholicism; he replied that he would sooner be
torn to pieces. When he was being taken to the place of execution,
the priests supposedly asked if he wanted to receive the eucharist
(though it seems unlikely that an obdurate heretic would have been
offered the viaticum), and he replied that they themselves did not
possess the body of Christ and could not give it to him. As he stood
before the stake, the priests allowed him to speak to the assembled
people, but stipulated that he could only say "good things." He
apparently began to proclaim his heretical beliefs, whereupon the
priests and monks started to drown him out with their singing. After
he had been burned, the priests went to the wives of those heretics
who had fled, and forced them to swear that if their husbands returned home they would report them at once to the clergy. For fear
of being apprehended, these fugitives thus had to take refuge through
the entire winter in the inhospitable environment of the woods. Even
at the time the letter was composed, they remained there in hiding.

Although this letter is written from a perspective entirely different
from that of the other documents accessible to historians, it confirms
many of the findings obtained from other sources. It is clear from
this missive that the initiative for prosecution lay with the parish
clergy, who had sustained familiarity with lay religious life. The
inquisitor who entered the case may have been a papal inquisitor,
though it is far from clear that this was the case.[40] Even if he was,
it was clearly not he who was responsible for getting the proceedings
under way. In the initial phases of the affair, the heretics received

protection from the secular authorities—not because these authorities were favorably disposed toward heresy, but because they were not convinced of the truth of the accusations. As soon as the charges became plausible, the secular powers immediately left the heretics to their own devices. Although one of the margraves attended Peter Weber's condemnation, he apparently took no measures to avert the outcome. That the "brethren" were in fact heretics is clear from the Donatist views attributed to Peter Weber in rejecting the eucharist. Once their allegiance was discovered, they could obtain security only in the woods—or across the border in Bohemia, where there was more sympathy for heterodox opinion.

The repression of Waldensian-Hussites during this period was in some respects similar to that of Waldensians in the late fourteenth century, and in other respects different. The campaign against Waldensians had been for the most part a tighly coordinated affair, largely because the majority of the trials were the work of only three inquisitors. In the fifteenth century the bishops did cooperate among themselves. There was a clear connection between the trials in Brandenburg and those in Misnia, and on at least one occasion a bishop sent records of his proceedings to other bishops to aid them in their maintenance of orthodoxy.[41] Yet the inquisitions during this period do not seem to have been interrelated as systematically as those of 1389–1404 were.

In one other respect the prosecution both in the 1420s and in the mid-fifteenth century repeated the pattern of the late fourteenth century: as in the earlier campaign, the inquisitions took place almost exclusively under episcopal auspices. One of the inquisitors at Heidelberg became a papal inquisitor, but only after the greater part of his known inquisitorial activity had been completed; the most important trials in which he participated, and the only ones that definitely involved Hussites, began on episcopal initiative.[42] The Dominican inquisitor at Strassburg may have been a papal delegate, but his name does not appear in the extant records from Rome or from the Dominican superiors, so it is more likely that he (like the Dominican at Magdeburg in 1420) was an episcopal appointee.[43] The inquisitor who condemned Peter Weber was apparently a Dominican, but once again it does not at all follow that he was a papal inquisitor.[44] There are thus only three exceptions. The Franciscan Jacob of Marchia was delegated by the pope in 1436 to act in Austria and Hungary, but his actual operation seems to have been limited to Hungary, and in any case he had no connection with the continua of Dominican inquisitors who served under papal commissions.[45] Similarly, Pope

Sixtus IV appointed Thomas Gognati as inquisitor for Vienna in 1479, and instructed him to act against "Nicolinist and Hussite heretics," but no record of his activity seems to survive, and in any event the danger of Hussitism in Austria had diminished, if not disappeared, by this date.[46] And John Botzin served as inquisitor for the dioceses of Brandenburg, Camin, Lebus, and Havelberg between 1491 and 1504; according to a later Dominican chronicle, he was so zealous in condemning heretics to death and intimidating others that no one dared anymore to profess heresy.[47] This rather vague encomium leaves the nature of the heresy and the precise scope of Botzin's work open to conjecture. One might speculate that at this late date a regular papal inquisitor did at last preoccupy himself with Hussites. But with these highly peripheral exceptions, all attempts to suppress the Hussites in Germany remained in episcopal hands.

As in earlier years, there is evidence in these trials that the Waldensians were willing to abjure their heresy only as long as they were in jeopardy, and tended to resume their former practices as soon as the inquisitor had departed.[48] Nonetheless, there is reason to think that the campaign of the late fourteenth century had depleted the sect, and that its strength had waned. In some towns the prosecution may have been fully effective. For example, the municipal authorities in Augsburg expressed the opinion in 1435 that the prosecution forty-two years earlier had eliminated Waldensians from their midst.[49] Indeed, there is no evidence of later Waldensians or Waldensian-Hussites in that town. Granted, proceedings at Würzburg in 1446 against 130 members of the sect suggest that in certain areas the heretics may not have diminished in numbers during the fifteenth century, but there were far fewer trials than in the late fourteenth-century.[50] Bernd Moeller cites in this connection a quotation from Frederick Reiser, the leader of Waldensian-Hussite communities in southern Germany in the 1450s. Reiser is supposed to have said of the heretics that "their cause is as a fire going out."[51] To be sure, the text from which this quotation comes is a highly romanticized paraphrase of the fifteenth-century document.[52] Reiser may or may not have made the statement, but in any case the assessment was probably correct. Though one cannot prove the point beyond all question, the Waldensians probably did suffer a decline in membership, and perhaps also in fervor.

One further development remains to be discussed, that being the participation of university faculties in the repression of Hussites. During the Great Schism (1378–1415), German scholars left Paris and other universities subject to the Avignonese papacy. Wishing to attend schools under Roman obedience, they found that the universities of Prague and Vienna were insufficient to meet their needs. For this reason, among others, five new universities sprang up in Germany during the schism, at Cologne, Heidelberg, Würzburg, Erfurt, and Leipzig.[53] In many ways these institutions were modeled after the University of Paris; most importantly, for present purposes, they imitated this older establishment in assuming antiheretical functions.[54] In Basel, too, one reason explicitly advanced for founding a university in 1460 was the need to strengthen Catholicism against heretical doctrine.[55]

Almost all of the German universities were active in the prosecution of heretics, usually in conjunction with episcopal authorities. The University of Heidelberg had the strongest tradition of antiheretical involvement. Although in 1394 its faculty cleared John Malkaw (a zealous advocate of the Roman papacy) of the charge of heresy, and early in the following century it stopped short of accusing the beguines of Basel of heretical doctrine, the Hussite threat seems to have persuaded its members that heresy was a real danger.[56] Thus, theologians from Heidelberg supported inquisitorial work against the leading Hussite Stanislas of Znaim; during the 1420s they participated in the episcopal trials of John Drändorf and others in the Rhineland; and as late as 1479 they aided, along with theologians from Cologne, in the proceedings at Mainz against John of Wesel.[57] In the case of the proceedings in the 1420s, the theologians not merely sat as judges but helped to draw up lists of questions and heretical articles. Furthermore, these trials gave an anonymous author (presumably an academician) cause to write a list of proposals for subsequent heresy trials. One of the suggestions was that lists of Hussite doctrines be sent to both archbishops and universities, so that Hussites could better be detected. Clearly this author anticipated future involvement of university faculties in the repression of heresy.[58] Likewise, the faculty at Vienna took action several times against Hussites and other heretics, the most noted of its subjects being Jerome of Prague.[59] Indeed, on one occasion this university was even cited as *apostolica auctoritate haereticae pravitatis inquisitrix*, which suggests a special papal mandate to act against subversive doctrine.[60] This papal "inquisitrix" appears to have taken more interest in the problem than did papal inquisitors. Other universities were less involved in such work, but in 1414 the faculty at Erfurt aided in the prosecution of flagellants, while as late as 1462 theologians from the University of Leipzig were aiding the bishop of Naumburg in his work against the Waldensian-Hussites of Misnia.[61]

It is not surprising that most of these cases involved persons suspect of Hussite or Waldensian-Hussite allegiance. After all, Hus and many of his followers had been academicians, and response to their teachings required some measure of sophistication. This is not to say that all of these heretics posed an intellectual challenge to their inquisitors; the characterization hardly applies to Helwig Dringenberger, a subject at Worms, who was utterly baffled by his judges' recondite questioning.[62] But once the academicians had begun to involve themselves in the problem of Hussite doctrine, their interest persisted.

MILLENARIAN HERETICS

The Hussite revolution surely was *"the* revolution" of the late Middle Ages, but the Hussites were not the only heretics who were feared as revolutionaries. Other heretics preached at least vaguely revolutionary millenarian doctrines: they anticipated the arrival, usually imminent, of that apocalyptic millennium in which there would be no distinction of social classes and no political authorities, and they conceived of themselves as heralds of that millennium. Although their long-range significance is problematic, they further exemplify the kind of religiopolitical threat against which the authorities reacted.[63]

Foremost among these movements was that of the flagellants, who either survived secretely after the prohibition of 1349 or developed shortly afterward in and around Thuringia.[64] Although they were the object of some attention in the later fourteenth century, the first major inquisition against them came in 1414, when the Dominican inquisitor Henry Schoneveld entered Thuringia, Misnia, and nearby territories.[65] One chronicler tells that the inquisitor imposed penances on numerous heretics, turning some over to the secular arm, but after the inquisitor's departure the secular authorities, fearing the dangers of this radical sect, grouped the penitent and obdurate heretics indiscriminately, and burned about three hundred in one day.[66] Other sources corroborate this report at least in part, with details of executions in various towns. Forty-four heretics were burned at Winkel, including one who, having been overlooked in the investigations, is supposed to have ridden voluntarily to the place of execution and leaped into the flames. There were eighty-three victims at Sangerhausen, and many more elsewhere.[67] The interest of both ecclesiastical and secular authorities remained great. On one occasion the entire town council of Sangerhausen attended the proceedings and provided armed guards.[68] A trial at Erfurt, conduced by the local provisor, took place before an assembly of clerics and university faculty members from the town.[69] Incidentally, historians repeatedly have stated that the dominant figure in this campaign, the inquisitor Henry Schoneveld, returned to the area two years later, but this is clearly an error, as is the identification of this inquisitor with Eylard Schoneveld.[70]

For some time afterward this sect went undisturbed, but the attacks resumed in the middle of the century, at roughly the same time as trials against the Waldensian-Hussites. In 1446 the papal inquisitor Frederick Müller tried thirteen flagellants at Nordhausen, in the presence of a nuncio and a commissary of the archbishop of Mainz, various other clerics, and witnesses from the town council.[71] The records of this case give vague references to earlier proceedings, about which very little can be ascertained.[72] Eight years later the same inquisitor took the unusual step of holding a public disputation with representatives of the heretical movement at Göttingen.[73] Even as late as 1481 the sect persisted, though probably with highly depleted forces. In that year Count George of Anhalt captured certain flagellants, whom he entrusted to the bishop of Halberstadt for trial, though the outcome of the case is not on record.[74]

The most striking aspect of these cases is the part that secular powers played in them. Even in 1414, before the Hussites had shown that radical religious ideology could pose a real threat to established powers, the secular authorities were far harsher in their proceedings than churchmen had been. All the more remarkably, the civil rulers preserved their concern about heresy even after the apocalyptic element in the flagellant doctrine had diminished, and the movement was reduced to a relatively harmless devotional cult.[75]

The importance of cooperation from secular powers was also evident in the proceedings against Janko and Livin of Wirsberg, members of a noble family from Franconia, who disseminated millenarian ideas around the border of Bohemia and Franconia.[76] According to the reports of their accusers, these brothers belonged to an extensive sect, headed by a runaway monk who was spreading an amalgam of Joachimite and Hussite doctrine.[77] Whatever the truth of this charge may have been, the Wirsberg brothers themselves were the ones who bore the brunt of the attack, primarily from the bishop of Regensburg. Livin was denounced to the bishop sometime around 1465, and before long both he and his brother were being sought for trial. For a time the antipapal king George of Bohemia apparently took the brothers under his protection. Likewise, suspicion arose that certain towns with which the brothers were connected were harboring them, though evidently the suspected communities cleared themselves of the charge. The fate of the heretics remains oddly obscure: Janko either died or absconded before the bishop could take him captive; Livin fell into the hands of a count who delivered him to the bishop, and within a few years he had died in prison.

In the case of the Wirsberg brothers, there is almost no information regarding the followers of the sect they are supposed to have fostered. If their heresy had fewer adherents than their opponents charged, however, this was not because millenarian ideals held no popular appeal. Nine years after the trial of Livin of Wirsberg, in 1476, anapocalyptic movement arose in Franconia under the influence of a shepherd named Hans Böhm.[78] His movement appears to have undergone progressive radicalization. Beginning as a penitential movement of pilgrims to a church in the town of Niklashausen, it soon assumed anticlerical, revolutionary, and millenarian traits, which culminated in armed conflict between the heretics and the bishop of Würzburg. The bishop was at the center of opposition to this movement: he was probably the first person to take official note of the pilgrimages, and the archbishop of Mainz left control over the affair in his suffragan's hands, even though Niklashausen was within the archdiocese of Mainz. It was also the bishop of Würzburg who attempted to strike at the heart of the matter soon after it had come to light. He prescribed that Böhm should be captured, tried, and (as a foregone conclusion) condemned; if he could not be approached, his preaching and related devotions were in any case forbidden. Similarly, the bishop arranged for the capture of the prophet when rumors of violence began to spread. When Böhm's followers marched on the episcopal fortress, it was the bishop who ordered negotiations with the mob, and who finally decided to disperse the assembled people with cannon-fire and cavalry. Later, an episcopal court had Böhm burned on the charge of heresy and sorcery. Although the bishop was always the leading figure in the opposition, he was by no means alone in resisting the movement. Numerous cities forbade their citizens to participate in the pilgrimages; some of them, such as Nürnberg, issued these prohibitions as early as a month before the violent confrontation at Würzburg. Similarly, Duke Louis of Bavaria issued such a prohibition, upon consultation with theologians and jurists of his university at Ingolstadt, and the bishop of Eichstätt made a similar order for all members of his diocese.[79]

The pilgrimages continued even after Böhm's death, and further prohibitions were required, even for so distant a region as Saxony.[80] The count of Wertheim, who had earlier offered his services for the suppression of the movement, viewed its later stages as harmless. The archbishop of Mainz did not share this view, and within two months of Böhm's death he ordered the church closed. He later placed the church under interdict, excommunicating all those who persisted in visiting it. Yet the pilgrimages continued, and in the following year the archbishop felt constrained to have the church demolished. Only then was the matter laid to rest.

The movement at Niklashausen shows clearly the dangers to which popular millenarian belief could lead. Even if the pilgrims to the shrine were not in fact plotting violence against the established authorities, as rumors had it, the rumors themselves could easily have inspired violence. And when the adherents stormed the episcopal fortress, this action surely seemed to confirm their opponents' worst suspicions. It is not at all surprising, therefore, that ecclesiastical and secular authorities joined in responding to this threat, as they did in measures against the Hussites. Nor is it altogether surprising that in these cases, where once again there was some form of genuinely heretical doctrine being upheld and where there was a very real threat to public order, the papal inquisitors played only an occasional role. They did take the lead in the prosecution of flagellants. Unfortunately, the obscurity of the sources makes it difficult to evaluate properly the character of these heretics and the extent of their threat to the established order. Likewise, it is difficult to discern precisely how the papal inquisitors became involved in these trials—whether on their own initiative or at others' request. What is clear is that these inquisitors had no role whatsoever in the most conspicuously volatile of all these affairs, that at Niklashausen. And in this respect they were true to their accustomed form.

PAPAL INQUISITORS

If papal inquisitors had virtually no role in the prosecution of Hussites, and if they were only tangentially preoccupied with millenarian heretics, one might well ask what they were doing during this period to eradicate heresy. In many cases, no doubt, the answer is that they were doing nothing. When papal inquisitors did bestir themselves to action, however, they showed a strong inclination to direct their efforts against political subjects and other nonheretics. This tendency was stronger in the fifteenth century than before, largely because the marginally heretical beghards and beguines no longer served as ready victims. The tendency was not wholly limited to papal inquisitors; the archiepiscopal trial of John of Wesel was in large part motivated by academic politics.[81] But in this period, as in others, papal inquisitors showed a stronger proclivity toward such action than did episcopal judges.

One issue that roused a papal inquisitor to proceedings early in this period was the traditional conflict between the mendicant orders and diocesan cleargy. In 1420 John Palborne, a secular priest of Soest, preached doctrines that gave rise to the accusation of heresy.[82] The first of these teachings was that bodies of the dead must be brought to the parish church where they had received the sacraments, so they could "give back" the sacraments bestowed. The second, correlative to the first, was that a body should not be taken out to another church (such as a Dominican or Franciscan church) for burial. Palborne declared these injunctions at a time when the city of Soest was undergoing an epidemic, and the number of deaths was too great for the parish churches to accommodate all the funerals. Still, when bodies were taken to other churches, the parish priests lost the burial stipends and other fees that accrued to the place of burial—which was the reason for Palborne's concern. This was also one reason for the interest of the Dominican inquisitor Jacob of Soest, who was eager to defend his order's right to perform burial services. It has been argued that the motive for prosecution was not exclusively one of institutional jealousy—that the inquisitor viewed Palborne's utterances as genuinely heretical, and that when the priest was denounced before him the inquisitor felt obliged to take action.[83] Yet it is difficult to believe that the inquisitor's affiliation with the Dominicans was wholly irrelevant to his action. A non-Dominican might have viewed Palborne's statements as erroneous and worthy of reprimand, but the extreme charge of heresy seems hardly explicable except in terms of tensions between secular and mendicant clergy.

The inquisitor summoned Palborne, ordering him to attend a hearing on the same day as the summons, and to bring with him a number of specified witnesses. The peremptory citation did not intimidate Palborne. Rather than come at the time prescribed, he agreed to present himself two days later, and delivered the inquisitor's summons only to some of the witnesses the inquisitor had demanded. On the first day of the proceedings, Palborne prepared a dinner for the witnesses and for several friends of his who had not received citations. He plied them all heavily with wine, and when they were sufficiently bereft of inhibitions he took them to the hearing. Predictably, they disrupted the trial so persistently that the inquisitor accomplished nothing. They even disputed his qualifications as an inquisitor, and refused to believe a letter from the archbishop of Cologne supporting him and his work.

Shortly afterward, Jacob of Soest left for Cologne, where as a member of the theological faculty he obtained the support of other members of the university, who agreed with him that Palborne's friends should stand trial as supporters of heresy. Further proceedings were delayed; on one occasion they were postponed because the episcopal official involved in the case was not on hand. A later hearing was apparently inconclusive, though some of the jurists in attendance took matters into their own hands and arranged for the accused to purge themselves of the charges. The inquisitor refused to accept this independent measure. Being unable to carry the affair further himself, he placed it in the hands of the pope. The issue of the case is not explicitly recorded, but in all probability it was favorable to the accused.

In view of the traditional rivalry between diocesan and mendicant clergy, it is perhaps surprising that conflicts of this sort did not result more often in judicial proceedings on charges of heresy. While the trial of Palborne was still under way, however, a trial of exactly the opposite sort began in the diocese of Worms, where the episcopal official conducted an inquisition against the Franciscan Peter Wyrach.[84] This Franciscan had purportedly preached various "heresies": that an illiterate priest cannot absolve from sin; that when a person is himself a public sinner he cannot correct the offenses of others; and other principles that seem to have been taken as prejudicial to the diocesan clergy. Wyrach's statements may have bordered on Donatism, if he in fact did make these remarks, but once again it is difficult to believe that jealously was not a primary stimulus to prosecution.[85] In short, episcopal courts were capable of undertaking politically motivated trials, though most of the overtly political inquisitions on record were begun by papal inquisitors. Even when the episcopal official at Worms did press charges against Wyrach, his handling of the affair was at least more regular and orderly than the proceedings of Jacob of Soest.[86] And the charge of heresy was somewhat more plausible in this instance.

Even local ecclesiastical conflicts could result in political trials, and during the fourteenth and fifteenth centuries German bishoprics were contested almost routinely by rival claimants, giving opportunity for such proceedings. Thus, in the 1430s there were two contenders for the episcopal see of Trier, and one of them received the dubious benefit of support from a woman who, like the recently executed Joan of Arc, went about in soldier's clothes.[87] Again it was a papal inquisitor, Henry Kalteisen, who took the initiative. He summoned the woman on the charge of magic. (She is supposed to have performed such magic tricks as restoring a severed cloth and a shattered glass through preternatural means.) But with the aid of a certain count, she managed to escape to France, where the inquisitor's sentence of excommunication was duly ignored.

Perhaps the most sensational political trial involving a papal inquititor during this era was that against John Reuchlin—an affair that began as a minor personal quarrel, but quickly developed into an intense conflict between scholastics and humanists, engaging the attention of pope, emperor, kings, princes, and several universities.[88] The confrontation proceeded in three stages. At first (1510–13), it was primarily a literary conflict over the question whether Jewish books should be confiscated. A converted Jew named John Pfefferkorn proposed this measure, and the emperor Maximilian asked Reuchlin to give his written opinion on the matter. In compliance with the request, Reuchlin wrote a defense of Jewish literature, which provoked the wrath of Pfefferkorn and led to a series of *ad hominem* attacks. The most famous product of this phase of the controversy was the *Epistolae obscurorum virorum*, written by Reuchlin's defenders as an anthology of slurs on his opponents. Evidently at Pfefferkorn's instigation, the theological faculty at Cologne issued a formal condemnation of Reuchlin's original treatise. The same faculty also procured an imperial decree against this work, and when Reuchlin published a defense, they obtained another edict condemning the defense.

As it happened, the dean of this faculty, Jacob Hochstraten, was also an inquisitor. In the later capacity he felt bound to bring charges against Reuchlin, who supposedly had lent illicit support to Jews, held the Fathers of the Church in disdain, and subscribed to a variety of errors in doctrine. Hochstraten therefore initiated the second stage of the conflict, the judicial proceedings (1513–16), by summoning Reuchlin to Mainz for trial. The case proceeded haltingly, with an appeal to Rome, then a referral to the bishop of Speyer, and finally a second appeal to Rome. Both parties solicited support for their positions. Reuchlin had friends in the Curia, and he persuaded them to use their influence in his favor; one of them, the pope's personal physician, was a Jew. Erasmus, other humanists, and even Maximilian I, despite his earlier condemnation of Reuchlin's work, wrote to the pope in his favor.[89] Maximilian's grandson Charles V, King Francis

I of France, and various universities supported the inquisitor. Reuchlin also endeavored to buttress his case at certain junctures by questioning the competence of Hochstraten to handle the case; the first and foremost objection was that Hochstraten, a leading scholastic theologian, was not a disinterested judge, but a party to the dispute that had led to judicial proceedings, and a personal enemy of the humanist Reuchlin. Even the way the inquisitor addressed Reuchlin in personal encounters revealed his disdain for the man. Still, Reuchlin expressed no intention of denying Hochstraten's competence in other heresy trials. The proceedings ended in favor of Reuchlin, and the humanists celebrated the victory jubilantly and arrogantly. One of the more subtle means of celebration, coming quite possibly from Reuchlin himself, was an edition of the acts of the trial, published ostensibly for the use of law students who needed specimens of inquisitorial procedure, citation, recusation, appeal, mandates *de supersedendo*, and so forth.[90] As a further upshot of the case, Hochstraten even lost his inquisitorial commission.

In following years (1516–20), however, events both in Rome and in Germany began to undermine Reuchlin's position. Many of his most influential supporters at the Curia either left or died, and the emergence of Luther, who paid Reuchlin the unwelcome compliment of recognizing him as a sort of precursor, made Pope Leo X increasingly suspicious of the humanist. Reuchlin's supporters in Germany were reduced to the expedient of force: in 1519 Franz von Sickingen made threatening gestures toward the Dominican superior in Germany to thwart a reversal of the earlier verdict. In response, the Dominicans placed full responsibility for the affair on Hochstraten's shoulders. At last, in 1520, Hochstraten succeeded in having Reuchlin condemned. Pope Leo issued a final verdict nullifying the earlier acquittal, declaring Reuchlin's original treatise offensive and forbidden (though not explicitly heretical), condemning Reuchlin to silence on the matter, and ordering him to pay all the costs of the proceedings.

Hochstraten attained his partial success (partial in the sense that he did not secure Reuchlin's condemnation as a heretic) only with great effort, and without the peculiar religiopolitical circumstances of 1520, he undoubtedly would never have attained even this much. At one point in the affair even his own order failed to support him. Thus, despite his eventual victory, what Hochstraten most clearly exemplifies is his weakness as a papal inquisitor—a quality that he shared with virtually all of his inquisitorial colleagues in the fifteenth century. How can one account for this widespread debility? One answer that the evidence clearly fails to bear out is the suggestion that papal inquisitors met local opposition on jurisdictional grounds. As in earlier periods, there was if anything cordial interaction between papal inquisitors and bishops. In the early 1420s Jacob of Soest worked in close conjunction with an episcopal official at Cologne, using the official's quarters as a courtroom, and refusing to engage in proceedings when the official was not available.[91] In 1425 Peter Turnau denied the right of the bishop of Speyer to try him without the cooperation of a papal inquisitor. (As a jurist, Turnau was familiar with the legislation on this point from the Council of Vienne.) The bishop circumvented this technicality by obtaining a letter from the papal inquisitor Giselbert of Maastricht (or of Utrecht), who willingly gave the bishop full powers.[92] In 1458 the bishop of Brandenburg delegated an episcopal inquisitor when heretics came to light, and stated explicitly in the commission that he was making this appointment because no papal inquisitor could be found.[93] If there had been a papal inquisitor on hand, the bishop, who was physically weak and had little relish for arduous proceedings himself, would presumably have been eager to divest himself of all responsibility for the affair. When the papal inquisitor Frederick Müller exercised his power against flagellants at Nordhausen in 1446, he acted in the presence of a nuncio and a commissary of the archbishop of Mainz, and there is no hint whatsoever of episcopal interference in his handling of the case.[94] Twelve years later the archbishop of Mainz had a beghard apprehended, but rather than try the subject independently, he entrusted the affair to the papal inquisitor Henry Kalteisen, who was to act along with an episcopal commission.[95] And again, in 1479, the archbishop of this city invited the papal inquisitor Gerhard of Elton to participate in the trial of John of Wesel.[96] It is noteworthy that most of these instances of close cooperation involved the Rhenish prelates—precisely the figures who, according to Lea and others, are supposed to have been adamant in upholding their jurisdictional rights.

There were two cases in which bishops did oppose papal inquisitors. One of these may be dismissed because the evidence does not permit detailed analysis: when a papal inquisitor named John Krähwinkel pursued a heretic named Hovet in 1477, the heretic entered the bishopric of Münster.[97] Krähwinkel appealed to the bishop there to deliver the fugitive to him, but the bishop denied the request, and with that the matter ended. Neither the nature of Hovet's doctrine nor the reasons for the bishop's refusal are on record. Hence, it is impossible to build any argument around this example.

The second case, that of Henry Institoris and his witch trials in Innsbruck, is infamous. The witch prosecutions in Innsbruck were not Institoris's only experience with this kind of inquisitorial action. He sought to eradicate the pestiferous practice of witchcraft in several areas of Upper Germany, particularly the diocese of Constance. At times he worked with his fellow Dominican, the papal inquisitor Jacob Sprenger, a professor at Cologne, who seems also to have been greatly interested in uprooting practitioners of witchcraft and related arts.[98] These two inquisitors collaborated on the *Malleus maleficarum*, the famous manual for witch hunters.[99] Apart from this magnum opus, Institoris produced several smaller works, which were also occasioned by his inquistorial practice. During the 1490s he wrote two treatises against certain erroneous opinions on the eucharist—one of these errors being the suggestion that a miraculous "bleeding host" at Augsburg was not a genuinely consecrated host.[100] In every way, these men fit the accustomed image of the papal inquisitor.

Although Institoris was a man of many accomplishments, he is especially well known for his trials at Innsbruck.[101] Because the reaction to his proceedings there has so often been cited as a classic example of resistance to a papal inquisitor, the affair warrants close examination. To begin with, armed with an endorsement from the pope, and with hopes of support from Archduke Sigismund of Austria, Institoris proceeded in 1485 to the bishop of Brixen to obtain consent for work in his diocese. (This request in itself suggests recognition of the need for cooperation.) Though not enthusiastic, the bishop granted the inquisitor a letter of introduction, ordering the people of the diocese to comply with the project of witch hunting, and offering forty days' indulgence to those who aided the inquisitor. Institoris then went to Innsbruck, where roughly five weeks of preliminary hearings yielded about fifty witches. The fate of most of these suspects remains mysterious. After a delay of about three weeks, the inquisitor drew up a second list of suspects, which included only seven of those from the first list. He then began to hear witnesses, in association with commissaries whom the bishop of Brixen had appointed in the meantime. After receiving testimony from witnesses, the inquisitor proceeded to an examination of the suspects themselves. At this point, however, his discretion failed him. At the beginning of the interrogation he posed questions of a personal character, pertaining to the sexual lives of the accused. From his viewpoint these questions were vital to the trial, since he maintained that witches were generally women who had been promiscuous from youth, and a history of sexual laxity would presumably support the charge of witchcraft. The other members of the tribunal took a dim view of Institoris's lurid interests, however; one episcopal commissary in particular dismissed these questions as irrelevant and frivolous. The charges were dismissed altogether when a defense attorney, apparently introduced into the proceedings by the episcopal representatives, found various technical flaws in the inquisitor's proceedings. The bishop, who had sought all along to terminate the affair swiftly and quietly, must have breathed a sigh of relief.

To the dismay of all, Institoris did not let matters rest. He remained in the city more than three months, attempting to press charges for a new trial, gathering evidence, and even taking certain women captive. The bishop wrote to the indefatigable inquisitor, urging him to abandon his efforts and return to his cloister. To frighten the aged Dominican, the bishop reminded him of the danger that he faced: the husbands of the accused women might rise up against him at any moment. (There is no further evidence, however, of popular uprising, despite historians' frequent statements to the contrary.)[102] The bishop also wrote to other persons, encouraging them to bring the ludicrous proceedings to an end, and describing the inquisitor as "quite childish on account of his old age."[103] He consistently agreed that Institoris had unquestionable authorization, and that it was incumbent upon local authorities to recognize a duly commissioned inquisitor. He does not even seem to have denied in principle that there might be such persons as witches. But even if there were witches who needed to be exterminated, the bishop was clearly convinced that Institoris was the wrong man for the job, and that the accusations set forth were groundless. Once again, therefore, the papal inquisitor was frustrated not because of political rivalry, but because of his own misguided zeal.

Can the decline of power among papal inquisitors be attributed to loss of political support? None of the successors of Charles IV appears to have fostered inquisitors to the extent that he did, and even if the emperors had wished to maintain their support, their power to do so was diminished. It is tempting to suggest that the dwindling political support explains why fifteenth-century papal inquisitors did not proceed as vigorously as their fourteenth-century predecessors had proceeded against beghards and beguines. The great majority of the fifteenth-century inquisitors appear to have done nothing for the cause of the faith.[104] Could this fact be the result of the loss of political backing? This explanation probably attributes too much significance to the support given by political figures in previous years. As was seen in chapter 3, prosecution of beghards and beguines seems to have been largely the work of individual inquisitors (especially Walter Kerlinger and, to a lesser extent, Eylard Schoneveld). Not all those inquisitors who enjoyed political aid can be shown to have taken advantage of this support; hence, highly placed support was not a sufficient condition for vigorous prosecution. And the anti-Waldensian campaign of the 1390s, which attained a fair measure of success in the absence of either papal or imperial acknowledgment, suggests that such help was not even a necessary condition for sustained and intensive antiheretical work.

The papal inquisitors' diminished vigor can be explained more compellingly on other grounds. These inquisitors had found their calling in the later fourteenth century in the attack on beghards and beguines. But after the first few years of the fifteenth century, the conventual beghards and beguines were no longer subject to prosecution as they had earlier been; there was no longer such a widespread tendency to consider them proper objects of prosecution either for their institutional irregularity or for their alleged heresy. And judging from the fact that Free Spirit literature comes mainly from the fourteenth century, and not the fifteenth, it seems that the genuine heresy so often associated with beghards and beguines had lost its former vitality.[105] Deprived of their earlier subjects, the papal inquisitors had neither the resources nor (apparently) even the inclination to seek out the difficult but more genuinely dangerous heretics, the Hussites. Hence, they tended to act, if at all, only against religious fanatics, political subjects, witches, and other fringe elements in the religious life of Germany. And the absence of effective institutional controls made it possible for them, more than for episcopal agents, to indulge their inclination toward such action. Once again, one may reasonably conjecture that if the papal inquisitors had belonged to a genuine Inquisition, this institution would have kept them from such diversions. One can readily imagine, for example, that a real institution might have kept Institoris within bounds more effectively than the bishop of Brixen was able to do. (When witch trials erupted on a much broader scale in the sixteenth and seventeenth centuries, and authorities throughout Europe, even great prince-bishops, succumbed to the mania, such trials were notably subdued in countries that had well-established Inquisitions, especially Spain, and the caution exercised by these institutions was at least partly responsible for the low rate of prosecution.)[106] For lack of such a restraining force, however, the inquisitors were free to proceed as they wished. The result was not so much diminution as dissipation of their power.

This dissipation of inquisitorial authority is nowhere more apparent than in the trial of John Reuchlin. H. C. Lea argued that this affair was largely responsible for the disfavor into which papal inquisitors fell, and that their disfavor in turn explains why Luther escaped the hands of inquisitors.[107] Yet Jacob Hochstraten, the inquisitor who proceeded against Reuchlin, was acting no differently from many preceding papal inquisitors. As we have seen, there was a long tradition of misdirected fervor among these inquisitors, and even at the height of their powers they lacked the organization bonds that might have made them an effective political tool. In the course of his proceedings against Reuchlin, Hochstraten lost his inquisitorial commission, but he regained his office two and a half months after Reuchlin's final condemnation. The restoration was in large part a formality, however, for the proceedings against Reuchlin were the last in which Hochstraten participated specifically as inquisitor. Apart from his attack on Reuchlin, he is best known for his opposition to Luther. Yet by the time Hochstraten or any other inquisitor became concerned about Luther, it was too late for inquisitorial proceedings. Caring little for ecclesiastical sanctions, and too firmly supported for effective measures against him, Luther posed a problem that exceeded the inquisitors' powers. Having frequently shown themselves ill-equipped to handle less problematic cases, the inquisitors could not be expected to present Luther and his supporters with significant opposition.

7

Conclusion

H. C. Lea wrote his *History of the Inquisition of the Middle Ages* during an era in which it was fashionable to seek explanations for historical events by probing the machinations of secular or ecclesiastical politicians. An interpretation that appealed to subjective factors, such as religious sentiment, was likely to be dismissed as if the interpretation itself were subjective—or, as one would now say, "soft." Later generations of historians shifted their emphasis to some degree away from political explanations and toward economic ones, for essentially similar reasons. It is only comparatively recently that fashions have again changed, and historians are given receptive hearing when they assign social or even cultural causes to events. And even in political history there has perhaps been an increased sophistication and awareness of the social element within political institutions. Rather than ask merely what a government did and what interests the action served, historians are more inclined to ask about the influence of institutional structures and their inner workings—whether in the consistory of sixteenth-century Geneva or in the committee structure of the United States Congress—upon the course of events. This trend has led historians to recognize what should perhaps be a truism: that the structure of judicial institutions is likely to have an impact upon judicial performance. In accordance with these historiographic developments, it is time to re-examine the topics that H. C. Lea treated roughly a century ago. Instead of accepting his presuppositions as fact, as historians have routinely done, one must question the presuppositions themselves.

The present study has attempted to make two essential points in this connection. First, it has endeavored to show that the motives for prosecution of heretics in medieval Germany were more complex than previous historians, including Lea, have recognized. Political considerations were of course important, in various ways. Heretics as such threatened the established ecclesiastical order; even the beghards and beguines, who did not usually advocate the total overthrow of the Church, upset the order of ecclesiastical polity. Indirectly, and at times directly, heretics also challenged the governance of secular authorities, as is seen most clearly in the cases of the Hussites and of the millenarian radicals. The repression of such groups clearly had *inherent* political implications. Furthermore, there could be *ulterior* political motives for prosecution; secular clergy could use the charge of heresy as an excuse for attacks on mendicants, members of one social class could brand members of another as heretical, adherents of one pope could institute inquisitorial proceedings against the followers of a rival papacy, and so forth. In some instances these political motives are transparent, while in other cases they are merely conjectural. Yet these political factors cannot satisfactorily account for all the trials. One must also recognize as significant the high valuation that medieval society (particularly, but not exclusively, at its upper levels) placed on religious orthodoxy. This ideological—or perhaps "socioreligious"—factor helps explain the fervor of those individual inquisitors who were responsible for much of the action against heretics. It also illuminates the widespread support that inquisitors appear to have received from the laity in their work against heretics. And the ideological element serves better than political considerations even in explaining the aid that Charles IV gave to inquisitors.

Second, this study has tried to clarify the reasons why, despite the multiple motives for prosecution of heretics, their extermination remained very much a haphazard endeavor, highly liable to distraction and marked by a strong degree of ineptitude. It has been argued that one cannot explain the data by the hypothesis that inquisitors met resistance from rival jurisdictions or from native authorities opposed in principle to repression of heresy. There is absolutely no evidence of such opposition. While local authorities often defended persons and groups they considered innocent of heresy (and in most cases their opinion appears to have been justified), there is no indication that they ever wilfully impeded prosecution when the accusation was plausible. Papal inquisitors did commonly provoke opposition, but not for demonstrable political reasons; in every known case, the reason for resistance seems clearly to be that these inquisitors were attacking orthodox or only marginally heretical subjects. One might hypothesize that these subjects were in fact heretical, and that for political reasons the extant sources have misrepresented them in a favorable light; but this suggestion would at best be mere speculation, and in numerous cases there are unimpeachable sources that exonerate the accused. Papal inquisitors were more susceptible to this kind of distraction than were episcopal judges precisely because there was no Inquisition, or judicial institution, to guide and control their efforts. Likewise, because there was no authority structure to keep them attentive to their inquisitorial task, many of these inquisitors evidently did nothing to eliminate genuine heretics, even when these were present. The business of dealing with these authentically heretical groups, especially the Waldensians and Hussites, thus fell to the episcopal authorities—who, having greater and more systematic contact with parochial affairs, were more likely to uncover such heretics. Beghards and beguines, religious enthusiasts, and political subjects tended to be well-known figures, easily apprehended even by papal inquisitors. But Waldensians and German Hussites were inclined to conceal their identity, thus requiring the more careful surveillance of diocesan authorities. Hence, it is episcopal judges who were more attentive to the genuinely radical groups that threatened the Church, while papal inquisitors dissipated their power in dubious and erratic activity or in sheer inactivity.

The irony is that during the later Middle Ages the Church was in general growing increasingly sophisticated and centralized in its bureaucratic and judicial structure. Ever since the administrative innovations of Urban II, in the late eleventh century, the papacy had sought to extend its control, largely for the sake of executing reforms throughout Christendom. And the attempt had met some degree of success, partly because it satisfied the specific needs of local churchman in various ways. During the fourteenth century, the centralization became even more pronounced as the Avignonese papacy sought to tighten its grasp on ecclesiastical taxes and appointments. Indeed, even the appointment of papal inquisitors was in some respects a measure that contributed toward centralization. Yet the results of this initiative serve as an important reminder that centralized authority had very definite limitations. Under some conditions papal inquisitors could be effective; in Germany, individual papal delegates seriously disrupted the movement of beghards and beguines for some time. But even in these cases the inquisitors seldom acted in the interests of a specifically papal policy. There was little direct control over these men by the Curia, and their activity was generally guided more by local than by international interests. And the lack of a real institution, an Inquisition, meant that the efficacy of these papal inquisitors was severely handicapped. The Church may have been refining its structure in many areas during the later Middle Ages. But seen in the perspective of later developments, its sophistication was greatly limited.

The conclusions to which this inquiry has led may in another way seem ironic, for it can be argued that the lack of institutional structure was a deficiency not only from the vantage point of medieval clerics, who were generally in favor of uprooting heresy effectively and expeditiously, but also from the perspective of a twentieth-century scholar personally committed to religious and political freedom. Indeed, it has been argued here that the brutality of repression might in some measure have been restrained if inquisitors had been more uniformly controlled within an institutional Inquisition. One might well ponder whether the same rule applies in our own era. Perhaps the contrary is now true; with present means for totalitarian control, perhaps institutional sophistication only enhances the brutality. This study has suggested that in certain contexts institutions can serve as checks upon the arbitrary will of individuals. Precisely when institutions can fulfill this function, and when they in turn require their own checks, is a much broader question that lies beyond the scope of this work.

Notes

In the following notes, the abbreviation *MGH* is used for *Monumenta Germaniae Historica*, with the further specification *SS* for *Scriptores in folio* (Stuttgart and Hanover, 1826–1934), *SS rer. Germ.* for *Scriptores rerum Germanicarum* (Stuttgart, etc., 1871–), and *SS rer. Germ., n.s.* for *Scriptores rerum Germanicarum*, new series (Berlin, etc., 1922–). *CDS* stands for *Chroniken der deutschen Städte*, ed. Historische Kommission bei der Bayerischen Akademie der Wissenschaften (Leipzig, etc., 1862–).

Chapter 1. Introduction

1. Translation in Roland H. Bainton, ed., *The Medieval Church* (New York, 1962), pp. 185f.

2. Henery Charles Lea, *A History of the Inquisition of the Middle Ages* (New York, 1887–88), esp. 1: 332; 2: 386–88, 396f.

3. Because there has been no systematic expression or development of Lea's thesis, a full-scale survey of the literature would contain nothing but a catalogue of essentially similar statements. All that one finds are incidental remarks reminiscent of Lea. For example: A. S. Turberville, *Mediaeval Heresy and the Inquisition* (New York and London, 1921), esp. p. 166; Ernest W. McDonnell, *The Beguines and Beghards in Medieval Culture* (New York, 1954), pp. 521, 560; Paul Flade, "Römische Inquisition in Mitteldeutschland," *Beiträge zur sächsischen Kirchengeschichte* 11 (1896): 67–69; Gerhard Ritter, *Die Heidelberger Universität* (Heidelberg, 1936), 1: 347; Dominique Villerot, *L'Inquisition* (Paris, 1973), pp. 154, 159. Not all

the elements of Lea's interpretation are present in all such passages, but the general presuppositions are the same as Lea's, or closely similar.

4. Hansen alluded to this project in his *Quellen und Untersuchungen zur Geschichte des Hexenwahns und der Hexenverfolgung im Mittelalter* (Bonn, 1901), p. 382 n. 1, and in Henry Charles Lea, *Geschichte der Inquisition im Mittelalter*, ed. Joseph Hansen (Bonn, 1909), 2: 483 n. 3. George Lincoln Burr, in his introduction to H. C. Lea, *Materials toward a History of Witchcraft* (Philadelphia, 1939), 1: xxxvi, indicated that Hansen already had in hand "both a narrative work and a collection of sources on this theme" before the turn of the century. In communication with the municipal archive at Cologne, where Hansen was archivist, I have ascertained that no such works are now known. Evidently Burr obtained his information from a source that was confusing Hansen's work on witchcraft with his work on repression of heresy.

5. H. R. Trevor-Roper, *Religion, the Reformation and Social Change* (London, 1967), p. 99.

6. It is true that this papal control had not been effected during the Avignonese period; see Guillaume Mollat, *The Popes at Avignon, 1305–1378* (New York and Evanston, 1965), pp. 224–28, 341. But the important point here is that the control which the papacy exerted later does not seem to have aided in establishing inquisitions.

7. Hermann Heimpel, in *Drei Inquisitions-Verfahren aus dem Jahre 1425* (Göttingen, 1969), p. 149, restricts the use of this term to papal inquisitions and bishops. But it clearly was used also by episcopal appointees; cf. Herbert Grundmann, "Ketzerverhöre des Spätmittelalters als quellenkritisches Problem," *Deutsches Archiv für Erforschung des Mittelalters* 21 (1965): 561; and Cod. Vindob. 3748, fol. 145^r for merely two examples.

8. Lea, *History of the Inquisition*, 1: 364.

9. Wilhelm Wattenbach, "Über die Inquisition gegen die Waldenser in Pommern und der Mark Brandenburg," *Abhandlungen der königlichen Akademie der Wissenschaften zu Berlin*, 1885, Philosophisch-historische Classe, Abhandlung 3, p. 72; *Monumenta Boica*, ed. Academia Scientiarum Boica (Munich, 1787), 15: 611f.; Carl Heinrich von Lang, ed., *Regesta, sive rerum Boicarum autographa* (Munich, 1843), 10: 15; Valentin Ferdinand von Guden, ed., *Codex diplomaticus anecdotorum, res Moguntinas . . . illustrantium* (Frankfurt and Leipzig, 1751), 3: 598–600; Heimpel, *Drei Inquisitions-Verfahren*; Grundmann, "Ketzerverhöre," pp. 535–50, 561–66.

10. One possible exception is John Wasmud of Homberg; see Robert E. Lerner, *The Heresy of the Free Spirit in the Later Middle Ages* (Berkeley, Los Angeles, and London, 1972), pp. 57–59.

11. For brief intervals there were cardinals appointed to oversee inquisitorial functions, but there is no indication that they exercised a centralizing influence. See Lea, *History of the Inquisition*, 1: 397f.

12. Yves Dossat, *Les Crises de l'Inquisition toulousaine au XIIIe siècle, 1233–1273* (Bordeaux, 1959), p. 89, argues that collegiality was inherent in

inquisitorial operation. Yet the pairing of inquisitors in thirteenth-century Languedoc was surely the result of immediate need for efficiency (and possibly also for protection), rather than the result of a decision in principle. When one views the totality of inquisitorial practice, collegiality appears to be the exception rather than the rule.

13. For example, the thirteenth-century documents in Kurt-Victor Selge, ed., *Texte zur Inquisition* (Gütersloh, 1967), refer occasionally to *inquisitores* (e.g., pp. 53, 60, 62, 66, 80); these same texts refer frequently to *inquisitiones* in the sense of specific trials in accordance with inquisitorial procedure (e.g., pp. 31, 40, 50, 56f., 65–67, 70–73), but never in the sense of an inquisitorial agency. The same holds true of the thirteenth-century texts in Célestin Douais, ed., *Documents pour servir à l'histoire de l'Inquisition dans le Languedoc*, Vol. 2 (Paris, 1900), with one possible exception on p. 230 (". . . hoc persoluto, bona predicta sint ex parte inquisitionis absoluta").

14. The term occurred occasionally as early as Clement IV; see c. 10 *Sext.*, lib. V, tit. 2 (e.g., ". . . an officium inquisitionis haereticae pravitatis . . . exspiret per mortem Romani Pontificis, qui commisit . . ."). Later it appears routinely, e.g., in Nicholas Eymericus, *Directorium inquisitorum* (Rome, 1585), p. 418 ("Ut autem Inquisitor . . . suum Inquisitionis officium securius et liberius exercere valeat"); p. 420 ("propter inquisitionis haereticorum nobis iniunctum officium"); p. 435 ("terris . . . nostrae Inquisitionis subiectis"); p. 605 ("statuta, per quae inquisitionis negotium seu officium . . . impediatur"); p. 622 ("provincia, in qua vobis inquisitionis officium est commissum"). Around 1320 papal officials charged that Matteo Visconti "manifeste officio inquisitionis se opposuerat," which could be construed as meaning that he had opposed an institution called the Inquisition; cf. Robert Michel, "Le Procès de Matteo et de Galeazzo Visconti," *Mélanges d'archéologie et d'histoire* 29 (1909): 322. But the same document speaks of prelates who "exerceant officium visitationis et correctionis" (ibid., p. 324), and no one has ever suggested that there were institutions called the Visitation and the Correction. Charles du Fresne, sieur DuCange, in *Glossarium mediae et infimae Latinitatis* (Niort, 1883–87), 6: 37f., devotes more than four columns to the term *officium*, largely in its liturgical employment; among the equivalents he lists *ministerium, districtus, territorium, jurisdictio,* and *pagus,* but none of his entries suggests that the term was used in the sense of an agency or institution.

15. Eymericus, *Directorium*, p. 439 ("ne inquisitionis officium deludatur"); p. 437 ("in opprobrium et iacturam officii inquisitionis, et verecundiam, et ruborem Inquisitoris"); Paul Fredericq, ed., *Corpus documentorum inquisitionis haereticae pravitatis Neerlandicae* (Ghent and The Hague, 1889), 1: 204f. ("hortamur . . . quatenus . . . consilium, auxilium, et favorem . . . impendatis, praestantes eidem [inquisitori] vestros carceres, quibus in eisdem partibus carere dicitur officium Inquisitionis hujusmodi, donec officio praedicto de certis carceribus sit provisum . . ."); Alexander Patschovsky, *Die Anfänge einer ständigen Inquisition in Böhmen* (Berlin and

New York, 1975), p. 149 ("privilegiorum officio inquisicionis a sede apostolica indultorum . . ."). In most such cases it is still possible to interpret *officium inquisitionis* in the sense of an activity, function, or jurisdiction, even if this is not the first meaning that comes to mind. In some instances the term can perhaps be better construed as an abstraction, analogous to *sacerdotium.*

16. Many such cases are cited in Fritz Bünger, *Beiträge zur Geschichte der Provinzialkapitel und Provinziale des Dominikanerordens* (Leipzig, 1919), pp. 39, 84, 84f., 95–97, 97–99, 101–3, 103–5. There are several further examples, such as the inquisitors mentioned in Hansen, *Quellen,* p. 382 n. 1.

17. Inquisitors were sometimes appointed for the entire "regnum Francie." But the scope of their work, at least in most cases, appears to have been limited to the traditional area of "Francia"—i.e., the territory now corresponding roughly to northern France, or the area that comprised the early Dominican province of Francia.

18. E.g., Walter Kerlinger, Gerhard of Elten, Jacob Hochstraten, Jacob Sprenger. On the Dominicans' reluctance to take on such extra burdens as the care of female religious houses, see the comments by Herbert Grundmann and Heribert Christian Scheeben in Kurt Ruh, ed., *Altdeutsche und altniederländische Mystik* (Darmstadt, 1964), pp. 82f., 106. The Dominicans were unable to avoid this task, and it undoubtedly consumed a great deal of their time. The inquisitorial office was one that could more readily be neglected, even if accepted.

19. See for example the long lists of blasphemers in various passages of the Augsburg *Achtbuch,* Stadtarchiv Augsburg.

20. Lea, *History of the Inquisition,* 2: 162–90.

21. Ibid., 2: 174–76.

22. Inquisitors in Germany seem for the most part to have limited themselves to attacks on individual heretics and specific heretical communities, and to have obtained their information about these subjects not through general inquisitions but through interrogation of heretics who sporadically (and often accidentally) came to light. There were occasions, however, on which they did carry out general inquisitions: see for example Walter Ribbeck, "Beiträge zur Geschichte der römischen Inquisition in Deutschland während des 14. und 15. Jahrhunderts," *Zeitschrift für vaterländische Geschichte und Altertumskunde* 46 (1888): 146.

23. Johann Lorenz von Mosheim, *De beghardis et beguinabus commentarius* (Leipzig, 1790), pp. 368–75.

24. Heinrich Volbert Sauerland, ed., *Urkunden und Regesten zur Geschichte der Rheinlande aus dem vatikanischen Archiv* (Bonn, 1902–13), 4: 26f., 27f., 102f., 170f.

25. Hermann Korner, *Chronica novella,* ed. Jakob Schwalm (Göttingen, 1895), pp. 99, 364f., 546.

26. Lea, *History of the Inquisition,* 1: 374–78, 381–84. The passage in Paul Hinschius, *Das Kirchenrecht der Katholiken und Protestanten in*

Deutschland (Berlin and Leipzig, 1869–97), 5: 465f., is not based on German materials.

27. Wilhelm Friedrich Volger, ed., *Urkundenbuch der Stadt Lüneburg* (Hanover, 1875), 2: 15–18; Herman Haupt, "Waldenserthum und Inquisition im südöstlichen Deutschland seit der Mitte des 14. Jahrhunderts," *Deutsche Zeitschrift für Geschichtswissenschaft* 3 (1890): 404f., 407f.

28. Some papal inquisitors were appointed with jurisdiction in the Dominican province of Saxony or that of Teutonia (southern Germany).

29. Gustav Schmidt, ed., *Päbstliche Urkunden und Regesten aus den Jahren 1353–1378, die Gebiete der heutigen Provinz Sachsen und deren Umlande betreffend* (Halle, 1889), pp. 173f.

Chapter 2.   Heresy and Repression in the High Middle Ages

1. An excellent point of departure for investigation of these early heresies is the brief sketch in Walter L. Wakefield and Austin P. Evans, *Heresies of the High Middle Ages* (New York and London, 1969), pp. 6–23. For longer surveys, see Jeffrey B. Russell, *Dissent and Reform in the Early Middle Ages* (Berkeley and Los Angeles, 1965); M. D. Lambert, *Medieval Heresy: Popular Movements from Bogomil to Hus* (New York, 1977), esp. 3–91; and R. I. Moore, *The Origins of European Dissent* (New York, 1977). Jeffrey B. Russell, "Interpretations of the Origins of Medieval Heresy," *Mediaeval Studies* 25 (1963): 26–53, is also very useful. For a very general statement on antiheretical measures, see Paul Braun, "Die Bekämpfung der Ketzerei in Deutschland durch die Päpste bis zum Laterankonzil von 1215," *Archiv für Kulturgeschichte* 9 (1911): 475–81.

2. *MGH SS*, 8: 228, translated in Wakefield and Evans, *Heresies*, p. 93; see Arno Borst, *Die Katharer* (Stuttgart, 1953), p. 79 (esp. n. 23); and Hermann Theloe, *Die Ketzerverhöre im 11. und 12. Jahrhundert* (Berlin and Leipzig, 1913), pp. 20f.

3. See R. I. Moore, "The Origins of Medieval Heresy," *History* 55 (1970): 21–36.

4. E.g., Herbert Grundmann, *Religiöse Bewegungen im Mittelalter*, 2d ed. (Hildesheim, 1961), p. 483.

5. *MGH SS*, 16: 741; *MGH SS*, 8: 193f.

6. Wakefield and Evans, *Heresies*, pp. 96–101, gives a good summary of the sources and literature, as well as an annotated translation of them.

7. The standard work is Borst, *Katharer*; but see also Wakefield and Evans, *Heresies*, pp. 6–23, 26–50, 64–67; Lambert, *Medieval Heresy*, pp. 108–50; and Moore, *Origins*, pp. 168–240.

8. *MGH SS*, 16: 727; see Borst, *Katharer*, p. 91; and Theloe, *Ketzerverhöre*, pp. 55–57.

9. Wakefield and Evans, *Heresies*, pp. 126–32, gives an introduction and an annotated translation of the source; see Borst, *Katharer*, p. 91; and Theloe, *Ketzerverhöre*, pp. 56f.

10. Theloe, *Ketzervorhöre*, pp. 57–59, esp. p. 57 n. 217.

11. Claus-Peter Clasen, in "Medieval Heresies in the Reformation," *Church History* 32 (1963): 406f., refers to a heretic arrested in Thuringia in 1564 as holding the heresies of the Cathars. To be sure, this heretic held (or is represented in the sources as holding) dualist beliefs, but it is far from clear that his doctrine was specifically that of the Cathars, and there is no indication that he belonged to a sect of fellow dualists. Even if one could grant that this man was a Cathar, it would be difficult to account for his presence in a region of Germany where Catharism had never before been known. Clasen's supposition raises more problems than it solves.

12. For general information, see Wakefield and Evans, *Heresies*, esp. pp. 50–53, 200–13; and Lambert, *Medieval Heresy*, pp. 67–91, 151–64.

13. Herman Haupt, "Waldenserthum und Inquisition im südöstlichen Deutschland bis zur Mitte des 14. Jahrhunderts," *Deutsche Zeitschrift für Geschichtswissenschaft* 1 (1889): 284–89, discusses the Waldensians in the southeast, where they were present by the beginning of the thirteenth century. Later sources render it likely that Waldensians had penetrated northward during the same century, but much of what has been written on this subject is now superseded by Alexander Patschovsky, *Die Anfänge einer ständigen Inquisition in Böhmen* (Berlin and New York, 1975), pp. 65–78.

14. Wilhelm Preger, "Ueber das Verhältnis der Taboriten zu den Waldesiern des 14. Jahrhunderts," *Abhandlungen der königlichen bayerischen Akademie der Wissenschaften*, Historische Classe, 18 (1889): 36f.

15. Ibid., p. 37.

16. Dietrich Kurze, "Zur Ketzergeschichte der Mark Brandenburg und Pommerns, vornehmlich im 14. Jahrhundert," *Jahrbuch für die Geschichte Mittel- und Ostdeutschlands* 16/17 (1968): 83–87.

17. Henri Maisonneuve, *Études sur les origines de l'Inquisition*, 2d ed. (Paris, 1960), pp. 151–98.

18. Franz Joseph Mone, ed., *Quellensammlung der badischen Landesgeschichte* (Karlsruhe, 1863), 3: 486f.; *CDS*, 9: 649.

19. Hermann Köhler, *Die Ketzerpolitik der deutschen Kaiser und Könige in den Jahren 1152–1254* (Bonn, 1913), pp. 55f.

20. For Germany, the most comprehensive treatment is Ludwig Förg, *Die Ketzerverfolgung in Deutschland unter Gregor IX.* (Berlin, 1932). H. C. Lea, *A History of the Inquisition of the Middle Ages* (New York, 1887), 1: 305–68; Maisonneuve, *Études*, pp. 243–86; and John B. Freed, *The Friars and German Society in the Thirteenth Century* (Cambridge, Mass., 1977), pp. 142–47, are also useful.

21. Wilhelm Wiegand, ed., *Urkundenbuch der Stadt Strassburg* (Strassburg, 1879), 1, pt. 1, p. 51; Förg, *Ketzerverfolgung*, pp. 62–64; Freed, *The Friars*, pp. 146f.; Gustav Roskoff, *Geschichte des Teufels* (Leipzig, 1869), 1: 328–32.

22. The best account is still Balthasar Kaltner, *Konrad von Marburg und die Inquisition in Deutschland* (Prague, 1882), esp. pp. 133–61; Förg,

Ketzerverfolgung, pp. 71–90, is in some ways useful as a corrective. For biographical details see Karl Hermann May, "Zur Geschichte Konrads von Marburg," *Hessisches Jahrbuch für Landesgeschichte* 1 (1951): 87–109. The basic sources are *MGH SS*, 17: 38–40, and *MGH SS*, 24: 400–402.

23. The notion occurs as early as Florianus Dalham, *Concilia Salisburgensia provincialia et dioecesana* (Augsburg, 1788), p. 157.

24. Kaltner, *Konrad von Marburg*, p. 136 n. 2.

25. Förg, *Ketzerverfolgung*, pp. 71–90.

26. *MGH SS*, 17: 39.

27. C. H. Haskins, "Robert le Bougre and the Beginnings of the Inquisition in Northern France," in C. H. Haskins, *Studies in Medieval Culture* (Oxford, 1929), pp. 193–244.

28. On the meaning of this story see Herbert Grundmann, "Ketzerverhöre des Spätmittelalters as quellenkritisches Problem," *Deutsches Archiv für Erforschung des Mittelalters* 21 (1965): 519–21.

29. The lull in proceedings was not uniformly maintained; see Walter L. Wakefield, "Friar Ferrier, Inquisition at Caunes, and Escapes from Prison at Carcassone," *Catholic Historical Review* 58 (1972): 222.

30. Haupt, "Waldenserthum bis zur Mitte des 14. Jahrhunderts," pp. 297–303; Alexander Patschovsky, *Der Passauer Anonymus* (Stuttgart, 1968).

31. On the general context of antiheretical action in southern France, see most recently Walter L. Wakefield, *Heresy, Crusade and Inquisition in Southern France, 1100–1250* (London, Berkeley, and Los Angeles, 1974).

32. Köhler, *Ketzerpolitik*, passim.

33. The relevant documents are placed in historical context in Köhler, *Ketzerpolitik*, pp. 5–14.

34. The basic documents are those in Johann Friedrich Böhmer, ed., *Regesta imperii*, 5, rev. Julius Ficker and Eduard Winkelmann (Innsbruck, 1881–1901), Nos. 4202, 4299a, and 6972. See Köhler, *Ketzerpolitik*, pp. 54–62; and Förg, *Ketzerverfolgung*, pp. 85–89.

35. Köhler, *Ketzerpolitik*, p. 61.

36. *MGH Leges*, sect. 4, vol. 2 (Hanover, 1896), p. 428.

Chapter 3. The War against Beghards and Beguines

1. Herman Haupt, "Beiträge zur Geschichte der Sekte vom freien Geiste und des Beghardentums," *Zeitschrift für Kirchengeschichte* 7 (1885): 565; also in J. J. I. von Döllinger, ed., *Beiträge zur Sektengeschichte des Mittelalters* (Munich, 1890), 2: 381.

2. See Norman Cohn, *The Pursuit of the Millennium*, 2d. ed., rev. (New York, 1970), pp. 148–86; Gordon Leff, *Heresy in the Later Middle Ages* (Manchester, 1967), 1: 308–407; and especially Robert E. Lerner, *The Heresy of the Free Spirit in the Later Middle Ages* (Berkeley, Los Angeles, and London, 1972). There is an extended review of Lerner's work by

Eleanor L. McLaughlin in *Speculum* 49 (1974): 747–51; cf. also Mc-Laughlin's "The Heresy of the Free Spirit and Late Medieval Mysticism," *Medievalia et Humanistica*, n.s. 4 (1973): 37–54. While McLaughlin has studied the Free Spirits from a perspective that shares much with Lerner's, she differs from him on various points of interpretation.

3. Herbert Grundmann, *Religiöse Bewegungen im Mittelalter*, 2d ed. (Hildesheim, 1961), pp. 503–12.

4. For reflections on this point see Gordon Leff, "Heresy and the Decline of the Medieval Church," *Past and Present* 20 (1961): 36–51.

5. See c. 1, *Clem.*, lib. 3, tit. 11, and c. 3, *Clem.*, lib. 5, tit. 3; see also Ernest W. McDonnell, *The Beguines and Beghards in Medieval Culture* (New York, 1954), esp. p. 524, and Lerner, *Free Spirit*, pp. 47, 81–83.

6. The question is a general theme of Lerner, *Free Spirit*, where reference to earlier literature may be found.

7. Martin Erbstösser and Ernst Werner, *Ideologische Probleme des mittelalterlichen Plebejertums* (East Berlin, 1960), p. 140; a heretic is represented here as claiming that for a Free Spirit "sensuality is so properly subject to the spirit and understanding, that such a man can rightfully concede to his body whatever pleases him."

8. Ibid., pp. 136–53; see Lerner, *Free Spirit*, pp. 135–39.

9. See esp. Wilhelm Wattenbach, "Über die Secte der Brüder vom freien Geiste," *Sitzungsberichte der königlichen preussischen Akademie der Wissenschaften zu Berlin*, 1887, pp. 524–26.

10. These measures are summarized in Lerner, *Free Spirit*, pp. 65–68.

11. Dayton Phillips, *Beguines in Medieval Strasburg* (Ann Arbor, Mich., 1941); the definitive account of the prosecutions is Alexander Patschovsky, "Strassburger Beginenverfolgungen im 14. Jahrhundert," *Deutsches Archiv für Erforschung des Mittelalters* 30 (1974): 92–109.

12. Patschovsky, "Strassburger Beginenverfolgungen," p. 101.

13. See esp. Josef Koch, "Kritische Studien zum Leben Meister Eckharts," *Archivum Fratrum Praedicatorum* 30 (1960): 16–50 ("Der Eckhart-Prozess"). The question of Eckhart's orthodoxy is discussed in historical context in Ingeborg Degenhardt, *Studien zum Wandel des Eckhartbildes* (Leiden, 1967).

14. *Monumenta Boica*, ed. Academia Scientiarum Boica (Munich, 1829), 27: 93 (on the dissolution of the community of beghards). On the identity of heretics at this time in the southeast generally, see Alexander Patschovsky, *Die Anfänge einer ständigen Inquisition in Böhmen* (Berlin and New York, 1975), pp. 65–78.

15. *MGH SS*, 14: 434; Lerner, *Free Spirit*, pp. 51f., 112–19 (trials directed against communities of beguines); *MGH SS rer. Germ.*, n.s., 3: 248–50; Johann Peter Ludewig, *Geschicht-Schreiber von dem Bischoffthum Wirtzburg* (Frankfurt, 1713), p. 626; *MGH SS*, 14: 435; Martin Erbstösser, *Sozialreligiöse Strömungen im späten Mittelalter* (East Berlin, 1970), pp. 160–63; Johannes Trithemius, *Annales Hirsaugienses* (St. Gall, 1690), 2: 231f.; Johannes Nauclerus, *Memorabilia omnis aetatis et omnium gentium*

chronici commentarii, 2 (Tübingen, 1516), fol. 257^r; *CDS*, 4: 68; Augsburg *Achtbuch*, Stadtarchiv Augsburg, fol. 116^v. See Lerner, *Free Spirit*, pp. 10f., 125–32. Following earlier discussions, Lerner suggests that Berthold of Rohrbach was tried by a papal inquisitor; it is at least as likely that he was the victim of an episcopal delegate.

16. Lerner, *Free Spirit*, pp. 29–31.

17. The three who definitely held papal commissions were Peregrinus of Oppeln, Nicholas "Hyspodinet," and John Schwenkenfeld; see Herman Haupt, "Waldenserthum und Inquisition im südöstlichen Deutschland bis zur Mitte des 14. Jahrhunderts," *Deutsche Zeitschrift für Geschichtswissenschaft* 1 (1889): 309, 313. Jordan of Quedlinburg and a Dominican named Arnold may have held such commissions; see *MGH SS*, 14: 434f.; and Haupt, "Waldenserthum bis zur Mitte des 14. Jahrhunderts," p. 306.

18. Gustav Schmidt, ed., *Päbstliche Urkunden und Regesten aus den Jahren 1295–1352, die Gebiete der heutigen Provinz Sachsen und deren Umlande betreffend* (Halle, 1886), p. 383; Heinrich Volbert Sauerland, ed., *Urkunden und Regesten zur Geschichte der Rheinlande aus dem vatikanischen Archiv* (Bonn, 1902–13), 4: 26–28, 102f., 170f. See McDonnell, *Beguines and Beghards*, pp. 558f.; and Lerner, *Free Spirit*, pp. 131f.

19. Gustav Schmidt, ed., *Päbstliche Urkunden und Regesten aus den Jahren 1353–1378* (Halle, 1889), pp. 173–75; see McDonnell, *Beguines and Beghards*, p. 561; and Lerner, *Free Spirit*, p. 132.

20. Johann Lorenz von Mosheim, *De beghardis et beguinabus commentarius* (Leipzig, 1790), pp. 343–75; Friedrich Wigger, "Urkundliche Mittheilungen über die Beghinen- und Begharden-Häuser zu Rostock," *Jahrbücher des Vereins für mecklenburgische Geschichte und Alterthumskunde* 47 (1882): 19–24; J. Caro, "Aus der Kanzlei Kaiser Sigismunds," *Archiv für österreichische Geschichte* 59 (1880): 168–72. See H. C. Lea, *A History of the Inquisition of the Middle Ages* (New York, 1888), 2: 387–91; McDonnell, *Beguines and Beghards*, pp. 563–65; and Lerner, *Free Spirit*, pp. 133f.

21. Mosheim, *De beghardis*, pp. 380–83; see McDonnell, *Beguines and Beghards*, p. 566.

22. On the conflicts among the southern Dominicans see Benedictus Maria Reichert, "Zur Geschichte der deutschen Dominikaner am Ausgange des 14. Jahrhunderts," *Römische Quartalschrift für christliche Altertumskunde und Kirchengeschichte* 14 (1900): 79–101; 15 (1901): 124–52. On the transfer of authority, see Mosheim, *De beghardis*, pp. 384–86; cf. Roger Wilmans, "Zur Geschichte der römischen Inquisition in Deutschland während des 14. und 15. Jahrhunderts," *Historische Zeitschrift* 41 (1879): 195 n. 1.

23. See, for example, the appointments listed in Benedictus Maria Reichert, ed., *Registrum litterarum Raymundi de Capua, 1386–1399 [et] Leonardi de Mansuetis, 1474–1480* (Leipzig, 1911).

24. E.g., Lucas Wadding, *Annales minorum* (Rome, 1734), 10: 269–73.

25. Erbstösser and Werner, *Ideologische Probleme*, pp. 136–53; *CDS*,

19: 539; Hermann Korner, *Chronica novella,* ed. *Jakob Schwalm* (Göttingen, 1895), pp. 66, 285; *MGH SS,* 14: 441; W. Rein, "Beguinen in Eisenach," *Zeitschrift des Vereins für thüringische Geschichte und Alterthumskunde* 4 (1860): 226f.; Benjamin Christoph Grasshof, *Commentatio de originibus atque antiquitatibus S.R.I. liberae civitatis Muhlhusae Thuringorum* (Leipzig and Görlitz, 1749), pp. 79f.; Georg May, *Die geistliche Gerichtsbarkeit des Erzbischofs von Mainz im Thüringen des späten Mittelalters* (Leipzig, 1956), p. 187 n. 9; Wilhelm Friedrich Volger, ed., *Urkundenbuch der Stadt Lüneburg* (Hanover, 1875), 2: 15–18; Wigger, "Urkundliche Mittheilungen," pp. 1–26. See the summaries in Erbstösser and Werner, *Ideologische Probleme,* pp. 108–10; and Lerner, *Free Spirit,* pp. 134–41.

26. Mosheim, *De beghardis,* pp. 356–62.

27. Korner, *Chronica,* p. 285; cf. Lerner, *Free Spirit,* p. 132 n. 20.

28. See esp. Patschovsky, "Strassburger Begininverfolgungen," pp. 109–18, for papal and episcopal inquisitions in Strassburg.

29. Leonard Ennen, ed., *Quellen zur Geschichte der Stadt Köln* (Cologne, 1875), 5: 88–90.

30. Conrad Justinger, *Die Berner-Chronik,* ed. Gottlieb Studer (Bern, 1871), pp. 147f.

31. Trial at Eichstätt—Herbert Grundmann, "Ketzerverhöre des Spätmittelalters als quellenkritisches Problem," *Deutsches Archiv für Erforschung des Mittelalters* 21 (1965): 535–50, 561–66; cf. Lerner, *Free Spirit,* pp. 141–45. Trial at Augsburg—*CDS,* 4: 68; Augsburg *Achtbuch,* fol. 116[v].

32. See above, n. 1.

33. Mosheim, *De beghardis,* pp. 383f., 409f., 653–56, 674f.; Gustav Schmidt, ed., *Urkundenbuch der Stadt Halberstadt* (Halle, 1878), 1: 565f.; Haupt, "Beiträge," p. 565; Döllinger, *Beiträge,* 2: 381.

34. Rostock—*Mecklenburgisches Urkundenbuch,* ed. Verein für mecklenburgische Geschichte und Altertumskunde (Schwerin, 1907), 22: 445; cf. Theodor Sohm, "Verbrennung der Ketzerin Helike Pors im Jahre 1394," in Karl Koppmann, ed., *Beiträge zur Geschichte der Stadt Rostock* (Rostock, 1899), 2, pt. 4: 98–101 (though Sohm's identification of this woman with one burned at Rostock in 1403 is purely conjecture, based on very slender connections). For references to papal inquisitors, see *Urkundenbuch der Stadt Lübeck,* ed. Verein für Lübeckische Geschichte und Alterthumskunde (Lübeck, 1873), 4: 12712; Fritz Bünger, *Beiträge zur Geschichte der Provinzialkapitel und Provinziale des Dominikanerordens* (Leipzig, 1919), p. 86; and *Mecklenburgisches Urbundenbuch,* 22: 204.

Austria—on the trial of Nicholas of Basel, see Haupt, "Beiträge," pp. 508–11; and Lerner, *Free Spirit,* pp. 151f; for the inquisitor John Stauder, see Reichert, *Registrum,* pp. 8f., 20.

Cologne—regarding the trial of Martin of Mainz, see Karl Schmidt, *Nicolaus von Basel: Leben und ausgewählte Schriften* (Vienna, 1866), pp. 66–69; for the MSS, see Lerner, *Free Spirit,* p. 151 n. 62. The inquisitor Adam of Gladbach was reappointed for the relevant area in 1395; cf. Reichert, *Registrum,* p. 18. Martin's trial is recorded in three MSS; one of these gives the name of the inquisitor as "Albertus," another gives "Anthonius," and the third gives merely the initial "A." Although the MS with the name Albertus is in general a superior text, it is entirely possible that both full names were constructed from an earlier MS that gave only the initial, and that this initial originally stood for "Adam." It would in any event be coincidental if Adam's successor at Cologne had the same initial.

35. The main source for Schoneveld's early activity is Dier de Muden, in Paul Fredericq, ed., *Corpus documentorum inquisitionis haereticae pravitatis Neerlandicae* (Ghent and The Hague, 1889), 1: 251; this chronicle is late, and Lerner, *Free Spirit*, p. 149 n. 55, has called its reliability into question. The chronicler placed this activity c. 1393–94, but there is some evidence for a later date: the first group of related documents (Fredericq, *Corpus* 2: Nos. 109–12, 119) shows that there was controversy in the Low Countries regarding the religious groups in question, but not that they underwent judicial proceedings. More important is a treatise (Mosheim, *De beghardis*, pp. 443–50; abbreviated in Fredericq, *Corpus*, 1: 251f., and in full in Fredericq, *Corpus* 2: 181–85) written by an "inquisitor Belgicus" in response to a favorable decision (of 1398) by a theological commission concerning the "beguines." The bulk of this treatise consists of extracts from the acts of Eylard Schoneveld, from an undiscernible year in the late fourteenth century. Mosheim, guided by a later bull favoring Eylard (Mosheim, *De beghardis*, pp. 225–28; for the dating see Wilmans, "Zur Geschichte," p. 205 n. 3), thought the year should be 1399; Fredericq, influenced by Dier de Muden, assigned the date c. 1393–94 in his vol. 1, but in vol. 2 gave the date as after 1398; W. Moll, *Kerkgeschiedenis van Nederland vóór de Hervorming* (Utrecht, 1869), 2, pt. 3: 91 n. 2, preferred the earlier date, on the grounds that Schoneveld's activity took place about ten years after the founding of the house in question. In any case, there is no evidence that Jacob of Soest acted in the diocese of Utrecht c. 1393–94, or at any other time. The source of this notion is again complex: Walter Ribbeck, "Beiträge zur Geschichte der römischen Inquisition in Deutschland während des 14. und 15. Jahrhunderts," *Zeitschrift für vaterländische Geschichte und Altertumskunde* 46 (1888): 138–41, published a treatise which bears a certain resemblance to the above-mentioned treatise of the "inquisitor Belgicus," though it is not simply another edition or version of the same treatise. The new treatise is anonymous and undated, but it appeared in a MS along with materials of the inquisitor Jacob of Soest. Evidently confused by this fact, Fredericq published this work as a list of "charges made by the inquisitor Jacob of Soest." To compound the confusion, Fredericq published this work under the date c. 1393–94, i.e., his original date for the treatise of the "inquisitor Belgicus." He thus led some historians to the impression that Jacob acted in the Low Countries during these years; e.g., C. Van der Wansem, *Het ontstaan en de geschiedenis der Broederschap van het Gemene Leven tot 1400* (Louvain, 1958), pp. 148–55.

On Schoneveld's Baltic campaign, see Korner, *Chronica*, pp. 99f., 364–66, 546; Fredericq, *Corpus*, 1: 264f. Günter Peters, "Norddeutsches Beginen- und Beghardenwesen im Mittelalter," *Niedersächsisches Jahrbuch für Landesgeschichte* 41/42 (1969–70): 113f., argues that a heretic at Stralsund was a flagellant, but takes his evidence from a derivative chronicle of the sixteenth century, and does not represent even this source altogether reliably; in arguing that the same inquisitor worked later against flagellants, Peters repeats a common error (see below, chap. 6, n. 70).

36. Apart from the works cited below, see now Jean-Claude Schmitt, *Mort d'une hérésie: L'Église et les clercs face aux béguines et aux béghards du Rhin supérieur du XIVe au XVe Siècle* (Paris, 1978), which appeared too late to be used for this study.

37. Franz Joseph Mone, ed., *Quellensammlung der badischen Landesgeschichte* (Karlsruhe, 1863), 3: 638; Karl Rieder, ed., *Regesten zur Geschichte der Bischöfe von Constanz* (Innsbruck, 1926), 3: 112, 132–34, 140, 145; Johannes Nider, *Formicarius* (Douai, 1602), pp. 191f. See Lerner, *Free Spirit*, p. 175.

38. See Georg Boner, "Das Predigerkloster in Basel," *Basler Zeitschrift für Geschichte und Altertumskunde* 34 (1935): 137–43; Brigitte Degler-Spengler, "Die Beginen in Basel," ibid. 69 (1969): 32–69; and Lerner, *Free Spirit*, pp. 151–57. The charge of heresy comes out most clearly in Max Straganz, "Zum Begharden- und Beghinenstreite in Basel zu Beginn des 15. Jahrhunderts," *Alemannia* 27 (1900): 20–28.

39. *CDS*, 18, pt. 1: 242; *MGH SS rer. Germ.*, 20: 82; Lerner, *Free Spirit*, pp. 104f., 156f.

40. Lerner, *Free Spirit*, pp. 162f.

41. Nider, *Formicarius*, pp. 191f.; Andreas of Regensburg, *Sämtliche Werke*, ed. Georg Leidinger (Munich, 1903), p. 484; Fritz Hermann, "Die letzte Ketzerverbrennung in Mainz," in *Beiträge zur Kunst und Geschichte des Mainzer Lebensraumes: Festschrift für Ernst Neeb* (Mainz, 1936), pp. 105–10; May, *Die geistliche Gerichtsbarkeit*, p. 189; Felix Hemmerlin, *Varie oblectationis opuscula et tractatus* (Basel, 1497), sig. c. 2^v; Mone, *Quellensammlung* (Karlsruhe, 1848), 1: 336. For a summary, see Lerner, *Free Spirit*, pp. 164–81.

42. Claus-Peter Clasen, "Medieval Heresies in the Reformation," *Church History* 32 (1963), esp. pp. 394–406, refers to certain sixteenth-century heretics as perpetuating the movement. These later antinomians certainly held notions akin to those of earlier Free Spirits, but the correspondence should not be exaggerated. Apart from the common idea that sexual acts could have religious significance (a notion that has arisen independently in many historical contexts, for obvious motives), there is little parallel. Clasen suggests that the sixteenth-century heretic Claus Fry was like the Free Spirits in his eschatological beliefs and in his rejection of all the sacraments. But eschatological motifs were never pronounced in the heresy of the Free Spirit, and rejection of some or all of the sacraments was a

natural, if not inevitable, consequence of any break with the Church that dispensed the sacraments.

43. Martin of Amberg, while mainly pursuing Waldensians, brought beghards to trial in Franconia and possibly also at Cham; see Augustin Neumann, *České sekty ve století XIV. a XV.* (Staré Brno, 1920), pp. 6f. of appendices; Herman Haupt, "Zwei Traktate gegen Beginen und Begharden," *Zeitschrift für Kirchengeschichte* 12 (1891): 85–90; and Ernst Werner, *Nachrichten über spätmittelalterliche Ketzer aus tschechoslovakischen Archiven und Bibliotheken* (Leipzig, 1963), pp. 256–59, 277–79. (Werner—who oddly persists in calling this treatise a protocol, as if all its contents necessarily derived from a single trial—gives a more specific dating than the sources permit. Apart from what Lerner has already said on this matter, in *Free Spirit*, p. 147 n. 51, it should be noted that there is no evidence that this Martin had anything to do with the trial in Strassburg in 1399–1400). John Wasmud of Homburg, who served on an episcopal commission against Waldensians in Mainz, wrote a treatise on beghards which, while it does not state explicitly that he sat in judgment upon them, certainly leaves that impression; see Aloys Schmidt, ed., "Tractatus contra hereticos Beckardos, Lulhardos et Swestriones des Wasmud von Homburg," *Archiv für mittelrheinische Kirchengeschichte* 14 (1962), esp. pp. 340, 352f.

44. See Mosheim, *De beghardis*, pp. 350–62, 364–66, 368–75, and references in the following note.

45. Sauerland, *Urkunden und Regesten*, 4: 27f.; Mosheim, *De beghardis*, pp. 336f., 343–50.

46. This is especially the case with the imperial decrees of 1369.

47. Schmidt, *Päbstliche Urkunden aus den Jahren 1353–1378*, p. 295 (campaign against flagellants). Thomas Ripoll, ed., *Bullarium Ordinis Fratrum Praedicatorum* (Rome, 1729–40), 2: 272f.; Alfred Overmann, ed., *Urkundenbuch der Erfurter Stifter und Klöster* (Magdeburg, 1926), p. 349 (against bishop). On the *Sachsenspiegel*, see Carl Gustav Homeyer, "Johannes Klenkok wider den Sachsenspiegel," *Abhandlungen der königlichen Akademie der Wissenschaften zu Berlin*, 1885, Philosophisch-historische Klasse, pp. 376–432, 432a–432d. Homeyer's dating is implausible. Accepting the authority of the chronicler Johannes Schiphower, who speaks of Klenkok as appealing the case to John XXII, Homeyer concludes that the affair must have occurred shortly after 1330, even though the participants are known to have been active much later. Discoveries made since publication of Homeyer's article have confirmed that all of Kerlinger's inquisitorial work took place c. 1370.

48. The heretics Kerlinger found at Nordhausen may well have been flagellants; see Ernst Günther Förstemann, *Die christlichen Geisslergesellschaften* (Halle, 1828), p. 177 n.

49. One could readily make an argument to this effect about such persons as Berthold of Rohrbach; see Lerner, *Free Spirit*, pp. 131f.

50. Rieder, *Regesten*, 3: 112, 132–34; see also p. 145.

51. See Richard Kieckhefer, *European Witch Trials: Their Foundations in Popular and Learned Culture, 1300–1500* (London, and Berkeley and Los Angeles, 1976), pp. 28, 90f.

52. See Antoine Dondaine, "Le Manuel de l'inquisiteur (1230–1330)," *Archivum fratrum praedicatorum* 17 (1947): 85–194.

53. C. Calvert and A. W. Gruner, *A Hangman's Diary* (London, 1928), pp. 17f.

54. Patschovsky, "Strassburger Beginenverfolgungen," pp. 182–84.

55. Stragnaz, "Zum Begharden- und Beghinenstreite," pp. 24f.

56. Erbstösser, *Sozialreligiose Strömungen*, pp. 161f.

57. Österreichische Nationalbibliothek, Cod. Vindob. 3748, fol. 146^r–146^v.

58. Trithemius and Nauclerus (as above, n. 15); see Lerner, *Free Spirit*, pp. 131f.

59. Erbstösser and Werner, *Ideologische Probleme*, pp. 136–53; see Lerner, *Free Spirit*, pp. 135–39.

60. Lerner, *Free Spirit*, p. 136.

61. Erbstösser, *Sozialreligiöse Strömungen*, p. 161; Grundmann, "Ketzerverhöre," p. 563.

62. Grundmann, "Ketzerverhöre," pp. 535–50, 561–66; see Lerner, *Free Spirit*, pp. 141–45.

63. This thesis is a corollary of Lea's general interpretation of repression in Germany.

64. See most recently Alois Schütz, *Die Prokuratorien und Instruktionen Ludwigs des Bayern für die Kurie (1331–1345): Ein Beitrag zu seinem Absolutionsprozess* (Kallmünz, 1973); and Hermann Otto Schwöbel, *Der diplomatische Kampf zwischen Ludwig dem Bayern und der römischen Kurie im Rahmen des kanonischen Absolutionsprozesses, 1330–1346* (Weimar, 1968).

65. Heinrich Friedjung, *Kaiser Karl IV. und sein Antheil am geistigen Leben seiner Zeit* (Vienna, 1876).

66. As above, n. 18.

67. Ferdinand Janner, *Geschichte der Bischöfe von Regensburg* (Regensburg, 1886), 3: 157f.

68. Lea, *History of the Inquisition*, 2: 388.

69. Urban V and Gregory XI appear to have maintained contact with Walter Kerlinger, though there is no reason to think that they conceived of him as an agent of their political policy, except in the sense that repression of beghards and beguines was a "political" undertaking. (And the impetus for this action appears to have come more from Germany than from the Curia, even when popes lent their sanction to German repression.)

70. E.g., Othmar Hageneder, *Die geistliche Gerichtsbarkeit in Ober- und Niederösterreich* (Graz, Vienna, and Cologne, 1967).

71. This policy was manifest primarily in the Golden Bull of 1356 and in Charles's later action relating to the election of his son Wenceslas. For the Golden Bull, see esp. Erling Ladewig Petersen, "Studien zur goldenen

Bulle von 1356," *Deutsches Archiv für Erforschung des Mittelalters* 22 (1966): 227–53. It is conceivable, to be sure, that Charles pursued a double policy with respect to the papacy: while reducing the pope's role in German electoral practice, he could have sought to augment papal powers in other fields. It is not clear, however, that Charles in fact carried out such a double policy, and in any event it is highly unlikely that he would have done so at the expense of the higher nobility and the hierarchy.

72. I am grateful to Alexander Patschovsky for reminding me of this aspect of the problem.

73. McDonnell, *Beguines and Beghards,* p. 562.

74. Howard Kaminsky, *A History of the Hussite Revolution* (Berkeley and Los Angeles, 1967), p. 8.

75. See Friedjung, *Kaiser Karl IV.,* on this general aspect of Charles's personality.

76. Patschovsky, *Anfänge,* pp. 73f.

77. Schmidt, *Päbstliche Urkunden aus den Jahren 1353–1378,* p. 175.

78. Some historians have argued that the campaign lasted longer, and ended only in 1378, with the death of Charles IV and the onset of the Great Schism; cf. most recently Lerner, *Free Spirit,* p. 141 n. 40. This interpretation is based largely on the fact that shortly before his death Charles was still lending support to a new papal inquisitor, John of Boland; cf. Mosheim, *De beghardis,* pp. 388–92. Yet the appointment and support of an inquisitor do not constitute evidence of inquisitorial vigor.

79. Unfortunately, the sources frequently do not specify which houses of beguines were attacked, or whether they were under the protection of one or another mendicant order.

80. Mosheim, *De beghardis,* pp. 356–62.

81. Volger, *Urkundenbuch,* 2: 15–18; Wigger, "Urkundliche Mittheilungen," pp. 13–26. Peters, "Norddeutsches Beginen- und Begardenwesen," 108, implies that the edicts were known at Hildesheim, but the source he refers to (dated 1386) merely pertains to an unspecified imperial letter. The context gives no indication of what the letter dealt with, and it is most unlikely that the edicts of 1369 would have been registered so long after the inquisitorial campaign had passed.

82. Schmidt, *Päbstliche Urkunden aus den Jahren 1353–1378,* pp. 320, 332–35.

83. For a plausible case of an inquisition motivated in part by financial considerations, see Georgene W. Davis, *The Inquisition at Albi, 1299–1300: Text of Register and Analysis* (New York, 1948), pp. 88f.

84. For general information on this case see Josef Koch, "Kritische Studien," pp. 16–50 ("Der Eckhart-Prozess"); and Degenhardt, *Studien zum Wandel des Eckhartbildes,* pp. 3–15. The primary sources, published now in diverse periodicals (and sometimes in divergent editions), are to be included in Meister Eckhart, *Die lateinischen Werke,* Vol. 5, now in progress under the auspices of the *Deutsche Forschungsgemeinschaft.*

85. Heinrich Denifle, "Acten zum Processe Meister Eckeharts," *Archiv*

für Literatûr- und Kirchengeschichte des Mittelalters 2 (1886): 636–40; translated in James M. Clark, *Meister Eckhart* (London, 1957), pp. 253–58.

86. For numerous examples of interpreters who have seen Eckhart as heretical, see the survey by Degenhardt.

87. Karl Kertz, "Meister Eckhart's Teaching on the Birth of the Word in the Soul," *Traditio* 15 (1959): pp. 327–63, furnishes one excellent example of such scholarship. General surveys of Eckhart-scholarship are given in Toni Schaller, "Die Meister Eckhart-Forschung von der Jahrhundertwende bis zur Gegenwart," *Freiburger Zeitschrift für Philosophie und Theologie* 15 (1968): 262–316, 403–26; and "Zur Eckhart-Deutung der letzten 30 Jahre," ibid. 16 (1969): 22–39.

88. G. Théry, "Ëdition critique des pièces relatives au procès d'Eckhart," *Archives d'histoire doctrinale et littéraire du moyen âge* 1 (1926–27): 218f.; translation is from *Meister Eckhart: A Modern Translation*, trans. Raymond Bernard Blakney (New York, 1941), p. 286.

89. Degenhardt, *Studien*, pp. 8–10, summarizes the evidence for this interpretation.

90. Ibid., pp. 10–13.

91. Ibid., p. 11 n. 1.

92. Denifle, "Acten," p. 628.

93. Ibid., pp. 13–15.

94. On this general question see M. D. Lambert, *Franciscan Poverty: The Doctrine of the Absolute Poverty of Christ and the Apostles in the Franciscan Order, 1210–1323* (London, 1961).

95. Master Eckhart, *Parisian Questions and Prologues*, trans. Armand A. Maurer (Toronto, 1974), pp. 12–28, 43–75.

96. James M. Clark, *The Great German Mystics: Eckhart, Tauler and Suso* (Oxford, 1949), p. 16, distinguishes sharply between the proceedings at Cologne and those at Avignon, and concludes that the latter were impartial. Clark is perhaps too willing to discount the possibility of political influence even at Avignon.

97. Fredericq, *Corpus*, 1: 188. The translation is McDonnell's.

98. McDonnell, *Beguines and Beghards*, p. 521.

99. Patschovsky, "Strassburger Beginenverfolgungen," pp. 164f.

100. McDonnell, *Beguines and Beghards*, p. 560.

101. See c. 1, *Clem.*, lib. V, tit. 3.

102. Patschovsky, *Anfänge*, pp. 29, 34–36.

103. Roger Aubenas, *Recueil de lettres des officialitées de Marseille et d'Aix* (Paris, 1937–38), pp. xiv ff.; cf. Aubenas, *La Sorcière et l'inquisiteur: Episode de l'Inquisition en Provence, 1439* (Aix-en-Provence, 1945), p. 35 n. 1.

104. E.g., Richard Wilder Emery, *Heresy and Inquisition in Narbonne* (New York, 1941), esp. pp. 77–102.

105. Célestin Douais, ed., *Documents pour servir à l'histoire de l'Inquisition dans le Languedoc* (Paris, 1900), 2: 302–49; see Ewald Müller, *Das Konzil von Vienne (1311–1312)* (Münster, 1934), pp. 302–49.

106. Ennen, *Quellen,* 5: 88–90.

107. They are referred to as "in civitate nostra . . . habiti pro veris christocolis."

108. See Johannes Asen, "Die Beginen in Köln," *Annalen des historischen Vereins für den Niederrhein* 111 (1927): 81–180; and Asen, "Die Begarden und die Sackbrüder in Köln," ibid. 115 (1929): 167–79.

109. The wording is "inquisitor . . . pauperibus hominibus laycis et omnino illiteratis proponit questiones. . . ."

110. Schimdt, "Tractatus contra hereticos," pp. 326–86; see Lerner, *Free Spirit,* p. 58 n. 70.

111. Eva Gertrud Neumann, *Rheinisches Beginen- und Begardenwesen* (Meisenheim am Glan, 1960), pp. 105–7.

112. Mosheim, *De beghardis,* pp. 364–66.

113. Volger, *Urkundenbuch,* 2: 15–18.

114. Hans-Joachim Behr, "Der Convent der blauen Beginen in Lüneburg," *Lüneburger Blätter* 11/12 (1961): 184. The argument is essentially this: the beguines' house founded by Albert van der Mölen and long patronized by the Lüneburg patriciate was found extant as late as 1383, and must therefore have been preserved or revived after the dissolution. It does not seem clear, though, that this particular convent was involved in the dissolution at all. The two houses that were dissolved are described in these words: "duas domos curias seu habitacula ipsorum, que ex opposito domus quondam magistri Theoderici Bromes ad partem orientem prope muros dicti opidi Luneborg situantur. . . ." Even if this places them in the same neighborhood as the convent of Albert van der Mölen (and I am not certain whether even this much is established), the case is not proved. Beguines' houses were commonly clustered together, and it is entirely possible that the two houses that were dissolved lay close by another that was left alone.

115. Mosheim, *De beghardis,* pp. 343–50.

116. See Walter L. Wakefield, *Heresy, Crusade and Inquisition in Southern France 1100–1250* (London, Berkeley, and Los Angeles, 1974), esp. pp. 207–36.

117. Patschovsky, *Anfänge,* esp. pp. 46–65.

118. Ibid., pp. 58–61.

119. Ibid., pp. 61–65.

120. Ibid., esp. pp. 54, 57f.

121. Patschovsky (ibid., p. 54 n. 208) cites a municipal violation of benefit of clergy—i.e., of ecclesiastical rights *ratione personae* rather than *ratione materiae.* Even if it could demonstrate resistance *in principle* to ecclesiastical claims (rather than merely failure to abide by these claims), and more specifically, even if it could show resistance to ecclesiastical jurisdiction, this instance would not by itself suffice to establish a general policy.

122. Ibid., p. 129 (my translation).

123. Ibid., p. 57.

124. Ibid., pp. 57f.
125. Ibid., p. 57 n. 223.
126. Emery, *Heresy and Inquisition,* esp. pp. 77–102.
127. Ibid., pp. 82–84.
128. Ibid., p. 90.
129. See Lea, *History of the Inquisition,* 1, esp. pp. 399–458; Patschovsky, *Anfänge,* pp. 54f.
130. See Kieckhefer, *European Witch Trials,* pp. 18f.
131. C. Kenneth Brampton, "Marsiglio of Padua," *English Historical Review,* 37 (1922): 501–15, pieces together the few facts known about Marsilius's life; see also Marsilius of Padua, *The Defender of the Peace,* trans. Alan Gewirth (New York, 1951), 1, esp. pp. 20–23; and John B. Morrall, *Political Thought in Medieval Times* (London, 1958), pp. 104–18.
132. Full accounts of Ockham's life are given in Léon Baudry, *Guillaume d'Occam: Sa vie, ses oeuvres, ses idées sociales et politiques,* 1 (Paris, 1949); and Jürgen Miethke, *Ockhams Weg zur Sozialphilosophie* (Berlin, 1969), pp. 1–136. For a brief English account, see Arthur Stephen McGrade, *The Political Thought of William of Ockham: Personal and Institutional Principles* (Cambridge, 1974), pp. 4–28.
133. Later, esp. in the fifteenth century, there was similar resistance to prosecution of witches and to political trials, for essentially the same reason —i.e., the conviction that the defendants were innocent.

Chapter 4. The Crisis of the Waldensians

1. On this point see, e.g., Wilhelm Wattenbach, "Über die Inquisition gegen die Waldenser in Pommerrn und der Mark Brandenberg," *Abhandlungen der königlichen Akademie der Wissenschaften zu Berlin,* 1886, Philosophisch-historische Classe, Abhandlung 3, pp. 47f.
2. E.g., Herman Haupt, "Waldenserthum und Inquisition im südöstlichen Deutschland seit der Mitte des 14. Jahrhunderts," *Deutsche Zeitschrift für Geschichtswissenschaft* 3 (1890): 404–11; Andreas Felix Oefele, ed., *Rerum Boicarum scriptores* (Augsburg, 1763), 1: 620.
3. Jean Groffier, *Qui sont les Vaudois?* (Apt-en-Provence, 1974); George B. Watts, *The Waldenses in the New World* (Durham, N.C., 1941).
4. Herman Haupt, "Waldenserthum und Inquisition im südöstlichen Deutschland bis zur Mitte des 14. Jahrhunderts," *Deutsche Zeitschrift für Geschichtswissenschaft* 1 (1889): 304–6, 309–15; Paul P. Bernard, "Heresy in Fourteenth Century Austria," *Medievalia et Humanistica* 10 (1956): 50–55; Valentin Prevenhueber, *Annales Styrenses* (Nürnberg, 1740), p. 47; Hieronymus Pez, ed., *Scriptores rerum Austriacarum* (Leipzig, 1725), 2: cols. 330, 533–36; Johann Losert, ed., *Fontes rerum Austriacarum,* sec. 1 (Vienna, 1875), 8: 365; Margaret Nickson, "The 'Pseudo-Reinerius' Treatise: The Final Stage of a Thirteenth-Century Work on Heresy from the Diocese of Passau," *Archives d'histoire doctrinale et littéraire du moyen*

âge 42 (1967): 303–14; Robert E. Lerner, *The Heresy of the Free Spirit in the Later Middle Ages* (Berkeley, Los Angeles, and London, 1972), pp. 25f., 28f., 107, 112–19; Augustin Theiner, ed., *Vetera monumenta historica Hungariam sacram illustrantia* (Rome, 1859), 1: 511–18; Herman Haupt, "Deutsch-böhmische Waldenser um 1340," *Zeitschrift für Kirchengeschichte* 14 (1894): 1–18; *MGH SS rer. Germ.*, 36, pt. 2: 130f.; *MGH SS rer. Germ.*, n.s., 3: 142, 144, 151; H. J. Zeibig, ed., "Die kleine Klosterneuburger Chronik (1322 bis 1428)," *Archiv für Kunde österreichischer Geschichtsquellen* 7 (1851): 232; Matthias Flacius Illyricus, *Catalogus testium veritatis* (Frankfurt, 1666), p. 638; *MGH SS*, 14: 434f.

    5. *MGH SS*, 9: 512.

    6. Dietrich Kurze, "Zur Ketzergeschichte der Mark Brandenburg und Pommerns, vornehmlich im 14. Jahrhundert," *Jahrbuch für die Geschichte Mittel- und Ostdeutschlands* 16/17 (1968): 56f.; Lerner, *Free Spirit*, pp. 27f.; Alexander Patschovsky, *Die Anfänge einer ständigen Inquisition in Böhmen* (Berlin and New York, 1975), pp. 65–80.

    7. Haupt, "Waldenserthum seit der Mitte des 14. Jahrhunderts," pp. 404f.; Augustin Neumann, *České sekty ve století XIV. a XV.* (Staré Brno, 1920), p. 6 of appendix (for activities in Hungary); Anton Weck, *Der Chur-Fürstlichen Sächsischen weitberuffenen Residenz- und Haupt-Vestung Dresden Beschreib- und Vorstellung* (Nürnberg, 1680), pp. 305f.; Roger Wilmans, "Zur Geschichte der römischen Inquisition in Deutschland während des 14. und 15. Jahrhunderts," *Historische Zeitschrift* 41 (1879): 203; Carl Heinrich von Lang, ed., *Regesta, sive rerum Boicarum autographa* (Munich, 1843), 10: 15.

    On the trials in Nürnberg see Werner Schultheiss, ed., *Die Acht-, Verbots-, und Fehdebücher Nürnbergs von 1285–1400* (Nürnberg, 1960), pp. 64f., 84, 150f., 157–59; Georg Andreas Will, *Kleine Beiträge zu der Diplomatik und deren Literatur* (Altdorf, 1739), pp. 109–25; Haupt, "Waldenserthum seit der Mitte des 14. Jahrhunderts," p. 350f.; *CDS*, 1: 362 n. 3. These heretics were sentenced along with their families and servants; beghards and beguines did not commonly live in family units. And there is no evidence for survival of flagellants or Cathars anywhere near Nürnberg. It is possible that the subjects were not heretics at all, but this hypothesis renders it difficult to account for such a sustained series of trials.

    8. Österreichische Nationalbibliothek, Cod. Vindob. 3748, fol. 154^r–154^v: "Item confitetur [Elizabeth conjux Conradi Huter] se taliter abjurasse domino Martino inquisitori tunc hic heretice pravitatis et domino Heinrico tunc plebano . . ."; cf. ibid., fol. 145^r, for further reference to Henrich, who is probably the same as the canon of that name appointed for the diocese in 1378 (see Lang, *Regesta*, 10: 15). The date of Martin's work is roughly ascertainable: Elizabeth Huter abjured before him, two years after joining the sect (Cod. Vindob. 3748, fol. 153^v), and had confessed to a heresiarch c. 1381 (ibid., fol. 153^r); her husband claimed to have been converted before his visit to Donauwörth in 1387 (ibid., fol. 147^v), and abjured two years before the death of the parish priest named Heinrich (ibid., fol. 145^r). Cf.

Heinrich Finke, "Waldenserprocess in Regensburg, 1395," *Deutsche Zeitschrift für Geschichtswissenschaft* 4 (1890): 345–46. Another heretic had abjured before Martin in Regensburg c. 1380; see Timotheus Wilhelm Röhrich, "Die Winkeler in Strassburg, sammt deren Verhöracten, um 1400," in Röhrich's *Mittheilungen aus der Geschichte der evangelischen Kirche des Elsasses* (Strassburg and Paris, 1855), 1: 63.

9. Kurze, "Ketzergeschichte," pp. 68f.; Dietrich Kurze, ed., *Quellen zur Ketzergeschichte Brandenburgs und Pommerns* (Berlin and New York, 1975), esp. pp. 91–93, 97.

10. Haupt, "Waldenserthum seit der Mitte des 14. Jahrhunderts," pp. 342f., 369; Caspar Brusch, *De Laureaco, veteri admodumque celebri olim in Norico, civitate, et de Patavio Germanico . . . libri duo* (Basel, 1553), p. 235; Constantin Höfler, ed., *Concilia Pragensia, 1353–1413* (Prague, 1862), pp. 26f.

11. As papal legate for the dioceses of Bamberg, Regensburg, and Misnia, the archbishop of Prague threatened to appoint inquisitors for these dioceses if the ordinaries did not prosecute the heretics present there (see Höfler, pages cited in preceding note). In a document of 1396, Martin of Amberg, writing from Prague to Regensburg, referred to himself as a papal inquisitor (Cod. Vindob. 3748, fol. 149ᵛ). One might speculate that in his work in the diocese of Regensburg Martin held an extraordinary papal commission, obtained through (or from?) the archbishop of Prague.

12. For Martin of Amberg, see the preceding note. There are two second-hand reports that corroborate the appointment of Martin as papal inquisitor. An anonymous notice prefixed to an episcopal edict from Strassburg of 1374 refers to a papal delegate named Martin who is almost certainly Martin of Amberg; see J. J. I. von Döllinger, ed., *Beiträge zur Sektengeschichte des Mittelalters* (Munich, 1890), 2: 378. And Johannes Trithemius, *Annales Hirsaugienses* (St. Gall, 1690), 2: 296, speaks of "Magister Martinus inquisitor . . . a sede apostolica deputatus"—though Trithemius is notoriously prone to inaccuracy. In all the extant protocols, however (see following note), Martin claimed only episcopal authority, and it is most unlikely that he would have neglected to cite a papal commission if he in fact held one. In all likelihood he was papal inquisitor only for the archdiocese of Prague, and possibly for those dioceses over which the archbishop of Prague was papal legate (see preceding note).

There is only one source that speaks of Peter Zwicker as a papal inquisitor, and it is most unreliable: his protocols were entrusted to Dominicans at Prenzlau, who (sometime before the mid-sixteenth century) added a notice speaking of Zwicker as "ad partes Almanie et dyocesim Caminensem specialiter destinatum per sedem apostolicam"; cf. Kurze, "Ketzergeschichte," pp. 67 n. 60, 72 n. 91. This information might conceivably have been drawn from a part of the records that no longer survives. But even assuming that the Dominicans bothered to read through the protocols carefully (and Kurze shows that they were incorrect in their dating), they may have drawn their conclusion from the knowledge that inquisitors in their own order were generally papal delegates. Of the extant protocols, all refer to Zwicker as having episcopal authority only. But even if one or more of these men did hold a papal commission, the essential point is that none of them had anything to do with the routine sequences of Dominican inquisitors who served under papal auspices.

13. The documents fall into seven groups. (1) One text speaks of a priest from Bohemia named Martin who took part in prosecution at Strassburg in 1374: see Döllinger, *Beiträge*, 2: 378; and Alexander Patschovsky, "Strassburger Beginenverfolgungen im 14. Jahrhundert," *Deutsches Archiv für Erforschung des Mittelalters* 30 (1974): 89f. (with reference to a supporting text). (2) Two records of inquisitions from the 1390s refer retrospectively to an inquisitor named Martin who acted at Regensburg in the early 1380s: see above, n. 8. (3) Two documents refer to an inquisitor named Martin active at Würzburg and Erfurt in 1391: Joseph M. Scheidt, *Thesaurus juris Franconici*, Abschnitt 1, Heft 17 (Würzburg, 1789), pp. 3263–66; and Herman Haupt, *Die religiösen Sekten in Franken vor der Reformation* (Würzburg, 1882), pp. 35f. (N.B.: the date is not 1392, as Haupt gives it). (4) Two texts mention a Martin active in Franconia in 1399: *Deutsche Reichstagsakten* (Munich, 1877), 3: 88; and Neumann, *České sekty*, p. 6 of appendices. (5) Three protocols refer to an inquisitor named Martin who worked in Hungary and eastern Austria in 1400–1401 along with Peter Zwicker: Haupt, "Waldenserthum seit der Mitte des 14. Jahrhunderts," pp. 401–3, 408–11; and Josef Truhlár, "Inkvisice Waldenských," *Česky časopis historický* 9 (1903): 196–98 (N.B.: there is no evidence that he worked in Austria earlier). (6) Two treatises were written by a Martin of Amberg, one of them "editus a domino Martino inquisitore hereticorum Amberge": Bayerische Staatsbibliothek, Munich, Clm 3764, fol. 35ʳ; and *Gewissensspiegel*, ed. Stanley N. Werbow (Berlin, 1958). (7) The inquisitor named Martin who had earlier dealt with heretics at Regensburg wrote a letter from Prague in 1396: see above, n. 11. That all of these references are to the same man can be demonstrated with reasonable certainty by the following links: in several cases the inquisitor is said to have been from Prague (2, 4, 5, 7); in 1391 at Erfurt, and in 1400–1401 in Hungary and Austria, he worked in connection with Peter Zwicker (3, 5); the inquisitor at Regensburg in the early 1380s was later called upon for information about Conrad Huter of Regensburg (2, 7); at Erfurt and in the treatises this inquisitor was named Martin of Amberg (3, 6); the inquisitors at Strassburg and Franconia both worked in conjunction with Bishop Lambert (1, 4; cf. Patschovsky, "Strassburger Beginenverfolgungen," p. 91). Historians have usually cited the inquisitor as Martin of Prague, but this surname is given only by a heretic about twenty years after his contact with the inquisitor, and in this case it is not even entirely certain that "of Prague" is intended as a surname (Röhrich, "Winkeler," p. 63). It is possible that Martin used "of Prague" as an alternative surname, but "of Amberg" is better authenticated.

14. Wattenbach, "Über die Inquisition," pp. 20–71; Kurze, "Ketzergeschichte," pp. 66–91; Haupt, "Waldenserthum seit der Mitte des 14.

Jahrhunderts," pp. 367–80, 401–11; Truhlár, "Inkvisice," pp. 196–98; Prevenhueber, *Annales*, p. 72; Pez, *Scriptores*, 1, col. 1244; Franz Xaver Pritz, *Geschichte der ehemaligen Benediktiner-Klöster Garsten und Gleink* (Linz, 1841), p. 32; Schneidt, *Thesaurus*, Absch. 1, H. 17, p. 3265; Trithemius, *Annales*, 2: 296; Haupt, *Die religiösen Sekten*, pp. 23–26; Herman Haupt, *Der Waldensische Ursprung des Codex Teplensis* (Würzburg, 1886), pp. 34–36; Döllinger, *Beiträge*, 2: 305–11, 330, 346–51; Margarinus de La Bigne, ed., *Maxima bibliotheca veterum patrum* (Lyon, 1677), 25: 281; Godfried Edmund Friess, "Patarener, Begharden und Waldenser in Oesterreich während des Mittelalters," *Oesterreichische Vierteljahresschrift für katholische Theologie* 11 (1872): 262–66; Giovanni Gonnet, "I Valdesi d'Austria nella seconda metà del secolo XIV," *Bollettino della società di studi valdesi* 82, no. 111 (1962): 5–41.

15. Oefele, *Rerum Boicarum scriptores*, 1: 620; Döllinger, *Beiträge*, 2: 363f.; *CDS*, 4: 96f., 249; Christian Bürckstümmer, "Waldenser in Dinkelsbühl," *Beiträge zur bayerischen Kirchengeschichte* 19 (1913): 272–75; Helmut Weigel, "Ein Waldenserverhör in Rothenburg im Jahre 1394," *Beiträge zur bayerischen Kirchengeschichte* 23 (1917): 81–86; Anton Philipp von Segesser, *Rechtsgeschichte der Stadt Lucern* (Lucerne, 1854), 2: 795 n. 2 (N.B.: there is no indication that the subject here was a Waldensian). The sources do not explicitly state that Angermeier was the inquisitor at Donauwörth, but the trial belongs in the complex of proceedings held in and around Augsburg in 1393, and it is probable that he was the inquisitor. There are several later chronicles for this complex of trials, some of them giving wildly divergent information, but there is no reason to prefer any of them (including *CDS*, 22: 40f., and 34: 221–23) to the contemporary records. The archival document cited in Maria Zelzer, *Geschichte der Stadt Donauwörth* (Donauwörth, 1958), 1: 382 n. 3, and Polykarp M. Siemer, *Geschichte des Dominikanerklosters Sankt Magdalena in Augsburg* (Vechta, 1936), p. 36 n. 41, is explicitly based on the derivative chronicles of Burkhard Zink (*CDS*, 5: 45f.) and the *Baumeister* Hector Mülich (*CDS*, 22: 40f.).

16. *CDC*, 18: 129f., 221; *MGH SS rer. Germ.*, 20: 63; Döllinger, *Beiträge*, 2: 620f.; Valentin Ferdinand von Guden, ed., *Codex diplomaticus anecdotorum, res Moguntinas . . . illustrantium* (Frankfurt and Leipzig, 1751), 3: 598–600; Österreichische Nationalbibliothek, Cod. Vindob. 3748, fol. 145ʳ–155ᵛ; Finke, "Waldenserprocess," pp. 345f.; Conrad Justinger, *Die Berner-Chronik*, ed. Gottlieb Studer (Bern, 1871), p. 186; Bernhard Rudolf Fetscherin, "Beitrag zur Geschichte der Waldenser," *Abhandlungen des historischen Vereins des Kantons Bern*, 2, pt. 2 (1854): 336f. Gottlieb Friedrich Ochsenbein, *Aus dem schweizerischen Volksleben des XV. Jahrhunderts* (Bern, 1881), pp. 95–126. Although Fribourg lies outside the bounds of this study, the case clearly belongs in this general campaign. The sources for Augsburg (*CDS*, 4: 96f., 249; Oefele, *Rerum Boicarum scriptores*, 1: 620) tell of a trial in Wemding, but according to Julius Sax, *Die Bischöfe und Reichsfürsten von Eichstätt, 745–1806* (Landshut, 1884), 1: 270, the inquisitor there was a Dominican named Berthold, appointed by the bishop of

Eichstätt. Since Wemding lies in the diocese of Eichstätt rather than that of Augsburg, this information is plausible.

17. The contrary information in *CDS*, 22: 40f., is clearly a misconstruction of an interpolation in *CDS*, 4: 96f. (in which the chronicler mentioned the burgomasters at the time). The later chronicler made almost exactly the same kind of error late in his text (*CDS*, 22: 54, drawn from *CDS*, 4: 111).

18. Haupt, "Waldenserthum seit der Mitte des 14. Jahrhunderts," p. 375; Döllinger, *Beiträge*, 2: 349f.

19. Friess, "*Patarener*," pp. 271f. The document does not even mention the inquisitor.

20. On the commission from the archbishop of Prague, see above, n. 11.

21. Regarding his commission, see above, n. 9.

22. *CDS*, 4: 96; on the proceedings at Rothenburg, see Weigel, "Waldenserverhör," pp. 81–86.

23. The proceedings at Mainz may have begun before any of the three leading inquisitors started working against Waldensians—though it is not possible to assign a definite date for the onset of Martin of Amberg's involvement, and it is at least conceivable that he set in motion the developments that led to prosecution even in the Middle Rhine.

24. See Albert Hauck, *Kirchengeschichte Deutschlands* (Leipzig, 1920), 5: 672–869.

25. Friess, "*Patarener*," pp. 262–66; Döllinger, *Beiträge*, 2: 305–11; *CDS*, 4: 96; Röhrich, "Winkeler," *passim*.

26. Wilmans, "Zur Geschichte der römischen Inquisition," p. 203.

27. Cod. Vindob. 3748; Weigel, "Waldenserverhör."

28. Wattenbach, "Über die Inquisition," p. 21; Kurze, "Ketzergeschichte," pp. 70f.

29. Cod. Vindob. 3748, fol. 150[r]; to be precise, it was Martin of Amberg, their correspondent, who consulted with the masters.

30. Döllinger, *Beiträge*, 2: 355–62; Röhrich, "Winkeler," pp. 28f., 43f., 50, 55, 57–62; see above, nn. 28, 29.

31. Haupt, *Der Waldensische Ursprung*, pp. 35f.; also in Döllinger, *Beiträge*, 2: 330f. There is another list of twelve masters, but it is unclear whether these are converts; the text is in Döllinger, *Beiträge*, 2: 367, and Friess, "*Patarener*," p. 257; cf. Haupt, "Waldenserthum seit der Mitte des 14. Jahrhunderts," pp. 346f.

32. Cf. John Weidenhofer and two masters from the undated list.

33. As above, n. 31.

34. Röhrich, "Winkeler."

35. Wilhelm Preger, "Über das Verhältnis der Taboriten zu den Waldesiern des 14. Jahrhunderts," *Abhandlungen der Königlichen bayerischen Akademie der Wissenschaften*, Historische Classe, 18 (1889): 36f.

36. Röhrich, "Winkeler," esp. p. 67.

37. *CDS*, 4: 97; Wattenbach, "Über die Inquisition," p. 27; Cod. Vindob. 3748.

38. As above, n. 1.

39. Röhrich, "Winkeler"; Paul Flade, "Deutsches Inquisitionsverfahren um 1400," *Zeitschrift für Kirchengeschichte* 22 (1901): 232–53.

40. He was present, with the title of papal inquisitor, at a hearing in Ulm in 1384; see Johann Georg Schelhorn, ed., *Amoenitates literariae* (Frankfurt and Leipzig, 1728), 8, esp. p. 514.

41. Röhrich, "Winkeler," passim.

42. Ibid.

43. Ibid.

44. Benedictus Maria Reichert, ed., *Registrum litterarum Raymundi de Capua, 1386–1399 [et] Leonardi de Mansuetis, 1474–1480* (Leipzig, 1911), p. 8. The dating is uncertain, and Reichert, in "Zur Geschichte der deutschen Dominikaner am Ausgange des 14. Jahrhunderts," *Römische Quartalschrift für christliche Altertumskunde und Kirchengeschichte* 15 (1901): 133, places the action in 1389. The evidence for the inquisitor's release is a letter from the Dominican general. The register in which it is listed gives a series of letters, dated in the following order: 2 Jan. 1390, 6 Feb. (no year specified), 20 Apr. 1389, 6 Feb., 29 Mar., 4 Apr., 11 Jan., 18 Mar., 6 Apr., and so on, in what then seems to be proper sequence. Apparently the only misplaced entries are those from 20 Apr. (1389), 11 Jan. (1390?), and 18 Mar. (1390?). If this is so, Arnoldi was released from office on 4 Apr. 1390.

45. Reichert, *Registrum*, p. 9. For dating, see Röhrich, "Winkeler," p. 66.

46. Herman Haupt, "Johannes Malkaw aus Preussen und seine Verfolgung durch die Inquisition zu Strassburg und Köln, 1390–1416," *Zeitschrift für Kirchengeschichte* 6 (1884): 323–89; Josef Hermann Beckmann, "Johannes Malkaw aus Preussen," *Historisches Jahrbuch* 48 (1928): 619–25.

47. Martin Erbstösser and Ernst Werner, *Ideologische Probleme des mittelalterlichen Plebejertums* (East Berlin, 1960), pp. 136–53; Haupt, *Der Waldensische Ursprung*, p. 36.

48. On Henry of Agro, see Patschovsky, "Strassburger Beginenverfolgungen," pp. 109–14, 164f. Patschovsky gives an ingenious argument to show that there were in fact at least two subjects. The present argument remains unaffected; Henry of Agro may have carried out more trials than are known now, but so presumably did Kerlinger, and it is not unreasonable to postulate that the proportion of extant documents is a rough measure of the extent of an inquisitor's activity. For John of Moneta, the only evidence is the letter of his appointment, in Gustav Schmidt, ed., *Päbstliche Urkunden und Regesten aus den Jahren 1353–1378* (Halle, 1889), pp. 173f.

49. Justinger, *Berner-Chronik*, p. 186; Ochsenbein, *Aus dem schweizerischen Volksleben*, pp. 95–126; *CDS*, 18: 129f.; *CDS*, 4: 96f., 249, Döllinger, *Beiträge*, 2: 363f.; and Röhrich, "Winkeler."

50. Pez, *Scriptores*, 2, col. 535, cites an Austrian heretic as claiming there were eighty thousand Waldensians in Austria. Bernard, "Heresy," p. 54, protests that this claim is fantastic, and that the number must be a misreading for "eight thousand." This adjustment would be more credible if the chronicler had been using Arabic numerals rather than Roman. In

any case, the claim may indeed have been fantastic, but that is certainly no proof that the heretic did not make it. Even if he knew how many co-believers there were, there is no reason to think that he would give unembellished census statistics to the orthodox authorities.

51. Kurze, "Zur Ketzergeschichte," p. 67.
52. La Bigne, *Maxima bibliotheca,* 25: 281.
53. Kurze, "Zur Ketzergeschichte," pp. 72–74.
54. Ibid., pp. 83–87; Wattenbach, "Über die Inquisition," esp. pp. 54–67.
55. Kurze, "Zur Ketzergeschichte," p. 67; Kurze, *Quellen,* pp. 73–77.
56. Compare Trithemius, *Annales,* 2: 296, with the superior account in Schneidt, *Thesaurus,* Absch. 1, H. 17, pp. 3263–66.
57. See H. C. Lea, *A History of the Inquisition of the Middle Ages* (New York, 1887), 1: 455f.
58. Wattenbach, "Über die Inquisition," pp. 26f., 34.
59. E.g., Hermann Heimpel, ed., *Drei Inquisitions-Verfahren aus dem Jahre 1425* (Göttingen, 1969), p. 85; Andreas Jung, "Friedrich Reiser: Eine Ketzergeschichte aus dem 15. Jahrhundert," *Timotheus* 2 (1822): 271–78.
60. The best general discussion of this phase of activity is still Haupt, "Waldenserthum seit der Mitte des 14. Jahrhunderts," pp. 367–80.
61. Friess, "Patarener," pp. 262–66; Döllinger, *Beiträge,* 2: 305–11.
62. Friess, "Patarener," p. 266. The date for the first incident is given as 1343, but the note seems to refer to recent events, and was evidently intended to be 1393, as Haupt, "Waldenserthum seit der Mitte des 14. Jahrhunderts," p. 372, read it.
63. Haupt, "Waldenserthum seit der Mitte des 14. Jahrhunderts," pp. 404f.
64. Lea, *History of the Inquisition,* 1: 541–49.
65. Haupt, "Waldenserthum seit der Mitte des 14. Jahrhunderts," pp. 405–8; given more fully (but less accurately) in Döllinger, *Beiträge,* 2: 346–51.
66. Haupt, *Der Waldensische Ursprung,* pp. 34f. There are other documents that one might dub vestigial protocols: acts that were once full protocols, but were copied (apparently as models for later use) without dates or names, or with abbreviations of names, and in any event without substantial or interesting information; see Döllinger, *Beiträge,* 2: 346; and Haupt, "Waldenserthum seit der Mitte des 14. Jahrhunderts," pp. 376f.
67. Cod. Vindob. 3748; and Finke, "Waldenserprocess."
68. As above, n. 8.
69. On the Waldensians' general reputation for deceitfulness, see, e.g., Walter L. Wakefield and Austin P. Evans, *Heresies of the High Middle Ages* (New York and London, 1969), pp. 397–402.
70. Wattenbach, "Über die Inquisition," p. 22; Kurze, *Quellen,* p. 204.
71. *CDS,* 4: 97.
72. Röhrich, "Winkeler," pp. 76f.
73. Stadtarchiv Augsburg, *Missivbücher,* 3, fol. 359^r.
74. Lerner, *Free Spirit,* pp. 36–44.

75. Eduard Osenbrüggen, *Das alamanische Strafrecht im deutschen Mittelalter* (Schaffhausen, 1860), pp. 289f., 375f.; cf. *CDS*, 22: 54.

76. Wattenbach, "Uber die Inquisition," p. 22.

77. "Piety in Germany around 1500," in Steven E. Ozment, ed., *The Reformation in Medieval Perspective* (Chicago, 1971), pp. 50–75; another translation in Gerald Strauss, ed., *Pre-Reformation Germany* (London and New York, 1972), pp. 13–42.

78. Ochsenbein, *Aus dem schweizerischen Volksleben*, pp. 95–126.

79. Gertrude Barnes Fiertz, "An Unusual Trial under the Inquisition at Fribourg, Switzerland, in 1399," *Speculum* 18 (1943): 340–57.

80. Ochsenbein, *Aus dem schweizerischen Volksleben*, pp. 126–396.

81. Regarding the sources, see above, n. 15.

82. Wilhelm Vischer, "Geschichte des schwäbischen Städtebundes der Jahre 1376–1389," *Forschungen zur deutschen Geschichte* 2 (1862): 1–201.

83. *CDS*, 4: 97.

84. Among the weavers burned was Konrad Stämlin (*CDS*, 4: 249); Hector Mülich (who, for all his inaccuracies, may usefully be consulted on Augsburg family names) transcribed the name as Stainlin (*CDS*, 22: 41). He may well be the same as the Konrad Steinlin or Steinlein who represented the guild of the *Lodweber* in the highly important constitutional documents, the two *Zunftbriefe* of 1368; cf. Christian Meyer, ed., *Urkundenbuch der Stadt Augsburg* (Augsburg, 1878), 2: 147, 152.

85. *CDS*, 34, esp. pp. 399–401.

86. Justinger, *Berner-Chronik*, p. 186.

87. Röhrich, "Winkeler," p. 57.

88. Kurze, "Zur Ketzergeschichte," pp. 68f.; Kurze, *Quellen*, p. 92.

89. Oefele, *Rerum Boicarum scriptores*, 1: 620; see Friedrich Zoepfel, *Geschichte des Bistums Augsburg und seiner Bischöfe*, 1: 338, 344.

90. Johannes Knebel, *Chronik der Stadt Donauwörth*, MS in the Fürstlich Oettingen-Wallerstein'sche Bibliothek und Kunstsammlung, Schloss Harburg über Donauwörth, Cod. III, 2, 2°, 18, fol. 131^v; discussed in Zelzer, *Geschichte*, 1: 76f., 167. The parents of two brothers had died in the plague, and the brothers donated their house to the hospital. Zelzer suggests that these brothers were descendants of the heretics; it is more likely that their family had acquired the house after its confiscation.

91. Oefele, *Rerum Boicarum scriptores*, 1: 620.

92. Esp. Cod. Vindob. 3748, fol. 146^r, 147^r, 147^v, 148^v.

93. Schultheiss, *Acht-, Verbots-, und Fehdebücher*, pp. 64f.; Will, *Kleine Beiträge*, pp. 109–25.

94. For similar results of investigation in a different context, see H. C. Erik Midelfort, *Witch Hunting in Southwestern Germany, 1562–1684* (Stanford, 1972), pp. 164–78.

95. Von Guden, *Codex diplomaticus*, 3: 599.

96. Lea, *History of the Inquisition*, 2: 396f.

97. Weigel, "Waldenserverhör."

98. Schubel had earlier gained familiarity with inquisitorial proceedings

at the trial of Conrad Kanner, to which he was a witness; see Herbert Grundmann, "Ketzerverhöre des Spätmittelalters als quellenkritisches Problem," *Deutsches Archiv für Erforschung des Mittelalters* 21 (1965): 564–66.

Chapter 5.   Heresy As Civil Disorder

1. As above, chap. 4, n. 7.
2. Rudolf His, *Das Strafrecht des deutschen Mittelalters* (Weimar, 1935), 2: 5, 27.
3. *Achtbuch*, Stadtarchiv Augsburg, fol. 71^r; the incident is given with a different dating in Rolf Kiessling, *Bürgerliche Gesellschaft und Kirche in Augsburg im Spätmittelalter* (Augsburg, 1971), p. 318.
4. *Achtbuch*, fol. 67^v. There were conventual beguines in the city, and in 1394 Bishop Burkhard of Ellerbach required that they adopt an approved religious rule; see Polykarp M. Siemer, *Geschichte des Dominikanerklosters Sankt Magdalena in Augsburg* (Vechta, 1936), pp. 59ff. The account in the *Achtbuch*, however, seems clearly to refer to nonconventual beguines.
5. One must bear in mind, however, that towns frequently kept more careful account of banished criminals than of executed ones. If a person was banished, there might be occasion in the future to verify the details of his sentence, especially if he returned to the city before he was supposed to do so. An executed man, on the other hand, might readily be forgotten.
6. On the prescription of exile, see Henri Maisonneuve, *Études sur les origines de l'Inquisition*, 2d ed. (Paris, 1960), pp. 76, 154.
7. The discussion of this topic by Paul Flade, *Das römische Inquisitionsverfahren bis zu den Hexenprozessen* (Leipzig, 1902), is unconvincing. In the cases that he cites, either city governments were responsible for the banishment, or the persons concerned were not actually banished, but merely driven from their religious houses. There are no instances of banishment by ecclesiastical courts during the period under discussion.
8. As above, chap. 4, n. 7.
9. Werner Schultheiss, ed., *Die Acht-, Verbots-, und Fehdebücher Nürnbergs von 1285–1400* (Nürnberg, 1960), p. 84.
10. Ibid., pp. 150f.; cf. Herman Haupt, "Waldenserthum und Inquisition im südöstlichen Deutschland seit der Mitte des 14. Jahrhunderts," *Deutsche Zeitschrift für Geschichtswissenschaft* 3 (1890): 350.
11. Schultheiss, *Acht-, Verbots-, und Fehdebücher*, pp. 158f.; cf. Haupt, "Waldenserthum seit der Mitte des 14. Jahrhunderts," p. 351.
12. See esp. Georg Wolfgang Karl Lochner, *Geschichte der Reichsstadt Nürnberg zur Zeit Kaiser Karls IV.* (Berlin, 1873).
13. Ibid., pp. 27, 62.
14. Wilhelm Vischer, "Geschichte des schwäbischen Städtebundes der Jahre 1376–1389," *Forschungen zur deutschen Geschichte* 2 (1862): 1–201.
15. CDS, 4: 68, and *Achtbuch*, fol. 116^v. There are numerous accounts in

derivative chronicles, including the very late one in Bayerische Staatsbibliothek, Cgm 2026, fol. 8ᵛ–9ʳ (where the reference to the "great wind" is an extraneous insertion, taken perhaps from *CDS*, 4: 26f. or 71f.).

16. *Achtbuch*, fol. 116ʳ (Ruff der Sturme); fol. 116ᵛ (cobbler).

17. Christian Meyer, ed., *Das Stadtbuch von Augsburg, insbesondere das Stadtrecht vom Jahre 1276* (Augsburg, 1872), pp. 106f.

18. E.g., Wilhelm Preger, ed., "Der Tractat des David von Augsburg über die Waldesier," *Abhandlungen der königlichen bayerischen Akademie der Wissenschaften*, Historische Classe, 14, pt. 2 (1879): 233f.

19. Lochner, *Geschichte*, pp. 27, 62.

20. *Achtbuch*, fol. 61ᵛ (blasphemers); fol. 62ʳ.

21. Kiessling, *Bürgerliche Gesellschaft*, p. 318, suggests that the doctrine is reminiscent of the heresy of the Free Spirit. The terms used do seem vaguely related to those of this heresy, but for lack of information as to the exact application of the terms, one cannot determine the substance of this heretic's belief.

22. *Achtbuch*, fol. 65ʳ.

23. Adolf Buff, "Verbrechen und Verbrecher zu Augsburg in der zweiten Hälfte des 14. Jahrhunderts," *Zeitschrift des historischen Vereins für Schwaben und Neuburg* 4 (1878), esp. pp. 200–207.

24. *Achtbuch*, fol. 89ᵛ. The term was applied in retrospect to Waldensians found in 1393 at Augsburg; see *CDS*, 4: 228, 315, and Stadtarchiv Augsburg, *Missivbücher*, 3, fol. 359ʳ. There seems to be no firm evidence that it applied specifically to Waldensians; it may have been synonymous with "heretic." For interpretation of the term, see Hermann Fischer, *Schwäbisches Wörterbuch* (Tübingen, 1911), 3: 864; Friedrich Zoepfel, *Das Bistum Augsburg und seine Bischöfe im Mittelalter* (Augsburg, 1955), p. 343; and Hermann Heimpel, *Zwei Wormser Inquisitionen aus den Jahren 1421 und 1422* (Göttingen, 1969), pp. 68 n. 19, 80.

25. Friedrich Wigger, "Urkundliche Mittheilungen über die Beghinen- und Begharden-Häuser zu Rostock," *Jahrbücher des Vereins für mecklenburgische Geschichte und Alterthumskunde* 47 (1882): 13.

26. See Richard Kieckhefer, "Radical Tendencies in the Flagellant Movement of the Mid-Fourteenth Century," *Journal of Medieval and Renaissance Studies* 4 (1974): 157–76, plus the works cited there, nn. 1, 5, and 6; and Gordon Leff, *Heresy in the Later Middle Ages* (Manchester, 1967), 2: 485–91. In my article I suggest that the character of the movement may have been influenced by whether it arose in a particular region before or after the onset of the plague. Stuart Jenks, "Die Prophezeiung von Ps.-Hildegard von Bingen: Eine vernachlässigte Quelle über die Geisslerzuge von 1348/49 im Lichte des Kampfes der Würzburger Kirche gegen die Flagellanten," *Mainfränkisches Jahrbuch für Geschichte und Kunst* 29 (1977): 21f., takes issue with this explanation, and proposes instead that the flagellants were radicalized where the clergy opposed them. Jenks's interpretation and mine are not, however, necessarily incompatible; it may well be that the chronological relationship between the plague and the flagellant movement influ-

enced clerical perceptions and reactions, as well as the attitudes of the flagellants themselves. Admittedly, my argument on this particular point remains conjectural, as I indicated when I first stated it.

27. Johann Losert, ed., *Die Konigsaaler Geschichts-Quellen* (Vienna, 1875), p. 599.

28. Gustav Adolf Stenzel, ed., *Scriptores rerum Silesiacarum* (Breslau, 1835), 1: 166f.; Albert Kaffler, ed., *"Annalista Silesiacus* und *Series episco-porum Wratislavensium* von J. 1382," *Zeitschrift des Vereins für Geschichte und Alterthum Schlesiens* 1 (1855): 221.

29. *CDS*, 19: 520f.

30. *MGH SS rer. Germ.*, 42: 180, 395.

31. Hugo Loersch, ed., *Achener Rechtsdenkmäler aus dem 13., 14., und 15. Jahrhundert* (Bonn, 1871), pp. 66–68. For the story that Charles IV's coronation was postponed because of the crowds of flagellants in Speyer, see Friedrich Haagen, *Geschichte Achens, von seinen Anfängen bis zur neusten Zeit* (Aachen, 1873), 1: 278.

32. Paul Fredericq, ed., *Corpus documentorum inquisitionis haereticae pravitatis Neerlandicae* (Ghent and The Hague, 1889), 1: 28.

33. Ibid., pp. 29–38.

34. *MGH SS*, n.s. 4: 272.

35. Fredericq, *Corpus*, 1: 199–201.

36. On the general problem see Decima L. Douie, *The Nature and the Effect of the Heresy of the Fraticelli* (Manchester, 1932).

37. J.-J. de Smet, ed., *Corpus chronicorum Flandriae* (Brussels, 1837), 1: 349–60.

38. Cf. the similar qualifying clause at the end of *Cum de quibusdam*; Robert E. Lerner, *The Heresy of the Free Spirit in the Later Middle Ages* (Berkeley, Los Angeles, and London, 1972), p. 47.

39. Fredericq, *Corpus*, 2, esp. pp. 112f., 117f., 120f.

40. *CDS*, 7: 204–7; *MGH SS*, 14: 487; Andreas Felix Oefele, *Rerum Boicarum scriptores* (Augsburg, 1763), 1: 212.

41. Lochner, *Geschichte*, p. 36.

42. Johann Friedrich Schannat and Josephus Hartzheim, eds., *Concilia Germaniae* (Cologne, 1761), 4: 471f., 485f.; Fredericq, *Corpus*, 2: 142.

43. "Versuch einer Conciliengeschichte des Bisthums Eichstätt," *Pastoral-blatt des Bisthums Eichstätt* 1 (1854): 138 n. 1; the author seems to have misconstrued 1351, the date, as the number of flagellants, transposing the event back to 1349.

44. See Kieckhefer, "Radical Tendencies," p. 168 n. 55; Gustav Schmidt, ed., *Päbstliche Urkunden und Regesten aus den Jahren 1353–1378* (Halle, 1889), p. 295; and Dietrich Kurze, "Märkische Waldenser und Böhmische Brüder," *Mitteldeutsche Forchungen* 74, pt. 2 (1974): 472 n. 62.

45. A mid-fifteenth century trial cites much earlier proceedings; Ernst Günther Förstemann, *Die christlichen Geisslergesellschaften* (Halle, 1828), p. 177 n. If one assumes that the flagellant leader Conrad Schmidt was executed, his death probably occurred in the later fourteenth century, but

see Martin Erbstösser, *Sozialreligiöse Strömungen in späten Mittelalter* (East Berlin, 1970), p. 76. Gregory XI directed Walter Kerlinger to proceed against flagelants and other heretics in 1372 or 1373 (Schmidt, as in preceding note). In 1391 certain flagellants appeared near Heidelberg and came to the authorities' attention, but there is no indication what action they took; Johann Friedrich Hautz, *Geschichte der Universität Heidelberg* (Mannheim, 1862), 1: 217–19. Johannes Trithemius, *Annales Hirsaugienses* (St. Gall, 1690), 2: 296, speaks of Martin of Amberg as proceeding against flagellants, but this identification is surely mistaken; the superior source (chap. 4, n. 56) speaks only of Waldensians. Gerhard Ritter, *Die Heidelberger Universität* (Heidelberg, 1936), 1: 432 n. 2, identifies Frederick of Brunswick as a flagellant, presumably because of his millenarian ideas, but this heretic's doctrines were quite different from those of the flagellants of Thuringia; see Carl Büttinghausen, *Beyträge zur pfälzischen Geschichte* (Mannheim, 1776), 1: 231–33; Gustav Toepke, ed., *Die Matrikel der Universität Heidelberg* (Heidelberg, 1884), 1: 643f.; and Friedrich Beyschlag, "Ein Speyerer Ketzerprozess vom Jahre 1392," *Blätter für pfälzische Kirchengeschichte* 3 (1927): 61–65.

Chapter 6.   Orthodox Reaction in an Age of Revolution

1. On the Hussite question generally see Frederick Heymann, *John Žižka and the Hussite Revolution* (Princeton, 1955); Howard Kaminsky, *A History of the Hussite Revolution* (Berkeley and Los Angeles, 1967); Josef Macek, *The Hussite Movement in Bohemia*, 2d ed. (Prague, 1958); and M. D. Lambert, *Medieval Heresy: Popular Movements from Bogomil to Hus* (New York, 1977), pp. 272–334. For the life of Hus himself, see Matthew Spinka, *John Hus: A Biography* (Princeton, 1968). For his doctrine, see Gordon Leff, *Heresy in the Later Middle Ages* (Manchester, 1967), 2: 606–707.

2. Kaminsky, *History*, p. 1.

3. Alexander Patschovsky, *Die Anfänge einer ständigen Inquisition in Böhmen* (Berlin and New York, 1975), pp. 65–78. I am here taking a more or less agnostic position, based in part on a suspicion that the heretics frequently did not belong to any specific and definable sect. For an effort to unravel the evidence that does exist, one must turn to Patschovsky.

4. S. Harrison Thomson, "Pre-Hussite Heresy in Bohemia," *English Historical Review* 48 (1933): 26f.

5. Ibid., p. 29 (synod); Patschovsky, *Anfänge*, pp. 30–46 (trial of 1315–16).

6. Patschovsky, *Anfänge*, esp. pp. 22f., 26–28.

7. Ibid., pp. 25–27.

8. Thomson, "Pre-Hussite Heresy," p. 40 and n. 4.

9. Ibid., p. 36.

10. Spinka, *John Hus*, pp. 3–20.

11. Kaminsky, *History*, pp. 98–126.

12. Macek, *Hussite Movement*, p. 25.

13. See esp. the sources and introduction in Matthew Spinka, ed., *John Hus at the Council of Constance* (New York, 1965).

14. Gerhard Schlesinger, *Die Hussiten in Franken* (Kulmbach, 1974); Edward Schröder, "Göttingen in der Hussitenfurcht," *Neues Göttinger Jahrbuch* 2 (1930): 73–80; and literature cited in these works.

15. Cesarini's role in the Hussite problem is a major concern of Gerald Christianson, "Cardinal Cesarini at the Council of Basel, 1431–1438" (Ph.D. diss., University of Chicago, 1972). Christianson analyzes the sources within a chronological framework. The most essential sources are in *Monumenta conciliorum generalium seculi decimi quinti*, ed. Oesterreichische Akademie der Wissenschaften (Vienna, 1857–86).

16. Herman Haupt, "Husitische Propaganda in Deutschland," *Historisches Taschenbuch*, ser. 6, 7 (1888), esp. pp. 241–69, 278–93.

17. Otto Clemen, "Ueber Leben und Schriften Johanns von Wesel," *Deutsche Zeitschrift für Geschichtswissenschaft* 8 (1897–98): *Vierteljahreshefte*, pp. 166f.

18. Gerald Strauss, ed., *Manifestations of Discontent in Germany on the Eve of the Reformation* (Bloomington, Ind., 1971), pp. 45f.

19. *Monumenta conciliorum*, 2: 100.

20. It is of course possible that the infiltration was continuous but not uniformly detected. Even if this was the case, though, it is likely that the decade of Hussite wars changed the nature of the proselytizing, and made it more of an adjunct to military activity than a normal missionary enterprise.

21. Kaminsky, *History*, passim, gives a great deal of information about Nicholas of Dresden.

22. Hans Freiherr von und zu Auffel, "Die Hussiten in Franken," *Archiv für Geschichte und Alterthumskunde von Oberfranken* 3, no. 1 (1845): 41; Franz Palacký, ed., *Urkundliche Beiträge zur Geschichte des Hussitenkrieges vom Jahre 1419 an* (Prague, 1873), 1: 120f.; Andreas of Regensburg, *Sämtliche Werke*, ed. Georg Leidinger (Munich, 1903), pp. 362f.; Joseph Heller, *Reformationsgeschichte des Bisthums Bamberg* (Bamberg, 1825), p. 11.

23. E.g., Rolf Kiessling, *Bürgerliche Gesellschaft und Kirche in Augsburg im Spätmittelalter* (Augsburg, 1971), p. 319 n. 23. For incidents of alleged violation see Palacký, *Urkundliche Beiträge*, 1: 163f., 189f., 367–69, 432, 447f.; see also Palacký, pp. 339f.

24. Haupt, "Hussitische Propaganda," p. 246; Andreas of Regensburg, *Sämtliche Werke*, pp. 350–404; Josef Riedmann, ed., *Die Fortsetzung der Flores Temporum durch Johann Spies* (Vienna, 1970), pp. 32–34.

25. Hermann Korner, *Chronica novella*, ed. Jakob Schwalm (Göttingen, 1895), pp. 427–29; *MGH SS*, 14: 458f.; *CDS*, 7: 350f.

26. Palacký, *Urkundliche Beiträge*, 1: 90; Herman Haupt, *Die religiösen Sekten in Franken vor der Reformation* (Würzburg, 1882), p. 32; Hermann

Heimpel, ed., *Zwei Wormser Inquisitionen aus den Jahren 1421 und 1422* (Göttingen, 1969), pp. 8–15, 37–43; Dietrich Kurze, "Märkische Waldenser und Böhmische Brüder," *Mitteldeutsche Forschungen 74*, pt. 2 (1974): 459, 463f.; Dietrich Kurze, ed., *Quellen zur Ketzergeschichte Brandenburgs und Pommerns* (Berlin, 1975), pp. 267–70.

27. Heimpel, *Zwei Wormser Inquisitionen*, pp. 37–43.

28. Ibid., pp. 40f.; cf. Clemen, "Ueber Leben," p. 168.

29. Hermann Heimpel, ed., *Drei Inquisitions-Verfahren aus dem Jahre 1425* (Göttingen, 1969); Horst Köpstein, "Das frühe Hussitentum in Deutschland—speziell Johann Drändorf," *Lětopis*, ser. B, 9/1 (1962): 133–61; Kurt-Victor Selge, "Heidelberger Ketzerprozesse in der Frühzeit der hussitischen Revolution," *Zeitschrift für Kirchengeschichte* 82 (1971): 167–202.

30. Heimpel, *Drei Inquisitions-Verfahren*, pp. 70, 75. Constantine is in fact venerated as a saint, but only in the Eastern Church; see F. L. Cross, ed., *Oxford Dictionary of the Christian Church* (London, 1958), p. 335.

31. For the prosecution at Fribourg in 1429–30, see Gottlieb Friedrich Ochsenbein, *Aus dem schweizerischen Volksleben des 15. Jahrhunderts* (Bern, 1881), pp. 126–396. Although the heretics' masters came from Germany and Bohemia, there is no indication that they or their masters had begun to absorb Hussite doctrine at this early date (*pace* Ochsenbein); even if the masters had converted to Hussitism, it is not indicated how recently these masters had visited the Swiss community. Thus, the heretics were probably Waldensians without Hussite influence. Also omitted here is the case of a priest and merchant taken prisoner at Frankfurt because of the report that they had come "from the Hussites"; see *Deutsche Reichstagsakten* (Gotha, 1887), 9: 123. The nature of the charges and of the proceedings is wholly unclear in this case.

32. Haupt, "Hussitische Propaganda," pp. 278–93.

33. Würzburg—Johann Peter Ludewig, ed., *Geschicht-Schreiber von dem Bischoffthum Wirtzburg* (Frankfurt, 1713), p. 801; cf. Haupt, *Die religiösen Sekten*, p. 44 (with incorrect date); and see also K. Schornbaum, "Zur Geschichte der Ketzer in Franken," *Zeitschrift für bayerische Kirchengeschichte* 8 (1933): 203f. Eichstätt—Franz Machilek, "Ein Eichstätter Inquisitionsverfahren aus dem Jahre 1460," *Jahrbuch für fränkische Landesforschung* 34/35 (1974–75): 417–46, supersedes all previous literature. Strassburg—Andreas Jung, "Friedrich Reiser: Eine Ketzergeschichte aus dem 15. Jahrhundert," *Timotheus* 2 (1882): 256; Horst Köpstein, "Über den deutschen Hussiten Friedrich Reiser," *Zeitschrift für Geschichtswissenschaft* 7, no. 2 (1959): 1068–81; Valdo Vinay, "Friedrich Reiser e la diaspora valdese di lingua tedesca nel XV secolo," *Bollettino della società di studi valdesi* 81, no. 109 (1961): 35–56.

34. Wilhelm Wattenbach, "Über die Inquisition gegen die Waldenser in Pommern und der Mark Brandenburg," *Abhandlungen der königlichen Akademie der Wissenschaft zu Berlin*, 1886, Philosophisch-historische Classe, Abhandlung 3, pp. 71–83; Kurze, "Märkische Waldenser"; Kurze, *Quellen*, esp. pp. 288–314.

35. Henricus Eckstormius, *Chronicon Walkenredense* (Helmstedt, 1617), p. 173; Jaroslav Goll, *Quellen und Untersuchungen zur Geschichte der Böhmischen Brüder* (Prague, 1878), 1: 30ff., 35, 100, 118, 120, 131, 136.

36. In this general subject see Kurze, "Märkische Waldenser."

37. Ibid., pp. 491–93.

38. Albert Achilles was margrave of Brandenburg from 1414 to 1486; during the later part of his life his son John Cicero was coregent.

39. This heretic's last name comes from other documents.

40. Kurze, "Märkische Waldenser," pp. 493 n. 156, 494, speculates that the judge was the papal inquisitor Clemens Lossow. The inquisitor referred to in the letter was a master of arts, while Lossow was a professor of theology (ibid., pp. 485f.); the two positions were not mutually exclusive, but since the references to Lossow and the inquisitor who condemned Peter Weber are nearly contemporary, the difference in title makes it prima facie unlikely that the two were the same man. It was quite common for bishops to delegate inquisitorial authority to Dominicans, and the choice of a man with an advanced university degree would be typical.

41. Johann Wolf, *Lectiones memorabiles* (Frankfurt, 1608), 2: 585; Machilek, "Ein Eichstätter Inquisitionsverfahren."

42. *Repertorium Germanicum* (Berlin, 1957), 2, col. 1903; Heimpel, *Zwei Wormser Inquisitionen*, p. 81; Marquard Freher, *De secretis judiciis olim in Westphalia aliisque Germaniae partibus usitatis* (Regensburg, 1762), p. 121.

43. Korner, *Chronica*, pp. 427–29; see chap. 4, n. 16.

44. As above, n. 40.

45. Lucas Wadding, *Annales minorum* (Rome, 1734), 10: 269–73.

46. Thomas Ripoll, ed., *Bullarium Ordinis Fratrum Praedicatorum* (Rome, 1729–40), 2: 577.

47. Kurze, "Märkische Waldenser." p. 486.

48. E.g., Heinrich Boehmer, "Die Waldenser von Zwickau und Umgegend," *Neues Archiv für sächsische Geschichte und Altertumskunde* 36 (1915): 34–38.

49. Stadtarchiv Augsburg, *Missivbücher*, 3, fol. 359^r; discussed also in Kiessling, *Bürgerliche Gesellschaft*, p. 317.

50. On the Würzburg proceedings, see above, n. 33.

51. "Piety in Germany around 1500," in Steven E. Ozment, ed., *The Reformation in Medieval Perspective* (Chicago, 1971), p. 52.

52. For the sources, see above, n. 33 (works listed for Strassburg). The original protocol is lost; Jung used a sixteenth-century copy of the protocol, though that copy has also vanished. Köpstein published an eighteenth-century excerpt from the latter part of the protocol. Comparison of the relevant parts of Jung's article with the excerpt in Köpstein suggests that Jung was accurate in paraphrasing the material he had, but allowed himself considerable latitude in making inferences from this material.

53. Useful for the general history of this development is Gerhard Ritter, *Die Heidelberger Universität* 1 (Heidelberg, 1936).

54. The attempt to imitate the University of Paris was conscious, and at

times was even expressed in the foundation charters of the German universities.

55. Robert E. Lerner, "Literacy and Learning," in Richard L. DeMolen, ed., *One Thousand Years* (Boston, 1974), p. 227.

56. On John Malkaw, see Eduard Winkelmann, ed., *Urkundenbuch der Universität Heidelberg* (Heidelberg, 1886), 1: 57f. On the beguines of Basel, see Johann Friedrich Hautz, *Geschichte der Universität Heidelberg* (Mannheim, 1863), 2: 364f.; and Robert E. Lerner, *The Heresy of the Free Spirit in the Later Middle Ages* (Berkeley, Los Angeles, and London, 1972), p. 156.

57. Ritter, *Die Heidelberger Universität*, 1: 354f. (Stanislas of Znaim); Heimpel, *Drei Inquisitions-Verfahren* (John Drändorf); and C. Ullmann, *Reformers before the Reformation*, trans. Robert Menzies (Edinburgh, 1855), 1: 341f. (John of Wesel).

58. Heimpel, *Drei Inquisitions-Verfahren*, pp. 96f.

59. Paul P. Bernard, "Jerome of Prague, Austria and the Hussites," *Church History* 27 (1958): 3–22; Johann Loserth, "Ueber die Versuche wiclif-husitische Lehren nach Oesterreich, Polen, Ungarn und Croatien zu verpflanzen," *Mittheilungen des Vereins für Geschichte der Deutschen in Böhmen* 24 (1885–86), esp. pp. 98–101; Rudolf Kink, *Geschichte der kaiserlichen Universität zu Wien*, 1, pt. 2 (Vienna, 1854), pp. 19–23; Ladislaus Klicman, "Der Wiener Process gegen Hieronymus von Prag, 1410–12," *Mitteilungen des Instituts für österreichische Geschichtsforschung* 21 (1900): 445–57.

60. Godfried Edmund Friess, "Geschichte der oesterreichischen Minoritenprovinz," *Archiv für österreichische Geschichte* 64 (1882): 154.

61. Augustin Stumpf, "Historia flagellantium, praecipue in Thuringia," *Neue Mittheilungen aus dem Gebiete historisch-antiquarischer Forschung* 2 (1835): 27 n. (Erfurt); Boehmer, "Die Waldenser," p. 3 (Leipzig).

62. Heimpel, *Zwei Wormser Inquisitionen*, esp. pp. 10f.

63. Robert E. Lerner is currently doing research that will attempt to place these isolated millenarian movements within a historical perspective.

64. There are surveys in Norman Cohn, *The Pursuit of the Millennium*, rev. ed. (New York, 1970), pp. 142–47; and Gordon Leff, *Heresy in the Later Middle Ages* (Manchester, 1967), 2: 492f. See esp. Siegfried Hoyer, "Die thüringische Kryptoflagellantenbewegung im 15. Jahrhundert," *Jahrbuch für Regionalgeschichte* 2 (1967): 148–74.

65. Korner, *Chronica*, p. 114f.; Stumpf, "Historia flagellantium," esp. pp. 26–35; Alexander Reifferscheid, ed., *Neue Texte der religiösen Aufklärung in Deutschland während des 14. und 15. Jahrhunderts* (Greifswald, 1905), pp. 32–39.

66. Korner, *Chronica*, pp. 114f.

67. Cyriacus Spangenberg, in Christian Gottlieb Buder, ed., *Nützliche Sammlung verschiedener meistens ungedruckter Schrifften* (Frankfurt and Leipzig, 1735), pp. 335–43; cf. Spangenberg, *Adels-Spiegel* (Schmalkalden, 1591), fol. 394^r–395^r.

68. Spangenberg, in Buder, *Nützliche Sammlung,* p. 342.

69. Stump, "Historia flagellantium," pp. 27 n.

70. Korner gave the incident under the year 1414 in the earlier editions of his chronicle, but in later editions shifted the account (along with the paragraph preceding it) to the year 1416. The former date is corroborated by other sources, and is clearly correct; the later date occurs nowhere else.

There are three reasons for denying the identification. (1) Eylard was dead by 1407; cf. Friedrich Crull, "Mag. Eilert Schönefeld," *Hansische Geschichtsblätter* 32 (1903): 138. (2) All the chronicles and documents give the name Henry, even the most reliable. Korner (who mentions Eylard in two other contexts, and thus did know him—as one might expect, since Eylard was a prominent member of Korner's order) gives this name; so also does Spangenberg, who (in Buder's ed.) gave names of witnesses and other information clearly derived from an inquisitorial protocol, and who (in *Adels-Spiegel,* fol. 394ʳ) claimed explicitly to have seen the original protocol. (3) There is independent record of at least one Dominican theologian named Henry Schonevelt, easily identifiable with the inquisitor; see esp. Fritz Bünger, *Beiträge zur Geschichte der Provinzialkapitel und Provinziale des Dominikanerordens* (Leipzig, 1919), p. 40 n. 3.

71. *Historische Nachrichten von der Kayserl. und des Heil. Röm. Reichs Freyen Stadt Nordhausen* (Leipzig and Nordhausen, 1740), pp. 616–25; Ernst Günther Förstemann, *Die christlichen Geisslergesellschaften* (Halle, 1828), pp. 278–91.

72. Förstemann, *Die christlichen Geisslergesellschaften,* p. 177 n.

73. *Zeit- und Geschichtsbeschreibung der Stadt Göttingen* (Hannover and Göttingen, 1736), 2: 256–61.

74. "Altes aus dem funfzehnten Seculo," in Johann Erhard Kapp, *Fortgesetzte Sammlung von alten und neuen theologischen Sachen* (Leipzip, 1747), pp. 475–83.

75. For further information on secular prosecution, see *MGH SS,* 14: 471; Förstemann, *Die christlichen Geisslergesellschaften,* pp. 172f.; and Samuel Müller, *Chronicka der Uralten Berg-Stadt Sangerhausen* (Leipzig and Frankfurt, 1731), pp. 233f.

76. Otto Schiff, "Die Wirsberger," *Historische Vierteljahrsschrift* 26 (1931): 776–86; Heinrich Gradl, "Die Irrlehre der Wirsperger," *Mittheilungen des Vereins für Geschichte der Deutschen in Böhmen* 19 (1881): 270–79.

77. Marjorie Reeves, *The Influence of Prophecy in the Later Middle Ages* (Oxford, 1969), esp. 476–78.

78. Ludewig, *Geschicht-Schreiber von dem Bischoffthum Wirtzburg,* pp. 852–54; Konrad Stolle, *Memoriale: Thüringisch-erfurtische Chronik,* ed. Richard Thiele (Halle, 1900), pp. 379–83; Johannes Trithemius, *Annales Hirsaugienses* (St. Gall, 1690), 2: 486–91; K. A. Barack, "Hans Böhm und die Wallfahrt nach Niklashausen im Jahre 1476," *Archiv des historischen Vereins von Unterfranken und Aschaffenburg* 14, no. 3 (1858): 1–108. See also Cohn, *Pursuit,* pp. 223–34.

79. Barack, "Hans Böhm," pp. 59, 63, 77f., 80.

80. Ibid., pp. 29–49.

81. Ullmann, *Reformers*, 1: 329–62; Clemen, "Ueber Leben," pp. 143–73.

82. Roger Wilmans, "Zur Geschichte der römischen Inquisition in Deutschland während des 14. und 15. Jahrhunderts," *Historische Zeitschrift* 41 (1879): 211–26; Walter Ribbeck, "Beiträge zur Geschichte der römischen Inquisition in Deutschland während des 14. und 15. Jahrhunderts," *Zeitschrift für vaterländische Geschichte und Altertumskunde* 46 (1888): 134–38, 151–53; Josef Hermann Beckmann, *Studien zum Leben und literarischen Nachlass Jakobs von Soest, O.P., 1360–1440* (Leipzig, 1929), pp. 33–51.

83. Beckmann, *Studien*, pp. 36f.

84. Heimpel, *Zwei Wormser Inquisitionen*, pp. 16–36, 43–66.

85. The protocol is inconclusive on the matter of whether Wyrach made the statements attributed to him. In any event, the articles were probably given in an extreme formulation for judicial purposes, so as to suggest the Donatist heresy.

86. The comparison is made by Heimpel, *Zwei Wormser Inquisitionen*, p. 71 n. 65.

87. Joseph Hansen, ed., *Quellen und Untersuchungen zur Geschichte des Hexenwahns und der Hexenverfolgung im Mittelalter* (Bonn, 1901), pp. 485f.

88. Ludwig Greiger, *Johann Reuchlin: Sein Leben und seine Werke* (Leipzig, 1871), esp. pp. 290–321, 436–54.

89. Ludwig Geiger, "Maximilian I. in seinem Verhältnisse zum Reuchlinschen Streite," *Forschungen zur deutschen Geschichte* 9 (1869): 203–16.

90. *Acta judiciorum inter F. Iacobum Hochstraten inquisitorem Coloniensium et Iohannem Reuchlin* (Hagenau, 1518).

91. Beckmann, *Studien*, pp. 41f., 46f.

92. Heimpel, *Drei Inquisitions-Verfahren*, pp. 107, 131f.

93. Wattenbach, "Uber die Inquisition," p. 72.

94. As above, n. 71.

95. Fritz Hermann, "Die letzte Ketzerverbrennung in Mainz," in *Beiträge zur Kunst und Geschichte des Mainzer Lebensraumes: Festschrift für Ernst Neeb* (Mainz, 1936), pp. 105–10.

96. Ullmann, *Reformers*, 1:341f.

97. J. F. Knapp, *Regenten- und Volks-Geschichte der Länder Cleve, Mark, Jülich, Berg und Ravensberg* (Crefeld, 1836), 3: 118f.

98. For these inquisitors see Hansen, *Quellen*, pp. 360–408; and Richard Kieckhefer, *European Witch Trials: Their Foundations in Popular and Learned Culture, 1300–1500* (London, and Berkeley and Los Angeles, 1976), pp. 141f.

99. Jacobus Sprenger and Henricus Institoris, *Malleus maleficarum* (Lyon, 1669); trans. Montague Summers, 2d ed. (London, 1948).

100. Hansen, *Quellen*, pp. 388f.

101. Hartmann Ammann, "Der Innsbrucker Hexenprocess von 1485," *Zeitschrift des Ferdinandeums für Tirol und Vorarlberg* ser. 3, 34 (1890): 1–87.

102. E.g., Henry Charles Lea, *Materials toward a History of Witchcraft* (Philadelphia, 1937), 1: 86.

103. Ammann, "Der Innsbrucker Hexenprocess," p. 86.

104. See chap. 1, n. 16.

105. Lerner, *Free Spirit*, pp. 200–227; cf. pp. 242f.

106. E.g., Julio Caro Baroja, *The World of the Witches* (Chicago, 1964), esp. pp. 152, 154, 180–89.

107. H. C. Lea, *A History of the Inquisition of the Middle Ages* (New York, 1887), 2: 423–26.

Selective Bibliography

The following list includes works chosen for their direct relevance to this study. Primary and secondary works are not separated because in many cases primary literature has been published in the form of appendices to secondary works.

Acta judiciorum inter F. Iacobum Hochstraten inquisitorem Coloniensium et Iohannem Reuchlin. Hagenau, 1518.

Barack, Karl August. "Hans Böhm und die Wallfahrt nach Niklashausen im Jahre 1476." *Archiv des historischen Vereins von Unterfranken und Aschaffenburg* 14, no. 3 (1858): 1–108.

Beckmann, Josef Hermann. "Johannes Malkaw aus Preussen." *Historisches Jahrbuch* 48 (1928): 619–25.

———. *Studien zum Leben und literarischen Nachlass Jakobs von Soest, O.P., 1360–1440.* Leipzig, 1929.

Behr, Hans-Joachim. "Der Convent der blauen Beginen in Lüneburg." *Lüneburger Blätter* 11/12 (1961): 181–93.

Bernard, Paul P. "Heresy in Fourteenth Century Austria." *Medievalia et Humanistica* 10 (1956): 50–63.

———. "Jerome of Prague, Austria and the Hussites." *Church History* 27 (1958): 3–22.

Beyschlag, Friedrich, "Ein Speyerer Ketzerprozess vom Jahre 1392." *Blätter für pfälzische Kirchengeschichte* 3 (1927): 61–65.

Boehmer, Heinrich. "Die Waldenser von Zwickau und Umgegend." *Neues Archiv für sächsische Geschichte und Altertumskunde* 36 (1915): 1–38.

Borst, Arno. *Die Katharer.* Stuttgart, 1953.

151

Bürckstümmer, Christian. "Waldenser in Dinkelsbühl." *Beiträge zur bayerischen Kirchengeschichte* 19 (1913): 272–75.

Clemen, Otto. "Ueber Leben und Schriften Johanns von Wesel." *Deutsche Zeitschrift für Geschichtswissenschaft* 8 (1897–98): Vierteljahreshefte, pp. 143–73.

Cohn, Norman. *The Pursuit of the Millennium.* rev. ed. New York, 1970.

Degenhardt, Ingeborg. *Studien zum Wandel des Eckhartbildes.* Leiden, 1967.

Degler-Spengler, Brigitte. "Die Beginen in Basel." *Basler Zeitschrift für Geschichte und Altertumskunde* 69 (1969): 5–83.

Döllinger, Johann Joseph Ignatz von, ed. *Beiträge zur Sektengeschichte des Mittelalters.* 2 vols. Munich, 1890.

Erbstösser, Martin. *Sozialreligiöse Strömungen im späten Mittelalter.* East Berlin, 1970.

Erbstösser, Martin, and Ernst Werner. *Ideologische Probleme des mittelalterlichen Plebejertums: Die freigeistige Häresie und ihre sozialen Wurzeln.* East Berlin, 1960.

Finke, Heinrich. "Waldenserprocess in Regensburg, 1395." *Deutsche Zeitschrift für Geschichtswissenschaft* 4 (1890): 345–46.

Flade, Paul. "Deutsches Inquisitionsverfahren um 1400." *Zeitschrift für Kirchengeschichte* 22 (1901): 232–53.

———. "Römische Inquisition in Mitteldeutschland, insbesondere in den sächsischen Ländern." *Beiträge zur sächsischen Kirchengeschichte* 11 (1896): 58–86.

———. *Das römische Inquisitionsverfahren in Deutschland bis zu den Hexenprozessen.* Leipzig, 1902.

Förg, Ludwig. *Die Ketzerverfolgung in Deutschland unter Gregor IX.* Berlin, 1932.

Förstemann, Ernst Günther. *Die christlichen Geisslergesellschaften.* Halle, 1828.

Fredericq, Paul, ed. *Corpus documentorum inquisitionis haereticae pravitatis Neerlandicae.* Ghent and The Hague, 1889–1906.

Friess, Godfried Edmund. "Patarener, Begharden und Waldenser in Oesterreich während des Mittelalters." *Oesterreichische Vierteljahresschrift für katholische Theologie* 11 (1872): 209–72.

Geiger, Ludwig. *Johann Reuchlin: Sein Leben und seine Werke.* Leipzig, 1871.

———. "Maximilian I. in seinem Verhältnisse zum Reuchlinschen Streite." *Forschungen zur deutschen Geschichte* 9 (1869): 203–16.

Gonnet, Giovanni. "I Valdesi d'Austria nella seconda metà del secolo XIV." *Bollettino della società di studi valdesi* 82, no. 111 (1962): 5–14.

Gradl, Heinrich. "Die Irrlehre der Wirsperger." *Mittheilungen des Vereins für Geschichte der Deutschen in Böhmen* 19 (1881): 270–79.

Grundmann, Herbert. "Ketzerverhöre des Spätmittelalters als quellenkritisches Problem." *Deutsches Archiv für Erforschung des Mittelalters* 21 (1965): 519–75.

Hansen, Joseph, ed. *Quellen und Untersuchungen zur Geschichte des Hexen-wahns und der Hexenverfolgung im Mittelalter.* Bonn, 1901.

Haupt, Herman. "Beiträge zur Geschichte der Sekte vom freien Geiste und des Beghardentums." *Zeitschrift für Kirchengeschichte* 7 (1885): 503–76.

———. "Deutsch-böhmische Waldenser um 1340." *Zeitschrift für Kirchengeschichte* 14 (1894): 1–18.

———. "Husitische Propaganda in Deutschland." *Historisches Taschenbuch,* ser. 6, 7 (1888): 233–304.

———. "Johannes Malkaw aus Preussen und seine Verfolgung durch die Inquisition zu Strassburg und Köln, 1390–1416." *Zeitschrift für Kirchengeschichte* 6 (1884): 323–89.

———. *Die religiösen Sekten in Franken vor der Reformation.* Würzburg, 1882.

———. "Waldenserthum und Inquisition im südöstlichen Deutschland bis zur Mitte des 14. Jahrhunderts." *Deutsche Zeitschrift für Geschichtswissenschaft* 1 (1889): 285–330.

———. "Waldenserthum und Inquisition im südöstlichen Deutschland seit der Mitte des 14. Jahrhunderts." *Deutsche Zeitschrift für Geschichtswissenschaft* 3 (1890): 337–411.

———. *Der Waldensische Ursprung des Codex Teplensis.* Würzburg, 1886.

———. "Zwei Traktate gegen Beginen und Begharden." *Zeitschrift für Kirchengeschichte* 12 (1891): 85–90.

Heimpel, Hermann, ed. *Drei Inquisitions-Verfahren aus dem Jahre 1425.* Göttingen, 1969.

———. *Zwei Wormser Inquisitionen aus den Jahren 1421 und 1422.* Göttingen, 1969.

Hermann, Fritz. "Die letzte Ketzerverbrennung in Mainz." In *Beiträge zur Kunst und Geschichte des Mainzer Lebensraumes: Festschrift für Ernst Neeb.* Mainz, 1936. Pp. 105–10.

Heymann, Frederick. *John Žižka and the Hussite Revolution.* Princeton, 1955.

Homeyer, Carl Gustav. "Johannes Klenkok wider den Sachsenspiegel." *Abhandlungen der königlichen Akademie der Wissenschaften zu Berlin,* 1885, Philosophisch-historische Klasse, pp. 376–432, 432a–432d.

Hoyer, Siegfried. "Die thüringische Kryptoflagellantenbewegung im 15. Jahrhundert." *Jahrbuch für Regionalgeschichte* 2 (1967): 148–74.

Jung, Andreas. "Friedrich Reiser: Eine Ketzergeschichte aus dem 15. Jahrhundert." *Timotheus* 2 (1882): 37ff.

Kaltner, Balthasar. *Konrad von Marburg und die Inquisition in Deutschland.* Prague, 1882.

Kaminsky, Howard. *A History of the Hussite Revolution.* Berkeley and Los Angeles, 1967.

Kapp, Johann Erhard. "Altes aus dem funfzehnten Seculo." In *Fortgesetzte*

Sammlung von alten und neuen theologischen Sachen. Leipzig, 1747.
Pp. 475–83.

Kieckhefer, Richard. *European Witch Trials: Their Foundations in Popular and Learned Culture, 1300–1500.* London, and Berkeley and Los Angeles, 1976.

———. "Radical Tendencies in the Flagellant Movement of the Mid-Fourteenth Century." *Journal of Medieval and Renaissance Studies* 4 (1974): 157–76.

Klicman, Ladislaus. "Der Wiener Process gegen Hieronymus von Prag, 1410–12." *Mitteilungen des Instituts für österreichische Geschichtsforschung* 21 (1900): 445–57.

Köhler, Hermann. *Die Ketzerpolitik der deutschen Kaiser und Könige in den Jahren 1152–1254.* Bonn, 1913.

Köpstein, Horst. "Das frühe Hussitentum in Deutschland—speziell Johann Drändorf." *Letopis,* ser. B, 9/1 (1962): 133–61.

———. "Uber den deutschen Hussiten Friedrich Reiser." *Zeitschrift für Geschichtswissenschaft* 7, no. 2 (1959): 1068–82.

Kurze, Dietrich. "Märkische Waldenser und Böhmische Brüder: Zur brandenburgischen Ketzergeschichte und ihrer Nachwirkung im 15. und 16. Jahrhundert." *Mitteldeutsche Forschungen* 74, pt. 2 (1974): 456–502.

———. "Zur Ketzergeschichte der Mark Brandenburg und Pommerns, vornehmlich im 14. Jahrhundert: Luziferianer, Putzkeller und Waldenser." *Jahrbuch für die Geschichte Mittel- und Ostdeutschlands* 16/17 (1968): 50–94.

———, ed. *Quellen zur Ketzergeschichte Brandenburgs und Pommerns.* Berlin and New York, 1975.

Lambert, Malcolm D. *Medieval Heresy: Popular Movements from Bogomil to Hus.* New York, 1977.

Lea, Henry Charles. *A History of the Inquisition of the Middle Ages.* 3 vols. New York, 1887–88.

Leff, Gordon. *Heresy in the Later Middle Ages.* 2 vols. Manchester, 1967.

Lerner, Robert E. *The Heresy of the Free Spirit in the Later Middle Ages.* Berkeley, Los Angeles, and London, 1972.

Loserth, Johann. "Ueber die Versuche wiclif-husitische Lehren nach Oesterreich, Polen, Ungarn und Croatien zu verpflanzen: Nach gleichzeitigen Correspondenzen." *Mittheilungen des Vereins für Geschichte der Deutschen in Böhmen* 24 (1885–86): 97–116.

McDonnell, Ernest W. *The Beguines and Beghards in Medieval Culture: With Special Emphasis on the Belgian Scene.* New York, 1954.

Macek, Josef. *The Hussite Movement in Bohemia.* 2d ed. Prague, 1958.

Machilek, Franz. "Ein Eichstätter Inquisitionsverfahren aus dem Jahre 1460." *Jahrbuch für fränkische Landesforschung* 34/35 (1974–75): 417–46.

Mosheim, Johann Lorenz von. *De beghardis et beguinabus commentarius.* Leipzig, 1790.

Neumann, Augustin. *České sekty ve století XIV. a XV., a základě archivních pramenu podává.* Staré Brno, 1920.

Neumann, Eva Gertrud. *Rheinisches Beginen- und Begardenwesen: Ein Mainzer Beitrag zur religiösen Bewegung am Rhein.* Meisenheim am Glan, 1960.

Patschovsky, Alexander. *Die Anfänge einer ständigen Inquisition in Böhmen.* Berlin and New York, 1975.

———. *Der Passauer Anonymus.* Stuttgart, 1968.

———. "Strassburger Beginenverfolgungen im 14. Jahrhundert." *Deutsches Archiv für Erforschung des Mittelalters* 30 (1974): 92–109.

Peters, Günter. "Norddeutsches Beginen- und Begardenwesen im Mittelalter." *Niedersächsisches Jahrbuch für Landesgeschichte* 41/42 (1969–70): 50–119.

Phillips, Dayton. *Beguines in Medieval Strasburg: A Study of the Social Aspect of Beguine Life.* Ann Arbor, Mich., 1941.

Preger, Wilhelm, "Ueber das Verhältnis der Taboriten zu den Waldesiern des 14. Jahrhunderts." *Abhandlungen der königlichen bayerischen Akademie der Wissenschaften,* Historische Classe, 18 (1889): 1–111.

———, ed. "Der Tractat des David von Augsburg über die Waldesier." *Abhandlungen der königlichen bayerischen Akademie der Wissenschaften.* Historische Classe, 14, pt. 2 (1879): 183–235.

Reifferscheid, Alexander, ed. *Neue Texte der religiösen Aufklärung in Deutschland während des 14. und 15. Jahrhunderts: Festschrift der Universität Greifswald.* Greifswald, 1905.

Rein, W. "Beguinen in Eisenach." *Zeitschrift des Vereins für thüringische Geschichte und Alterthumskunde* 4 (1860): 226f.

Ribbeck, Walter. "Beiträge zur Geschichte der römischen Inquisition in Deutschland während des 14. und 15. Jahrhunderts." *Zeitschrift für vaterländische Geschichte und Altertumskunde* 46 (1888): 129–56.

Röhrich, Timotheus Wilhelm. "Die Winkeler in Strassburg, sammt deren Verhöracten, um 1400." In *Mittheilungen aus der Geschichte der evangelischen Kirche des Elsasses.* Strassburg and Paris, 1855. 1: 3–77.

Schiff, Otto. "Die Wirsberger." *Historische Vierteljahresschrift* 26 (1931): 776–86.

Schmidt, Karl. *Nicolaus von Basel: Leben und ausgewählte Schriften.* Vienna, 1866.

Schornbaum, K. "Zur Geschichte der Ketzer in Franken." *Zeitschrift für bayerische Kirchengeschichte* 8 (1933): 203f.

Selge, Kurt-Victor. "Heidelberger Ketzerprozesse in der Frühzeit der hussitischen Revolution." *Zeitschrift für Kirchengeschichte* 82 (1971): 167–202.

Sohm, Theodor. "Verbrennung der Ketzerin Helike Pors im Jahre 1394." In Karl Koppmann, ed., *Beiträge zur Geschichte der Stadt Rostock,* 2, sect. 4. Rostock, 1899.

Spinka, Matthew, ed. *John Hus at the Council of Constance.* New York, 1965.

Straganz, Max. "Zum Begharden- und Beghinenstreite in Basel zu Beginn des 15. Jahrhunderts." *Alemannia: Zeitschrift für Sprache, Kunst und Altertum, besonders des alemannisch-schwäbischen Gebiets* 27 (1900): 20–28.

Stumpf, Augustin. Historia flagellantium, praecipue in Thuringia." *Neue Mittheilungen aus dem Gebiete historisch-antiquarischer Forschung* 2 (1835): 1–37.

Theloe, Hermann. *Die Ketzerverhöre im 11. und 12. Jahrhundert: Ein Beitrag zur Geschichte der Entstehung des päpstlichen Ketzerinquisitionsgerichts.* Berlin and Leipzig, 1913.

Truhlář, Josef. "Inkvisice Waldenských v Trnavě r. 1400." *Český časopis historicky* 9 (1903): 196–98.

"Versuch einer Conciliengeschichte des Bisthums Eichstätt." *Pastoralblatt des Bisthums Eichstätt* 1 (1854), in sections throughout the volume, esp. pp. 138–40.

Vinay, Valdo. "Friedrich Reiser e la diaspora valdese di lingua tedesca nel XV secolo." *Bollettino della società di studi valdesi* 81, no. 109 (1961): 35–56.

Wasmud von Homburg, Johann. "Tractatus contra hereticos Beckardos, Lulhardos et Swestriones des Wasmud von Homburg," ed. Aloys Schmidt. *Archiv für mittelrheinische Kirchengeschichte* 14 (1962): 336–86.

Wattenbach, Wilhelm," Über die Inquisition gegen die Waldenser in Pommern und der Mark Brandenburg." *Abhandlungen der königlichen Akademie der Wissenschaften zu Berlin*, 1886, Philosophisch-historische Classe, Abhandlung 3.

———. "Über Ketzergerichte in Pommern und der Mark Brandenburg." *Sitzungsberichte der königlichen preussischen Akademie der Wissenschaften zu Berlin*, 1886, pp. 47–58.

———. "Über die Secte der Brüder vom freien Geiste." *Sitzungsberichte der königlichen preussischen Akademie der Wissenschaften zu Berlin*, 1887, pp. 517–44.

Weigel, Helmut. "Ein Waldenserverhör in Rothenburg im Jahre 1394." *Beiträge zur bayerischen Kirchengeschichte* 23 (1917): 81–86.

Werner, Ernst. *Nachrichten über spätmittelalterliche Ketzer aus tschechoslovakischen Archiven und Bibliotheken.* Leipzig, 1963.

Wigger, Friedrich. "Urkundliche Mittheilungen über die Beghinen- und Begharden-Häuser zu Rostock." *Jahrbücher des Vereins für mecklenburgische und Alterthumskunde* 47 (1882): 1–26.

Wilmans, Roger. "Zur Geschichte der römischen Inquisition in Deutschland während des 14. und 15. Jahrhunderts." *Historische Zeitschrift* 41 (1879): 193–228.

Index

157

THE MIDDLE AGES

Edward Peters, General Editor